Bloom's Modern Critical Views

AMERICAN MODERNIST POETS

Edited and with an introduction by
Harold Bloom
Sterling Professor of the Humanities
Yale University

BLOOM'S
LITERARY CRITICISM
An imprint of Infobase Publishing

Bloom's Modern Critical Views: American Modernist Poets
Copyright © 2011 by Infobase Learning
Introduction © 2011 by Harold Bloom

Bloom's Literary Criticism
An imprint of Infobase Learning
132 West 31st Street
New York NY 10001

Library of Congress Cataloging-in-Publication Data
American modernist poets / edited and with an introduction by Harold Bloom.
    p. cm. — (Bloom's modern critical views)
  Includes bibliographical references and index.
  ISBN 978-1-60413-275-5 (hardcover)
  1. American poetry—20th century—History and criticism. 2. Modernism (Literature)—United States. I. Bloom, Harold.
  PS310.M57A64 2011
  811'.509112—dc22

                         2010041435

Contributing editor: Pamela Loos
Cover designed by Takeshi Takahashi
Composition by IBT Global, Troy NY
Cover printed by IBT Global, Troy NY
Book printed and bound by IBT Global, Troy NY
Date printed: February 2011
Printed in the United States of America

10 9 8 7 6 5 4 3 2 1

This book is printed on acid-free paper.

Contents

Editor's Note

My introduction surveys the major modernist poets, from the Emersonian religion of Frost to the late flowering of Stevens.

Peter Schmidt views *Paterson* as an epical summation of the various modes of writing Williams explored throughout his life, followed by Jerome J. McCann's suggestion that the *Cantos* are the greatest achievement of modern poetry in any language.

Robert Pinsky turns his attention to the sociable writings of Marianne Moore, after which Mark Van Wienen detects the socialist bent in the early work of Sandburg.

Roger Mitchell provides an overview of moderism's influence on the century's early decades, followed by Eleanor Cook's examination of puns and word play primarily in the work of Stevens and Bishop.

Jay Parini offers a shrewd assessment of Frostian poetics, after which Suzanne Clark unlocks the uncanny endurance of Millay's high modernist strivings. The volume concludes with Martin Heusser's analysis of the multiple selves present in the poetry of Cummings.

Introduction

Robert Frost

Frost died two months short of his eighty-ninth birthday in 1963. That he was the major poet of twentieth-century America can be both affirmed and disputed. But even the admirers of his strongest rivals—Wallace Stevens, T.S. Eliot, Hart Crane, Elizabeth Bishop—concede Frost's unique eminence as a poet both popular and sophisticated. There is a mountain in Ripton, Vermont, named after Robert Frost; no one is going to name a mountain after Wallace Stevens or Thomas Stearns Eliot.

Frost, read by hundreds of thousands, is a great poet by all the aesthetic and cognitive standards that have been crucial to the Western canon at least since Dante and Petrarch. Robert Frost's poetry, invulnerable to the tides of resentment, becomes stronger with each passing year. Its values indeed are aesthetic and cognitive: It gives difficult pleasure, implicitly urging us to abandon easier pleasures, and it educates us up to Frost's own high standards. Frost himself, whom I met a few times, at Yale and at Breadloaf, was a difficult personality, at least in his old age. A superb monologist, he held one by his bursts of eloquence and his poetic authority. Some of the later poetry is self-indulgent, but always there are moments of vitalizing realization, as here in "Pod of the Milkweed," the opening poem in Frost's final volume, *In the Clearing* (1962):

> But waste was the essence of the scheme.
> And all the good they did for man or god
> To all those flowers they passionately trod
> Was leave as their posterity one pod
> With an inheritance of restless dream.

1

If a single pod is of the essence, the vision might seem minimalist, but Frost is too shrewd and too large for such ironic reductiveness, even when it is his own. Like Walt Whitman, with whom he has nothing else in common, he was an Emersonian. Frost placed Emerson's "Uriel" first among Western poems. That is sublime overpraise, but reading "Uriel" now, one uncannily hears the poetic voice of Robert Frost:

> Line in nature is not found;
> Unit and universe are round;
> In vain produced, all rays return;
> Evil will bless, and ice will burn.

Frost's voice, at its strongest, can be found in a plethora of his poems: "A Servant to Servants," "The Wood-Pile," "The Oven Bird," "Putting in the Seed," "Two Watches," "Once by the Pacific," "The Flower Bust," "Two Tramps in Mud Time," "Design," "Provide, Provide," "The Most of It," "Never Again Would Birds' Song Be the Same," "The Subverted Flower," "A Cabin in the Clearing." That is a personal list of 14; the fifteenth and best seems to me "Directive," for it has the whole of Frost in it.

"Directive" is the fourth poem in the later volume, *Steeple Bush* (1947). It is a retrospective vision of his life by a man of 73 and is animated by an astonishing harshness, both toward the poet and the reader. Opening with a powerfully monosyllabic line—"Back out of all this now too much for us"—Frost takes his reader and himself on a journey to the interior, past and inward:

> Back in a time made simple by the loss
>
> Of detail, burned, dissolved, and broken off
> Like graveyard marble sculpture in the weather.

We go back to a house, farm, town all now obliterated by time, and we take a road that is more like a quarry. The going back is a "serial ordeal," an Arthurian testing to see if we are worthy to quest for the Holy Grail, a quest wholly ironized in "Directive":

> Your destination and your destiny's
> A brook that was the water of the house,
>
> I have kept hidden in the instep arch
> Of an old cedar at the waterside

A broken drinking goblet like the Grail
Under a spell so the wrong ones can't find it,
So can't get saved, as Saint Mark says they mustn't.

The Gospel of Mark (4:11–12) gives us, just this once, a Jesus incredibly harsh:

That seeing they may see, and not perceive, and hearing they may hear, and not understand, lest at any time, they should be converted, and their sins should be forgiven them.

But if we *are* among Frost's elect, to be saved by the poet, then:

Here are your waters and your watering place.
Drink and be whole again beyond confusion.

The poem is only a "momentary stay against confusion," Frost had said elsewhere. With a desperate irony, he hopes for something more, for himself and for us, here at the conclusion of "Directive."

Wallace Stevens

Since I find myself in what William Butler Yeats called "the Autumn of the Body," I write this introduction as a conscious farewell to the poet who formed my mind, as I am not likely ever to find occasion to meditate again in print upon him.

I will confine these remarks to what may be Stevens's masterwork, the magnificent *The Auroras of Autumn*, composed when Stevens was 68, in 1947. One could argue that *Notes Toward a Supreme Fiction* (1942) is Stevens's formal attempt at his major poem, and I have moods when I favor *An Ordinary Evening in New Haven* (1949). And yet, on balance, *The Auroras of Autumn* is Stevens's version of the American sublime, a worthy companion to the Walt Whitman of the great elegies "Out of the Cradle Endlessly Rocking," "As Ebb'd with the Ocean of Life," and "When Lilacs Last in the Dooryard Bloom'd."

I have been teaching, and writing about, *The Auroras of Autumn* for nearly a half century and will not attempt a comprehensive commentary here. Walter Pater called a superb volume of critical essays *Appreciations*, and in my old age increasingly I want to write "appreciations" of the great works of imaginative literature.

The Auroras of Autumn, at first, can seem a rather difficult poem, though after so many decades of possessing it by memory, the complexities smooth

out, and something like a total coherence prevails. My students generally find
Canto I of the poem the most immediately hard to absorb, particularly the
now famous three opening tercets:

> This is where the serpent lives, the bodiless.
> His head is air. Beneath his tip at night
> Eyes open and fix on us in every sky.
>
> Or is this another wriggling out of the egg,
> Another image at the end of the cave,
> Another bodiless for the body's slough?
>
> This is where the serpent lives. This is his nest,
> These fields, these hills, these tinted distances,
> And the pines above and along and beside the sea.

Stevens, in this most personal and dramatic of all his poems, sets the scene
carefully but obliquely. An extraordinary conflagration of the aurora borealis or
Northern Lights bursts above him in the evening sky, even as summer yields
to autumn. Looking up, the aging poet beholds the auroras lashing across the
heavens like a giant serpent extending and then withdrawing. He walks the
beach, with fields, hills, pines behind him, while (implicitly) he alternately surveys sky, sea, and land. Since the illumination of the auroras is pervasive, the
entire scene is the serpent's nest, while the eyes opening beneath the serpent's
tip are the stars, captive to the aurora—serpent's reign. Yet, in the second ter-
cet the poet allows himself a momentary skepticism: Are the great lights only
another mythic origin (wriggling out of the egg), or another illusion on the wall
of Plato's cave, or a wish fulfillment of an old man heavily caught in the body's
slough, and identifying with the serpent's bodilessness?

Cantos II–IV of *The Auroras of Autumn* all begin with the phrase: "Farewell
to an idea." Stevens relies on the reader's knowledge of *Notes Toward a Supreme
Fiction*, where "the first idea" or snowman's reality is perpetually reimagined. It
is the idea of reimagining the first idea to which the poet now says farewell.
Canto II is so brilliant that I need to appreciate it very closely here:

> Farewell to an idea. . . . A cabin stands,
> Deserted, on a beach. It is white,
> As by a custom or according to
>
> An ancestral theme or as a consequence
> Of an infinite course. The flowers against the wall

Are white, a little dried, a kind of mark
Reminding, trying to remind, of a white
That was different, something else, last year
Or before, not the white of an aging afternoon,

Whether fresher or duller, whether of winter cloud
Or of winter sky, from horizon to horizon.
The wind is blowing the sand across the floor.

Here, being visible is being white,
Is being of the solid of white, the accomplishment
Of an extremist in an exercise . . .

The season changes. A cold wind chills the beach.
The long lines of it grow longer, emptier,
A darkness gathers though it does not fall

And the whiteness grows less vivid on the wall.
The man who is walking turns blankly on the sand.
He observes how the north is always enlarging the change,

With its frigid brilliances, its blue-red sweeps
And gusts of great enkindlings, its polar green,
The color of ice and fire and solitude.

A great and frightening metaphorical tradition of the "blank" culminates as Stevens walks the beach: "The man who is walking turns *blankly* on the sand" (my italics). John Milton, blindly invoking the Holy Light, laments "a universal blank/of Nature's works to me expunged and razed." Samuel Taylor Coleridge, confronting his dejection, stares on a foreboding sky: "And still I gaze—and with how blank an eye!" Coleridge alludes to Milton, and Ralph Waldo Emerson, in his *Nature*, subsumes them both: "The ruin or blank that we see when we look at nature is in our own eye." Emily Dickinson, obsessed with the metaphor of the blank, sees herself as going "From Blank to Blank" in a labyrinth without a guiding thread. In Stevens, the sinister white of his reductions to a first idea modulates into a blank that his own imagination has created. The man who is walking the sands, the 68-year-old poet, turns blankly, because he observes a blank, with an eye that is blank, in the context of a universal blank, while knowing that all the poems he has composed now seem blank. The Northern Lights enlarge the change, confronting him with ruin.

    A strong poet, Stevens fights back against the auroras in cantos III and IV, summoning up the images of his late mother and father. But memory dissolves in the glare of the Northern Lights:

> And yet she too is dissolved, she is destroyed.
> She gives transparences. But she has grown old.
> The necklace is a carving not a kiss
>
> The soft hands are a motion not a touch.

    It is at the close of canto VI that Stevens achieves the apotheosis of this crisis poem. A lifetime of imaginative discipline courageously attempts to unname the auroras but is defeated by the uncanny terror brought about by the responsive flaming-up of the Northern Lights:

> This is nothing until in a single man contained,
> Nothing until this named thing nameless is
> And is destroyed. He opens the doors of his house
>
> On flames. The scholar of one candle sees
> An Arctic effulgence flaring on the frame
> Of everything he is. And he feels afraid.

    The scholar is Emerson's "Man thinking," but thought cannot prevail when the house of the spirit opens its door on the flames of the auroras. Subtly, Stevens works through his dilemmas until in canto VIII he can affirm the innocence of the auroras:

> So, then, these lights are not a spell of light,
> A saying out of a cloud, but innocence.
> An innocence of the earth and no false sign
>
> Or symbol of malice.

    It is, from Hamlet through Milton on to the High Romantics and Wallace Stevens, the poetic enterprise proper to affirm the power of the mind over a universe of death. In *The Auroras of Autumn*, Stevens paradoxically experiences the defeat of that enterprise and yet continues it even in apparent defeat. If the sublime poem exists in twentieth-century American English, *The Auroras of Autumn*, in my judgment, joins Hart Crane's *The Bridge* as one of its leading exemplars.

William Carlos Williams

In his critical biography *William Carlos Williams: A New World Naked*, Paul Mariani wisely asserts the lasting influence of John Keats's poetry on even the late phases of Williams:

> The voice he was listening to, and the voice that struck paydirt for him, was a matter of a complex crossing with Keats, especially the Keats of the *Hyperion* fragments and the odes. Why this should have been so is difficult to say with any exactness, for Williams himself probably did not understand why. What *he* thought he was "capturing" was the voice of the classics—the stately rhythms and sharp straightforward idiom of the Greeks as he thought they must sound should they be discovered walking the streets of his Paterson. But there was something more, a kinship Williams had felt with Keats for over half a century, the plight of the romantic poet who would have spoken as the gods speak if only he had had the power to render their speech in the accents of his own debased language. *Hyperion* is in part the portrait of the dying of the ephebe into the life of the major poet, and Keats had aborted it at the very moment that his poet was undergoing that transformation.
>
> And so with Williams, opting for the step-down line as his "classic" signature as he surfaced from the realization of his mortality, the new rhythm providing a stately, slow saraband to echo Keats's Miltonic and Dantesque phase with a difference. The crossing with Keats is there too in the nature of Williams's late iconography, in the stasis of his late images, frozen for eternity in the realized artifact, as in Williams's translation from Theocritus's first idyll, with its images limned on a "two-eared bowl / of ivy-wood," a girl and two young men, an ancient fisherman, and a small boy preoccupied with "plaiting a pretty / cage of locust stalks and asphodel." The images of *Asphodel* too belong to the same strain: sharply realized but without Williams's earlier breathlessness and jagged line cuttings.

Poetic influence, an intensely problematical process, normally brings together a strong poet's earliest and final phases. Williams's true precursor, necessarily composite and in some sense imaginary, was a figure that fused Keats with Walt Whitman. Such a figure has in it the potential for a serious splitting of the poetic ego in its defense against the poetic past. The "negative capability" of Keats sorts oddly with Whitman's rather positive capability for conveying the powerful press of himself. "Memory is a kind / of

accomplishment," Williams wrote in "The Descent," a crucial poem in his
The Desert Music (1954). The descent to dying beckons to a return of the dead
precursors in one's own colors, even as Keats and Whitman beckoned Williams to ascend into his own poetry. But the poem "The Descent" Williams
shrewdly quarried from book 2 of his own major long poem, *Paterson*, a quar-
rying that suggests his pride in his own continuities.

Those continuities are massive throughout Williams's best work, which
can be cataloged (against the numerous Williams idolators) as a limited yet still
remarkably diverse canon: *Paterson* (book I), *Kora in Hell*, *Spring and All*, "The
Widow's Lament in Springtime," "To Waken an Old Lady," "The Trees," "The
Yachts," "A Coronal," "These," "The Poor," "A Marriage Ritual," "Raleigh Was
Right," "Burning the Christmas Greens," "A Unison," and the grand return of
Keats-as-Williams in *Asphodel, That Greeny Flower*. Every critic I have chosen
for this volume would select more, much more, but I am of the school of Wallace Stevens, rather than of Williams, and the Williams I honor is the author of
about a dozen shorter poems and four remarkable long poems and prose or verse
sequences. I write this introduction not to dissent but as an experiment. If you
believe—as I do—that Williams is not of the eminence of Stevens and Robert
Frost, of Hart Crane and even of T.S. Eliot, then what is the irreducible achievement that survives even an extreme skepticism as to Williams's poetic greatness?

Of the volumes that collect Williams, I return most often to *Imaginations*,
edited by Webster Schott (1979), which gathers together four weird American
originals—*Kora in Hell*, *Spring and All*, *The Great American Novel*, *The Descent of
Winter*—as well as some miscellaneous prose. *Kora in Hell* was subtitled *Improvisations* by Williams, who had a particular fondness for it. He analogized its
astonishing "Prologue" to *On the Sublime* by the pseudo-Longinus, a comparison not so far-fetched as he himself asserted it to be. Essentially it, and all
of *Kora*, is a collection of what Emerson (following Plutarch and Cudworth)
called "lustres" (Ezra Pound's *lustra*), aphoristic impressions drawn either from
others or from the self. Its center is in Williams's characteristic polemic against
Pound and Eliot, with an ironizing boost from Stevens:

> E.P. is the best enemy United States verse has. He is interested,
> passionately interested—even if he doesn't know what he is talking
> about. But of course he does know what he is talking about. He
> does not, however, know everything, not by more than half. The
> accordances of which Americans have the parts and the colors but
> not the completions before them pass beyond the attempts of his
> thought. It is a middle-aging blight of the imagination.
>
> I praise those who have the wit and courage, and the con-
> ventionality, to go direct toward their vision of perfection in an

objective world where the signposts are clearly marked, viz., to London. But confine them in hell for their paretic assumption that there is no alternative but their own groove.

Dear fat Stevens, thawing out so beautifully at forty! I was one day irately damning those who run to London when Stevens caught me up with his mild: "But where in the world will you have them run to?"

The shrewd link to *On the Sublime* is that Williams (admirably and accurately) shares the conviction of Longinus that the sublime or strong poetry either is agonistic or it is nothing. Williams, too, seeks to persuade the reader to forsake easier pleasures (Eliot and Pound) for more difficult pleasures (*Kora in Hell*). And his quest is frankly Emersonian, an overt instance of American cultural nationalism. Unfortunately, *Kora*'s considerable verve and vivacity is shadowed by the immense power of James Joyce's *Ulysses*, still incomplete then but appearing in magazine installments even as Williams wrote and read. Williams's use of mythology is essentially Joyce's, and to fight Joyce on any ground, let alone his prepared killing field, was beyond Williams's talents:

Giants in the dirt. The gods, the Greek gods, smothered in filth and ignorance. The race is scattered over the world. Where is its home? Find it if you've the genius. Here Hebe with a sick jaw and a cruel husband,—her mother left no place for a brain to grow. Herakles rowing boats on Berry's Creek! Zeus is a country doctor without a taste for coin jingling. Supper is of a bastard nectar on rare nights for they will come—the rare nights! The ground lifts and out sally the heroes of Sophokles, of Æschylus. They go seeping down into our hearts, they rain upon us and in the bog they sink again down through the white roots, down—to a saloon back of the railroad switch where they have that girl, you know, the one that should have been Venus by the lust that's in her. They've got her down there among the railroad men. A crusade couldn't rescue her. Up to jail—or call it down to Limbo—the Chief of Police our Pluto. It's all of the gods, there's nothing else worth writing of. They are the same men they always were—but fallen. Do they dance now, they that danced beside Helicon? They dance much as they did then, only, few have an eye for it, through the dirt and fumes.

The question becomes: Who shall describe the dance of the gods as it is danced now in America? The answer is: Dr. Williams, who brings American babies into the world and who sees exquisitely what we cannot see without him, which is how differently the gods come to dance here in America:

> This is a slight stiff dance to a waking baby whose arms have been lying curled back above his head upon the pillow, making a flower—the eyes closed. Dead to the world! Waking is a little hand brushing away dreams. Eyes open. Here's a new world.

This dance figures again in the concluding improvisation of *Kora in Hell*, as an American seasonal rhythm akin to the natural year of Stevens's "Credences of Summer" and Emerson's "Experience":

> Seeing the leaves dropping from the high and low branches the thought rises: this day of all others is the one chosen, all other days fall away from it on either side and only itself remains in perfect fullness. It is its own summer, of its leaves as they scrape on the smooth ground it must build its perfection. The gross summer of the year is only a halting counterpart of those fiery days of secret triumph which in reality themselves paint the year as if upon a parchment, giving each season a mockery of the warmth or frozenness which is within ourselves. The true seasons blossom or wilt not in fixed order but so that many of them may pass in a few weeks or hours whereas sometimes a whole life passes and the season remains of a piece from.

The world is largest in the American summer, for Williams and Stevens, even as it was for their forefather, Emerson. *Spring and All* celebrates not this world but the more difficult American skepticism of a hard spring, imperishably rendered in its magnificent opening lyric, "By the road to the contagious hospital," with its harsh splendor of inception, at once of vegetation, infants, and of Whitmanian or American poems:

> Lifeless in appearance, sluggish
> dazed spring approaches—
>
> They enter the new world naked,
> cold, uncertain of all
> save that they enter. All about them
> the cold, familiar wind—
>
> Now the grass, tomorrow
> the stiff curl of wildcarrot leaf

one by one objects are defined—
It quickens: clarity, outline of leaf

But now the stark dignity of
entrance—Still, the profound change
has come upon them: rooted, they
grip down and begin to awaken

The ancient fiction of the leaves, a continuous tradition from Homer
and Virgil, through Dante and on to Spenser and Milton, Shelley and Whitman, receives one culmination in Stevens and a very different apotheosis here
in Williams. In the prose of *Spring and All*, Williams protests too emphati-
cally that: "THE WORLD IS NEW," a protest that has been taken too much
at its own self-mystifying evaluation by the most distinguished of the decon-
structive critics of Williams, J. Hillis Miller and Joseph Riddel. But when the
best poems in *Spring and All* unfold themselves, the reader can be persuaded
that Williams has invented freshly the accurate metaphors for our American sense of imaginative belatedness: "There is / an approach with difficulty
from / the dead—" and "The rose is obsolete / but each petal ends in / an
edge." Except for "By the road to the contagious hospital," the best poems in
Spring and All are the justly famous ones: "The pure products of America / go
crazy—," and "so much depends / upon / a red wheel / barrow."

More problematical are *The Great American Novel* and *The Descent of
Winter*, pugnacious assaults on Williams's own formal limits, yet assaults
masked as ironies directed against the literary conventionalities of others. I
prefer *The Descent of Winter*, where the authentic anxiety of belatedness, the
only legitimate point of origin for any American literature, is expressed in
relation to that most impossible of all influences, Shakespeare:

By writing he escaped from the world into the natural world of his
mind. The unemployable world of his fine head was unnaturally
useless in the gross exterior of his day—or any day. By writing he
made this active. He melted himself into that grossness, and colored
it with his powers. The proof that he was right and they passing,
being that he continues always and naturally while their artificiality
destroyed them. A man unable to employ himself in his world.

Therefore his seriousness and his accuracies, because it was
not his play but the drama of his life. It is his anonymity that is
baffling to nitwits and so they want to find an involved explanation—to defeat the plainness of the evidence.

When he speaks of fools he is one; when of kings he is one,
doubly so in misfortune.

He is a woman, a pimp, a prince Hal—

Such a man is a prime borrower and standardizer—No inventor. He lives because he sinks back, does not go forward, sinks back into the mass—

He is Hamlet plainer than a theory—and in everything.

You can't buy a life again after it's gone, that's the way I mean.

He drinks awful bad and he beat me up every single month while I was carrying this baby, pretty nearly every week.

As an overview of Shakespeare, this is unquestionably the weakest commentary available since Tolstoy; but as a representation of Williams's dilemmas, it has a curious force, including the weird parody of Hemingway's agonistic stance in the last sentence I have just quoted. Despite his army of hyperbolic exegetes, Williams's nakedness in relation to the literary past is not so much that of "a new world naked" as it is that of a no longer so very new world awkwardly wrapped round by too many fine rags.

The best lyrics and book I of *Paterson* are of a higher order, though they also betray darker anxieties of influence than even Williams's defiances dared to confront. They display also another kind of agon, the anxiety as to contemporary rivals, not so much Pound and Eliot as Wallace Stevens and Hart Crane, heirs to Keats and to Whitman, even as Williams was. No two readers are likely to agree on just which shorter poems by Williams are his strongest, but the one that impresses and moves me most is "A Unison," where the title seems to comprehend most of the dictionary meanings of "unison": an identity of pitch in music; the same words spoken simultaneously by two or more speakers; musical parts combined in octaves; a concord, agreement, harmony. Thomas R. Whitaker, one of Williams's best and most sympathetic critics but no idolator, gives the best introduction to "A Unison":

> It is like an improvisation from *Kora in Hell*—but one with the quiet maturity of vision and movement that some three decades have brought.... As the implicit analogies and contrasts accumulate, we discover (long before the speaker tells us) that we are attending a "unison and a dance." This "death's festival"— *memento mori* and celebration of the "*Undying*"—evades neither the mystery of transience nor that of organic continuance, though neither can be "parsed" by the analytical mind.... In this composed testament of acceptance, Williams's saxifrage ("through metaphor to reconcile / the people and the stones") quietly does its work.... Not since Wordsworth has this natural piety been rendered so freshly and poignantly.

I would not wish to quarrel with Whitaker's judgment, yet there is very little Wordsworth and (inevitably) much Whitman and considerable Keats in "A Unison." Indeed, the poem opens with what must be called an echo from Whitman, in what I assume was a controlled allusion:

> The grass is very green, my friend,
> And tousled, like the head of—
> your grandson, yes?

We hear one of the uncanniest passages in Whitman, from *Song of Myself* 6:

> This grass is very dark to be from the white heads of old mothers,
> Darker than the colorless beards of old men,
> Dark to come from under the faint red roofs of mouths.

Whitman's great fantasia answers a child's question: "*What is the grass?*" As an Epicurean materialist, Whitman believed that the *what* was unknowable, but his remarkable troping on the grass takes a grand turn after his Homeric line: "And now it seems to me the beautiful uncut hair of graves." Williams simply borrows the trope, and even his "very green" merely follows Whitman's hint that a "very green" becomes a "very dark" color in the shadow of mortality. "A Unison" insists on:

> —what cannot be escaped: the
> mountain riding the afternoon as
> it does, the grass matted green,
> green underfoot and the air—
> rotten wood. *Hear! Hear them!*
> *the Undying.* The hill slopes away,
> then rises in the middleground,
> you remember, with a grove of gnarled
> maples centering the bare pasture,
> sacred, surely—for what reason?

Williams does not know whether he can or cannot say the reason, but the allusion is to Keats's characteristic, Saturnian shrine in *Hyperion*. For Williams it is "a shrine cinctured there by / the trees," the girdling effect suggested by the natural sculpture of Keats's shrine. Where Keats as the quester in *The Fall of Hyperion* pledges "all the mortals of the world, / And all the dead whose names are in our lips," and where Whitman insists, "The smallest sprout shows there is really no death," Williams neither salutes the living and the dead, nor folds the two into a single figuration. Rather, he *hears* and urges us to: "*Hear the unison of their voices. . . .*" How are we to interpret such an imaginative gesture? Are we hearing more, or enough more, than the unison of the voices of John Keats and Walt Whitman? Devoted Williamsites doubtless would reject the question, but it always retains its force, nevertheless. It is not less true of *The Waste Land* than it is of Williams. Eliot revises Whitman's "When Lilacs Last in the Dooryard Bloom'd" by fusing it with Tennyson (among others but prime among those others). Image of voice or the trope of poetic identity then becomes a central problem.

Whitman once contrasted himself to Keats by rejecting "negative capability" and insisting instead that the great poet gave us the "powerful press of himself." Admirable as *Paterson* is (particularly its first book), does even it resolve the antithesis in Williams between his "objectivism," or negative capability, and his own agonistic, powerful press of himself? Mariani ends his vast, idealizing biography by asserting that Williams established "an American poetic based on a new measure and a primary regard for the living, protean shape of the language as it was actually used." Hillis Miller, even more generously, tells us that Williams gave us a concept of poetry transcending both Homer and Wordsworth, both Aristotle and Coleridge:

> The word is given reality by the fact it names, but the independence of the fact from the word frees the word to be a fact in its own right and at the same time "dynamizes" it with meaning. The word can then carry the facts named in a new form into the realm of imagination.

Mariani and Miller are quite sober compared to more apocalyptic Williamsites. Not even Whitman gave us "a new measure," and not Shakespeare himself freed a single word "to be a fact in its own right." William Carlos Williams was, at his best, a strong American poet, far better than his hordes of imitators. Like Ezra Pound's, Williams's remains a fairly problematical achievement in the traditions of American poetry. Some generations hence, it will become clear whether his critics have canonized him permanently or subverted him by taking him too much at his own intentions. For now he abides, a live influence perhaps with even more fame to come.

H.D.

There is something quaintly archaic about H.D.'s *Tribute to Freud,* where the professor's interventions are so accurate, his spiritual efficacy so instantaneous, as to suggest the advent of a new age of faith, the Freud era. A prose memorial provokes our resistances when it seems too pious or too amiably earnest. The pre-Raphaelite aura, hieratic and isolated, with its characteristic effect of a hard-edged phantasmagoria, rescues "The Master" from the cloying literalism of the *Tribute*. "The old man," of the poem is God's prophet, since "the dream is God," and Freud, therefore, is heard as one who speaks with authority: "his command / was final" and "his tyranny was absolute, / for I had to love him then." The command, at least as H.D. interpreted it, was to accept her own bisexuality as being one with her poethood:

I do not know what to say to God,
for the hills
answer his nod,
and the sea
when he tells his daughter,
white Mother
of green
leaves
and green rills
and silver,
to still
tempest
or send peace
and surcease of peril
when a mountain has spit fire:

I did not know how to differentiate
between volcanic desire,
anemones like embers
and purple fire
of violets
like red heat,
and the cold
silver
of her feet:

I had two loves separate;
God who loves all mountains,
alone knew why
and understood
and told the old man

to explain
the impossible,

which he did.
    ("The Master")

The phallic or volcanic is evidently preferred by this male God, at least rhetorically, but of the "two loves separate" the "cold / silver / of her feet" triumphs with the reentry of the dancer in section 5. The force that comes with celebration of the dancer depends on H.D.'s vision of herself as wrestling Jacob, arguing till daybreak, and of Freud as God or His angel, giving further rhetorical primacy to "the man-strength" rather than to the dancer's leapings:

I was angry with the old man
With his talk of the man-strength,
I was angry with his mystery, his mysteries,
I argued till day-break

O, it was late,
and God will forgive me, my anger,
but I could not accept it.

I could not accept from wisdom
what love taught,
woman is perfect.
    ("The Dancer")

That would appear to have meant that a woman's bisexuality or her perfection (in the sense of completeness) was of a different and more acceptable order than a man's bisexuality. The ecstasy of section 5 gently mocks the Freudian "man-strength" even as it salutes the dancer for needing no male, since at least as dancer (or poet) woman is indeed pragmatically perfect. Section 5 has a kind of uncanny force, akin to Yeatsian celebrations of the dancer as image. But the authentic strength of the poem centers elsewhere, in its elegiac identification of the dead father, Freud, with the earth, and with all the dead fathers. Freud is Saturn, ancient wisdom, and the rock that cannot be broken—a new earth. His temples will be everywhere, yet H.D. cries out: "only I, I will escape," an escape sanctioned by Freud as the freedom of the woman poet. Though D.H. Lawrence is not even alluded to in "The Master," he enters the poem by negation, since it is transformed into a fierce hymn against Lawrence's vision of sexual release:

no man will be present in those mysteries,
yet all men will kneel,
no man will be potent,
important,
yet all men will feel
what it is to be a woman,
will yearn,
burn,
turn from easy pleasure
to hardship
of the spirit,

men will see how long they have been blind,
poor men
poor man-kind
how long
how long
this thought of the man-pulse has tricked them,
has weakened them,
shall see woman,
perfect.
   ("The Master")

The blindness is precisely Lawrence's in H.D.'s judgment, and it is
hinted at, in muted form, in "The Poet," not so much an elegy for Lawrence
as for her failed relationship with him. What seems clear is that her sexual
self-acceptance, whether Freudian or not, gave her the creative serenity that
made possible the wonderfully controlled, hushed resignation of her wisely
limited farewell to Lawrence:

No,
I don't pretend, in a way, to understand,
nor know you,
nor even see you;

I say,
"I don't grasp his philosophy,
and I don't understand,"

but I put out a hand, touch a cold door,
(we have both come from so far);

I touch something imperishable;
I think,
why should he stay there?
why should he guard a shrine so alone,
so apart,
on a path that leads nowhere?

he is keeping a candle burning in a shrine
where nobody comes,
there must be some mystery
in the air
about him,

he couldn't live alone in the desert,
without vision to comfort him,
there must be voices somewhere.
   ("The Poet")

The wistfulness of that tribute, if it is a tribute, veils the harshness of the critique. A woman can be perfect, but a man cannot, though Lawrence would not learn this. One can imagine his response to H.D.; it would have been violent, but that perhaps would have confirmed her stance, whether sanctioned or unsanctioned by her father and master, Freud.

Ezra Pound

I have brought the great ball of crystal; who can lift it?

—Canto 116

Pound's prime explainer, Hugh Kenner, commenting on the *Cantos*, writes of "the paradox that an intensely topical poem has become archaic without ever having been contemporary: archaic in an honorific sense." Kenner accounts for the paradox by insisting that: "There is no substitute for critical tradition: a continuum of understanding, early commenced. . . . ! Precisely because William Blake's contemporaries did not know what to make of him, we do not know either . . ." As the greatest of antiquarian modernists, Kenner's authority in these judgments is doubtless unassailable. His Pound may well be *the* Pound, even if his Joyce somehow seems less Dublin's Joyce than T.S. Eliot's Joyce. I, in any case, would not care to dispute any critic's Pound. They have their reward, and he has them.

   I do not know many readers who have an equal affection for the *Cantos* and for, say, Wallace Stevens's *An Ordinary Evening in New Haven* or *The*

Auroras of Autumn. Doubtless, again, such differences in poetic taste belong to the accidents of sensibility or to irreconcilable attitudes concerning the relation of poetry to belief. They may indeed belong to more profound distinctions; in judgments as to value that transcend literary preferences. I do not desire to address myself to such matters here. Nor will I consider Pound's politics. The *Cantos* contain material that is not humanly acceptable to me, and if that material is acceptable to others, then they themselves are thereby less acceptable, at least to me.

My subject here, in necessarily curtailed terms, is Pound's relation to poetic tradition in his own language and to Whitman, in particular. Pound's critics have taken him at his word in this regard, but no poet whatsoever can be trusted in his or her own story of poetic origins, even as no man or woman can be relied on to speak with dispassionate accuracy of his or her parents. Perhaps Pound triumphed in his agon with poetic tradition, which is the invariable assertion of all of his critical partisans. But the triumph, if it occurred, was a very qualified one. My own experience as a reader of the *Cantos*, across many years, is that the long poem or sequence is marred throughout by Pound's relative failure to transume or transcend his precursors. Their ancestral voices abound and indeed become more rather than less evident as the sequence continues. Nor is this invariably a controlled allusiveness. Collage, which is handled as metaphor by Marianne Moore and by the Eliot of *The Waste Land*, is a much more literal process in Pound, is more scheme than trope, as it were. The allusive triumph over tradition in Moore's "Marriage" or *The Waste Land* is fairly problematical yet nowhere near so dubious as it is in the *Cantos*. Confronted by a past poetic wealth in figuration, Pound tends to resort to baroque elaborations of the anterior metaphors. What he almost never manages is to achieve an ellipsis of further troping by his own inventiveness at metaphor. He cannot make the voices of Whitman and Browning seem belated, while his own voice manifests what Stevens called an "ever early candor."

I am aware that I am in apparent defiance of the proud Poundian dictum: *Make It New*. Whitman made it new in one way and Browning in another, but Pound's strength was elsewhere. Anglo-American poetic "modernism" was Ezra Pound's revolution, but it seems now only another continuity in the long history of romanticism. Literary history may or may not someday regard Pound as it now regards Abraham Cowley, John Cleveland, and Edmund Waller, luminaries of one era who faded into the common light of another age. But, as a manneristic poet, master of a period style, Pound has his deep affinities to Cowley, Cleveland, and, above all, Waller. He has affinities also though to Dante Gabriel Rossetti, a permanent poet who suffered from belatedness in a mode strikingly akin to that of Pound. Poundian critics tend to regard Rossetti as a kind of embarassing prelude to their hero, but I certainly intend only a tribute to Pound in comparing him to Rossetti. It is, after all, far better to be called the Dante Gabriel Rossetti than the Edmund Waller of your era.

> *Mr. Eliot and I are in agreement, or "belong to the same school of critics," in so far as we both believe that existing works form a complete order which is changed by the introduction of the "really new" work.*
> —Pound, *Active Anthology*

Timeless, or complete, orders are beautiful idealizations and have not the slightest relevance to the actual sorrows of literary influence. Time's disorders are the truth of poetic tradition. Eliot, child of Whitman and Tennyson, preferred to see himself in the timeless order of Virgil and Dante, Pascal and Baudelaire. Pound, brash and natural child of Whitman and Browning, found his idealized forerunners in Arnaut Daniel and Cavalcanti, Villon and Landor. Oedipal ambivalence, which marks Pound's stance toward Whitman, never surfaces in his observations on Cavalcanti and Villon, safely remote not only in time and language but more crucially isolated from the realities of Pound's equivocal relation to his country and compatriots.

I find Whitman quite unrecognizable in nearly every reference Pound makes to him. Our greatest poet and our most elusive, because most figurative, Whitman consistently is literalized by Pound, as though the Whitmanian self could be accepted as a machine rather than as a metaphor. What can be construed in the weird piece of 1909, "What I Feel about Walt Whitman," is a transference so ambivalent that the positive and negative elements defy disentanglement:

> From this side of the Atlantic I am for the first time able to read Whitman, and from the vantage of my education and—if it be permitted a man of my scant years—my world citizenship: I see him America's poet. The only Poet before the artists of the Carmen-Hovey period, or better, the only one of the conventionally recognised 'American Poets' who is worth reading.
>
> He *is* America. His crudity is an exceeding great stench, but it *is* America. He is the hollow place in the rock that echoes with his time. He *does* 'chant the crucial stage' and he is the 'voice triumphant.' He is disgusting. He is an exceedingly nauseating pill, but he accomplishes his mission.
>
> Entirely free from the renaissance humanist ideal of the complete man or from the Greek idealism, he is content to be what

he is, and he is his time and his people. He is a genius because he has vision of what he is and of his function. He knows that he is a beginning and not a classically finished work.

I honour him for he prophesied me while I can only recognise him as a forebear of whom I ought to be proud.

In America there is much for the healing of the nations, but woe unto him of the cultured palate who attempts the dose.

As for Whitman, I read him (in many parts) with acute pain, but when I write of certain things I find myself using his rhythms. The expression of certain things related to cosmic consciousness seems tainted with this maramis.

I am (in common with every educated man) an heir of the ages and I demand my birth-right. Yet if Whitman represented his time in language acceptable to one accustomed to my standard of intellectual-artistic living he would belie his time and nation. And yet I am but one of his 'ages and ages' encrustations' or to be exact an encrustation of the next age. The vital part of my message, taken from the sap and fibre of America, is the same as his.

Mentally I am a Walt Whitman who has learned to wear a collar and a dress shirt (although at times inimical to both). Personally I might be very glad to conceal my relationship to my spiritual father and brag about my more congenial ancestry— Dante, Shakespeare, Theocritus, Villon, but the descent is a bit difficult to establish. And, to be frank, Whitman is to my fatherland (*Patriam quam odi et amo* for no uncertain reasons) what Dante is to Italy and I at my best can only be a strife for a renaissance in America of all the lost or temporarily mislaid beauty, truth, valour, glory of Greece, Italy, England and all the rest of it.

And yet if a man has written lines like Whitman's to the *Sunset Breeze* one has to love him. I think we have not yet paid enough attention to the deliberate artistry of the man, not in details but in the large.

I am immortal even as he is, yet with a lesser vitality as I am the more in love with beauty (if I really do love it more than he did). Like Dante he wrote in the 'vulgar tongue,' in a new metric. The first great man to write in the language of his people.

Et ego Petrarca in lingua vetera scribo, and in a tongue my people understood not.

It seems to me I should like to drive Whitman into the old world. I sledge, he drill—and to scourge America with all the old beauty. (For Beauty *is* an accusation) and with a thousand thongs from Homer to Yeats, from Theocritus to Marcel Schwob. This desire is because I am young and impatient, were I old and wise I should content myself in seeing and saying that these things will come. But now, since I am by no means sure it would be true prophecy, I am fain set my own hand to the labour.

It is a great thing, reading a man to know, not 'His Tricks are not as yet my Tricks, but I can easily make them mine' but 'His message is my message. We will see that men hear it.'

Whitman is at once crude, disgusting, nauseating, and to be read with acute pain but also America's poet, indeed America itself, a genius more vital than the equally immortal Pound and a father one has to love. Let us read this Oedipal fragment just a touch more closely. Its subject is hardly Whitman at all, but rather the United States in 1909, viewed as a country that does not acknowledge its self-exiled bard, Ezra Pound, who had taken up residence in London the year before. As a country that needs to be scourged with/by beauty (a conceit perhaps more Sacher-Masoch than Whitman), the United States (or Whitman) becomes a castrated father, even as the passionate Pound assumes the male function of driving the American vitality into the old world. If this seems crude, it is, but the crudity is certainly not Walt Whitman's.

Though he once assured the world that "Whitman goes bail for the nation," Pound seems to have meant that no one could bail out the nation. Many Poundians have quoted as evidence of their hero's esteem of Whitman a bad little poem of 1913:

A Pact

I make a pact with you, Walt Whitman—
I have detested you long enough.
I come to you as a grown child
Who has had a pig-headed father;
I am old enough now to make friends.
It was you that broke the new wood,
Now is a time for carving.
We have one sap and one root—
Let there be commerce between us.

Truce, the original word in the first line, is more accurate than *pact,* because truly there was a failure in commerce between Whitman and Pound. Whether Pound remembered that Whitman's father was a carpenter, and that Whitman himself had worked with his father at the trade, is beyond surmise.

The root, as Pound perhaps knew, was Emerson. It is no accident that Whitman and Emerson return to Pound together in *The Pisan Cantos*, with Whitman central in the eighty-second and Emerson in the eighty-third of the *Cantos*. Emerson, I think, returns in his own trope of self-identification, the Transparent Eyeball, yet in Pound's voice, since Emerson was at most Pound's American grandfather. But Whitman returns in Whitman's own voice and even in his own image of voice, the "tally," because the obstinate old father's voice remains strong enough to insist on itself:

> "Fvy! in Tdaenmarck efen dh' beasantz gnow him,"
> meaning Whitman, exotic, still suspect
> four miles from Camden
> "O troubled reflections
> "O Throat, O throbbing heart"
> How drawn, O GEA TERRA,
> what draws as thou drawest
> till one sink into thee by an arm's width
> embracing thee. Drawest,
> truly thou drawest.
> Wisdom lies next thee,
> simply, past metaphor.
> Where I lie let the thyme rise
> . . . .
> fluid ΧΘΟΝΟΣ, strong as the undertow
> of the wave receding
> but that a man should live in that further terror, and live
> the loneliness of death came upon me
> (at 3 P.M., for an instant)
> δακρυων
> εντευθεν
> three solemn half notes
> their white downy chests black-rimmed
> on the middle wire
> periplum

Pound begins by recalling his German teacher at the University of Pennsylvania, 40 years before, one Richard Henry Riethmuller, author of *Walt Whitman and the Germans*, an identification I owe to Roy Harvey Pearce. Riethmuller (Pound got the spelling wrong) had contrasted Whitman's fame in the professor's native Denmark to the bard's supposed obscurity in the America of 1905, a contrast that leads Pound to a recall of Whitman's "Out

of the Cradle Endlessly Rocking." Whitman's poem is an elegy for the poetic
self so powerful that any other poet ought to be wary of invoking so great
a hymn of poetic incarnation and disincarnation. Whitman's "O troubled
reflection in the sea! / O throat! O throbbing heart!" is revised by Pound into
"O troubled reflection / O throat, O throbbing heart," with "in the sea" omitted. These are the last two lines of the penultimate stanza of the song of the
bird lamenting his lost mate:

> *O darkness! O in vain!*
> *O I am very sick and sorrowful.*
> *O brown halo in the sky near the moon, drooping upon the sea!*
> *O troubled reflection in the sea!*
> *O throat! O throbbing heart!*
> *And I singing uselessly, uselessly all the night.*

Canto 82 rather movingly has shown the incarcerated poet studying the
nostalgias of his early literary life, while meditating on the unrighteousness
of all wars. A vision of the earth now comes to him, in response to his partly
repressed recall of Whitman's vision of the sea. Marrying the earth is Pound's
counterpart to Whitman's marrying the sea, both in "Out of the Cradle Endlessly Rocking" and in "When Lilacs Last in the Dooryard Bloom'd," and
both brides are at once death and the mother. "Where I lie let the thyme rise,"
perhaps repeating William Blake's similar grand pun on "thyme" and "time,"
is a profound acceptance of the reality principle, with no more idealization
of a timeless order. Whitman returns from the dead even more strongly in
the closing lines of canto 82, where Pound lies down in a fluid time "strong
as the undertow / of the wave receding," which invokes another great elegiac
triumph of Whitman's, "As I Ebb'd with the Ocean of Life." The two song-
birds of "Out of the Cradle," with Whitman their brother making a third,
utter "three solemn half notes" even as the loneliness of death came, for an
instant, on Whitman's son, Pound. Most powerful, to me, is Pound's recall
of Whitman's great image of voice, the tally, from "Lilacs," "Song of Myself,"
and other contexts in the poet of night, death, the mother, and the sea. In
Whitman, the tally counts up the poet's songs as so many wounds, so many
autoerotic gratifications that yet, somehow, do not exclude otherness. Pound,
marrying the earth, realizes his terrible solitude: "man, earth: two halves of
the tally / but I will come out of this knowing no one / either they me."

Kenner is able to read this as commerce between Whitman and Pound
and insists that "the resources in the Canto are Pound's, as are those of Canto
1." But Homer, ultimate ancestor in canto 1, was safely distant. Whitman is
very close in canto 82, and the resources are clearly his. Pound does better
at converting Emerson to his own purposes, a canto later, than he is able to

do with Whitman here. Would the following judgment seem valid to a fully informed and dispassionate reader?

> Pound's faults are superficial, he does convey an image of his time, he has written *histoire morale*, as Montaigne wrote the history of his epoch. You can learn more of twentieth-century America from Pound than from any of the writers who either refrained from perceiving or limited their record to what they had been taught to consider suitable literary expression. The only way to enjoy Pound thoroughly is to concentrate on his fundamental meaning.

This is Pound on Whitman from the *ABC of Reading*, with Pound substituted for Whitman and the twentieth for the nineteenth century. Pound was half right about Whitman; Whitman does teach us his country in his century, but his form and his content are not so split as Pound says, and his fundamental meaning resides in nuance, beautifully shaped in figurative language. Pound's faults are not superficial, and absolutely nothing about our country in this century can be learned from him. He conveys an image only of himself, and the only way to enjoy him is not to seek a fundamental meaning that is not there but to take his drafts and fragments one by one, shattered crystals, but crystalline nevertheless. He had brought the great ball of crystal, of poetic tradition, but it proved too heavy for him to lift.

Marianne Moore

For Plato the only reality that mattered is exemplified best for us in the principles of mathematics. The aim of our lives should be to draw ourselves away as much as possible from the unsubstantial, fluctuating facts of the world about us and establish some communion with the objects which are apprehended by thought and not sense. This was the source of Plato's asceticism. To the extent that Miss Moore finds only allusion tolerable she shares that asceticism. While she shares it she does so only as it may be necessary for her to do so in order to establish a particular reality or, better, a reality of her own particulars.

—Wallace Stevens

Allusion was Marianne Moore's method, a method that was her self. One of the most American of all poets, she was fecund in her progeny—Elizabeth Bishop, May Swenson, and Richard Wilbur being the most gifted among them. Her own American precursors were not Emily Dickinson and Walt Whitman—still our two greatest poets—but the much slighter Stephen Crane, who is echoed in her earliest poems, and, in an oblique way, Edgar Poe, whom she parodied. I suspect that her nearest poetic father, in English, was Thomas Hardy, who seems to have taught her lessons in the mastery of incongruity, and whose secularized version of biblical irony is not far from her own. If we compare her with her major poetic contemporaries—Frost, Stevens, Eliot, Pound, Williams, Aiken, Ransom, Cummings, H.D., Hart Crane—she is clearly the most original American poet of her era, though not quite of the eminence of Frost, Stevens, and Crane. A curious kind of devotional poet, with some authentic affinities to George Herbert, she reminds us implicitly but constantly that any distinction between sacred and secular poetry is only a shibboleth of cultural politics. Someday she will remind us also of what current cultural politics obscure: that any distinction between poetry written by women or poetry by men is a mere polemic, unless it follows on an initial distinction between good and bad poetry. Moore, like Bishop and Swenson, is an extraordinary poetas-poet. The issue of how gender enters into her vision should arise only after the aesthetic achievement is judged as such.

Moore, as all her readers know, to their lasting delight, is the visionary of natural creatures: the jerboa, frigate pelican, buffalo, monkeys, fish, snakes, mongooses, the octopus (actually a trope for a mountain), snail, peacock, whale, pangolin, wood weasel, elephants, racehorses, chameleon, jellyfish, arctic ox (or goat), giraffe, blue bug (another trope, this time for a pony), all of La Fontaine's bestiary, not to mention sea and land unicorns, basilisks, and all the weird, fabulous roster that perhaps only Borges also, among crucial modern writers, celebrates so consistently. There is something of Blake and of the Christopher Smart of *Jubilate Agno* in Moore, though the affinity does not result from influence but rather is the consequence of election. Moore's famous eye, like that of Bishop after her, is not so much a visual gift as it is visionary, for the beasts in her poems are charged with a spiritual intensity that doubtless they possess but that I myself cannot see without the aid of Blake, Smart, and Moore.

I remember always in reading Moore again that her favorite poem was the book of Job. Just as I cannot read Ecclesiastes without thinking of Dr. Johnson, I cannot read certain passages in Job without recalling Marianne Moore:

> But ask now the beasts, and they shall teach thee; and the fowls
> of the air, and they shall tell thee:
> Or speak to the earth, and it shall teach thee: and the fishes of
> the sea shall declare unto thee.
> Who knoweth not in all these that the hand of the Lord hath
> wrought this?
> In whose hand is the soul of every living thing.

This, from chapter 12, is the prelude to the great chant of Yahweh, the voice out of the whirlwind that sounds forth in the frightening magnificence of chapters 38 through 41, where the grand procession of beasts comprehends lions, ravens, wild goats, the wild ass, the unicorn, peacocks, the ostrich, the sublime battlehorse who "saith among the trumpets, Ha, ha," the hawk, the eagle, and at last behemoth and leviathan. Gorgeously celebrating his own creation, Yahweh through the poet of Job engendered another strong poet in Marianne Moore. Of the book of Job, she remarked that its agony was veracious and its fidelity of a force "that contrives glory for ashes."

"Glory for ashes" might be called Moore's ethical motto, the basis for the drive of her poetic will toward a reality of her own particulars. Her poetry, as befitted the translator of La Fontaine and the heir of George Herbert, would be in some danger of dwindling into moral essays, an impossible form for our time, were it not for her wild allusiveness, her zest for quotations, and her essentially anarchic stance, the American and Emersonian insistence on seeing everything in her own way, with "conscientious inconsistency." When her wildness or freedom subsided, she produced an occasional poetic disaster like the patriotic war poems "In Distrust of Merits" and "'Keeping Their World Large.'" But her greatest poems are at just the opposite edge of consciousness: "A Grave," "Novices," "Marriage," "An Octopus," "He 'Digesteth Harde Yron,'" "Elephants," the deceptively light "Tom Fool at Jamaica."

Those seven poems by themselves have an idiosyncratic splendor that restores my faith, as a critic, in what the language of the poets truly is: diction, or choice of words, playing endlessly on the dialectic of denotation and connotation, a dialectic that simply vanishes in all structuralist and poststructuralist ruminations on the supposed priority of "language" over meaning. "The arbitrariness of the signifier" loses its charm when one asks a Gallic psycholinguistifier whether denotation or connotation belongs to the signifier, as opposed to the signified, and one beholds blank incredulity as one's only answer. Moore's best poems give the adequate reply: The play of the signifier is answered always by the play of the signified, because the play of diction, or the poet's will over language, is itself constituted by the endless interchanges of denotation and connotation. Moore, with her rage to order allusion, echo, and quotation in ghostlier demarcations, keener sounds, helps us to realize that the belated modernism of the Gallic proclamation of the death of the author was no less premature than it was, always already, belated.

> Marriage, through which thought does not penetrate, appeared to Miss Moore a legitimate object for art, an art that would not halt from using thought about it, however, as it might want to.

> Against marriage, "this institution, perhaps one should say enter-
> prise"—Miss Moore launched her thought not to have it appear
> arsenaled as in a textbook on psychology, but to stay among apples
> and giraffes in a poem.
>
> —William Carlos Williams

If I had to cite a single poem by Moore as representing all of her powers working together, it would be "Marriage" (1923), superficially an outrageous collage but profoundly a poignant comic critique of every society's
most sacred and tragic institution. As several critics have ventured, this is
Moore's *The Waste Land*, a mosaic of fragments from Francis Bacon, the *Scientific American*, Baxter's *The Saint's Everlasting Rest*, Hazlitt on Burke, William
Godwin, Trollope, *The Tempest*, a book on *The Syrian Christ*, the Bible, Ezra
Pound, and even Daniel Webster (from an inscription on a statue!), and 20
sources more. Yet it is a poem and perhaps is more ruggedly unified than any
other poem of such ambition by Moore.

The poet's own headnote to "Marriage" could not be more diffident:
"Statements that took my fancy which I tried to arrange plausibly." The
arrangement is more than plausible; it is quite persuasive, though it begins
with a parody of the societal *apologia* for marriage:

> This institution,
> perhaps one should say enterprise
> out of respect for which
> one says one need not change one's mind
> about a thing one has believed in,
> requiring public promises
> of one's intention
> to fulfil a private obligation.

No one, I believe, could interpret that opening stance with any exactitude. The substitution of "enterprise" for "institution" qualifies the wryness of
"public promises / of one's intention / to fulfil a private obligation" but adds a
note both of commerce and of the human virtue of taking an initiative. Who
could have anticipated that the next movement of the poem would be this?

> I wonder what Adam and Eve
> think of it by this time,
> this fire-gilt steel
> alive with goldenness;

how bright it shows—
"of circular traditions and impostures,
committing many spoils,"
requiring all one's criminal ingenuity
to avoid!

Like nearly every other quotation in this poem, the two lines from Sir Francis Bacon gain nothing for Moore's own text by being restored to their own context. Steel burned by fire does not exactly brighten into a golden bough, so the "gilt" is there partly as anticipation of "criminal ingenuity." Yet "gilt" is in cognitive sequence with "goldenness" and "bright," even if we rightly expect to behold blackened steel. All who have known marriage (as Moore declined to do) will register an unhappy shudder at the force the Baconian phrases take on when Moore appropriates them. Traditions as treasons become circular and together with impostures can be read here either as performing many despoilments or as investing many gains of previous despoilments. Either way, it might seem as though an ingenuity avoiding this equivocal enterprise could only be taken as criminal by some dogmatist, whether societal or theological.

The poem proceeds to dismiss psychology, since to explain everything is to explain nothing, and then meditates on the beauty, talents, and contrariness of Eve, a meditation that suddenly achieves Paterian intensity:

Below the incandescent stars
below the incandescent fruit,
the strange experience of beauty;
its existence is too much;
it tears one to pieces
and each fresh wave of consciousness
is poison.

The detachment of Moore as watcher is not totally lost but seems (by design) never fully recovered again in the poem. A woman's fine bitterness against the West's endless assault on Eve is felt in Moore's description of the universal mother as "the central flaw" in the experiment of Eden, itself "an interesting impossibility" ecstatically described by Richard Baxter as "the choicest piece of my life." If Baxter's ecstasy (though not his eloquence) is qualified shrewdly by Moore's contextualizations, Eden is nowhere near so scaled down by her as is Adam, whose male pomp is altogether undermined. He is pretty well identified with Satan and like Satan is: "alive with words, / vibrating like a cymbal / touched before it has been struck."

Moore's genius at her method allows her the joy of exemplifying her
borrowings even as she employs them in a corrective polemic against male
slanderings of women:

> "Treading chasms
> on the uncertain footing of a spear,"
> forgetting that there is in woman
> a quality of mind
> which as an instinctive manifestation
> is unsafe,
> he goes on speaking
> in a formal customary strain.

In the first quotation, Hazlitt is praising his precursor Edmund Burke
for a paradoxically certain footing: for power, energy, truth set forth in the
sublime style. Burke is a chasm treader, surefooted as he edges near the abyss.
But men less given to truth than Burke have very uncertain footing indeed,
whether they forget or remember their characteristic brutalities in regard to
a woman's "quality of mind." The poem's "he" therefore goes on speaking of
marriage in Richard Baxter's ecstatic terms, as though marriage itself somehow could become "the saints' everlasting rest." Fatuously joyous, the male is
ready to suffer the most exquisite passage in the poem and perhaps in all of
Moore:

> Plagued by the nightingale
> in the new leaves,
> with its silence—
> not its silence but its silences,
> he says of it:
> "It clothes me with a shirt of fire."
> "He dares not clap his hands
> to make it go on
> lest it should fly off;
> if he does nothing, it will sleep;
> if he cries out, it will not understand."
> Unnerved by the nightingale
> and dazzled by the apple,
> impelled by "the illusion of a fire
> effectual to extinguish fire,"
> compared with which
> the shining of the earth

is but deformity—a fire
"as high as deep
as bright as broad
as long as life itself,"
he stumbles over marriage,
"a very trivial object indeed"
to have destroyed the attitude
in which he stood—.

I hardly know of a more unnerving representation of the male fear and distrust of the female, uncannily combined with the male quandary of being obsessed with, fascinated by, not only the female but the enterprise of marriage as well. Moore imperishably catches the masterpiece of male emotive ambivalence toward the female, which is the male identification of woman and the taboo. Here the nightingale, perhaps by way of Keats's erotic allusions, becomes an emblem of the female, while the male speaker, ravished by the silences of the emblem, becomes Hercules suicidally aflame with the shirt of Nessus. The poor male, "unnerved by the nightingale / and dazzled by the apple," stumbles over the enterprise that is Adam's experiment, marriage:

its fiddlehead ferns,
lotus flowers, opuntias, white dromedaries,
its hippopotamus—
nose and mouth combined
in one magnificent hopper—
its snake and the potent apple.

We again receive what might be called Moore's Paradox: marriage, considered from either the male or female perspective, is a dreadful disaster but as a poetic trope gorgeously shines forth its barbaric splendors. The male, quoting Trollope's *Barchester Towers*, returns us to the image of Hercules and commends marriage "as a fine art, as an experiment, / a duty or as merely recreation." I myself will never get out of my memory Moore's subsequent deadpan definition of marriage as "the fight to be affectionate." With a fine impartiality, the poet has a vision of the agonists in this eternal dispute:

The blue panther with black eyes,
the basalt panther with blue eyes,
entirely graceful—
one must give them the path—.

But this mutual splendor abates quickly, and a rancorous humor emerges:

> He says, "What monarch would not blush
> to have a wife
> with hair like a shaving brush?"
> The fact of woman
> is "not the sound of the flute
> but very poison."
> She says, "Men are monopolists
> of 'stars, garters, buttons
> and other shining baubles'—
> unfit to be the guardians
> of another person's happiness."
> He says, "These mummies
> must be handled carefully—
> 'the crumbs from a lion's meal,
> a couple of shins and the bit of an ear';
> turn to the letter M
> and you will find
> that 'a wife is a coffin.'

This marvelous exchange of diatribes is weirdly stitched together from outrageously heterogeneous "sources," ranging from a parody of *The Rape of the Lock* (in which Moore herself took a hand) to a women's college president's denunciation of the male love of awards and medals on to a surprising misappropriation of a great moment in the prophet Amos, which is then juxtaposed to a brutal remark of Ezra Pound's. Amos associates the lion with Yahweh:

> The lion hath roared, who will not fear? the Lord GOD hath spoken, who can but prophesy?
> Thus saith the LORD; As the shepherd taketh out of the mouth of the lion two legs, or a piece of an ear; so shall the children of Israel be taken out that dwell in Samaria in the corner of a bed, and in Damascus in a couch.

Moore slyly revises the roaring prophet, making the lion every male and the children of Israel every woman. Pound's dictum, that "a wife is a coffin," is presumably placed under the letter *M* for "male" and sorts well with Moore's unfair but strong revision of Amos, since the revision suggests that a wife is a corpse. In order to show that her revisionary zeal is savagely if suavely directed against both sexes (or rather their common frailties), Moore proceeds to dissect the narcissism of men and women alike, until she concludes with the most ironic of her visions in the poem:

"I am such a cow,
if I had a sorrow
I should feel it a long time;
I am not one of those
who have a great sorrow
in the morning
and a great joy at noon";

which says: "I have encountered it
among those unpretentious
protégés of wisdom,
where seeming to parade
as the debater and the Roman,
the statesmanship
of an archaic Daniel Webster
persists to their simplicity of temper
as the essence of the matter:

'Liberty and union
now and forever';
the Book on the writing table;
the hand in the breast pocket."

Webster, hardly unpretentious and wise only in his political cunning, is indeed the message inscribed on his statue: "Liberty and union / now and forever." As a judgment on marriage, it would be a hilarious irony, if we did not wince so much under Moore's not wholly benign tutelage. That book on the writing table, presumably the Bible, is precisely like Webster's hand in the breast pocket, an equivocal emblem, in this context, of the societal benediction on marriage. Moore's own *The Waste Land*, "Marriage" may outlast Eliot's poem as a permanent vision of the West in its long, ironic decline.

T.S. Eliot

The Waste Land, though something less than a unified poem, is Eliot's masterwork, by common agreement. Where few agree is on the question as to just what *The Waste Land* is doing as a poetic performance. Is it a lament for Western cultural decline, for a Europe in retreat from Christianity? Or is it a very American elegy for the self, in direct descent from Walt Whitman's magnificent "When Lilacs Last in the Dooryard Bloom'd"? Clearly the second, I would insist, though mine remains a minority view.

Eliot's own notes to *The Waste Land* are frequently outrageous, never more so than when they explicate the song of the hermit thrush by remarking, "Its 'water-dripping song' is justly celebrated." Why yes, particularly when the hermit thrush sings its Song of Death in Whitman's "Lilacs" elegy. Ostensibly mourning the martyred Lincoln, "Lilacs" more pervasively both celebrates and laments the Whitmanian poetic self. Eliot's poethood, and not Western civilization, is the elegiac center of *The Waste Land*. Personal breakdown is the poem's true subject, shrewdly masked as the decline and fall of Christian culture in post–World War I Europe.

Such a judgment, on my part, hardly renders *The Waste Land* a less interesting or aesthetically eminent poem (or series of poems, or fragments). Hardly an escape from either emotion or from personality, *The Waste Land* seems a monument to the emotional despair of a highly individual romantic personality, one in full continuity with Shelley, Tennyson, and Whitman, who are far closer to the poem than are Eliot's chosen precursors: Dante, Baudelaire, and Jules Laforgue.

Northrop Frye followed Eliot himself in reading *The Waste Land* as a poem of Christian redemption. I think that Eleanor Cook is more accurate in her subtle emphasis on the poem as a representation of exile and of private grief. No one is saved in *The Waste Land*, any more than Lincoln or Whitman is saved in "When Lilacs Last in the Dooryard Bloom'd." Both grand elegies for the self are American songs of death, including the death-in-life of poetic crisis.

The Waste Land is an American self-elegy masking as a mythological romance, a romantic crisis poem pretending to be an exercise in Christian irony. Mask and pretense, like the invention of more congenial fathers and ancestors, are customary poetic tropes and certainly not to be censured. They are part of any poet's magic or personal superstition, and they help to get authentic poems written. *The Waste Land*, rather than *Four Quartets* or the verse dramas, is Eliot's major achievement, a grand gathering of great fragments and indisputably the most influential poem written in English in our century. I read it, on evidence internal and external, as being essentially a revision of Whitman's final great achievement, "When Lilacs Last in the Dooryard Bloom'd," ostensibly an elegy for Lincoln but more truly the poet's lament for his own poethood. Elegy rather than brief epic or quest-romance, *The Waste Land* thus enters the domain of mourning and melancholia, rather than that of civilization and its discontents. Many of the links between Eliot's and Whitman's elegies for the poetic self have been noted by a series of exegetes starting with S. Musgrove and continuing with John Hollander and myself and then younger critics, including Gregory S. Jay and Cleo McNelly Kearns. Rather than repeat Cleo Kearns, I intend to speculate here on the place of *The Waste Land* in romantic tradition, particularly in regard to its inescapable precursor, Whitman.

In his essay, "The *Pensées* of Pascal" (1931), Eliot remarked on Pascal's adversarial relation to his true precursor, Montaigne:

> One cannot destroy Pascal, certainly; but of all authors Montaigne is one of the least destructible. You could as well dissipate a fog by flinging hand-grenades into it. For Montaigne is a fog, a gas, a fluid, insidious element. He does not reason, he insinuates, charms, and influences.

Walt Whitman, too, is "a fluid, insidious element," a poet who "insinuates, charms, and influences." And he is the darkest of poets, despite his brazen self-advertisements and his passionate hopes for his nation. *Song of Myself,* for all its joyous epiphanies, chants also of the waste places:

> Of the turbid pool that lies in the autumn forest,
> Of the moon that descends the steeps of the soughing twilight,
> Toss, sparkles of day and dusk—toss on the black stems that
> decay in the muck,
> Toss to the moaning gibberish of the dry limbs.

I turn to the most rugged of his self-accusations, in the astonishing "Crossing Brooklyn Ferry":

> It is not upon you alone the dark patches fall,
> The dark threw its patches down upon me also,
> The best I had done seem'd to me blank and suspicious,
> My great thoughts as I supposed them, were they not in reality
> meagre?
> Nor is it you alone who know what it is to be evil,
> I am he who knew what it was to be evil,
> I too knotted the old knot of contrariety,
> Blabb'd, blush'd, resented, lied, stole, grudg'd,
> Had guile, anger, lust, hot wishes I dared not speak,
> Was wayward, vain, greedy, shallow, sly, cowardly, malignant,
> The wolf, the snake, the hog, not wanting in me,
> The cheating look, the frivolous word, the adulterous wish, not
> wanting,

Refusals, hates, postponements, meanness, laziness, none of these
wanting,
Was one with the rest, the days and haps of the rest,
Was call'd by my nighest name by clear loud voices of young men
as they saw me approaching or passing,
Felt their arms on my neck as I stood, or the negligent leaning of
their flesh against me as I sat,
Saw many I loved in the street or ferry-boat or public assembly,
yet never told them a word,
Lived the same life with the rest, the same old laughing, gnawing,
sleeping,
Play'd the part that still looks back on the actor or actress,
The same old role, the role that is what we make it, as great as we
like,
Or as small as we like, or both great and small.

The barely concealed allusions to Milton's Satan and to *King Lear*
strengthen Whitman's catalog of vices and evasions, preparing the poet
and his readers for the darker intensities of the great *Sea-Drift* elegies and
"Lilacs," poems that are echoed everywhere in Eliot's verse but particularly
in "The Death of Saint Narcissus," *The Waste Land*, and "The Dry Salvages."
Many critics have charted these allusions, but I would turn consideration of
Eliot's agon with Whitman to the question: Why Whitman? It is poetically
unwise to go down to the waterline or go to the headland with Walt Whitman, for then the struggle takes place in an arena where the poet who found
his identifying trope in the sea drift cannot lose.

An answer must be that the belated poet does not choose his trial by
landscape or seascape. It is chosen for him by his precursor. Browning's
quester in "Childe Roland to the Dark Tower Came" is as overdetermined
by Shelley as Eliot is overdetermined by Whitman in *The Waste Land*,
which is indeed Eliot's version of "Childe Roland," as it is Eliot's version
of Percivale's quest in Tennyson's "The Holy Grail," a poem haunted by
Keats in the image of Galahad. "Lilacs" is everywhere in *The Waste Land*:
in the very lilacs bred out of the dead land, in the song of the hermit
thrush in the pine trees, and most remarkably in the transumption of
Whitman walking down to where the hermit thrush sings, accompanied
by two companions walking beside him, the thought of death and the
knowledge of death:

Then with the knowledge of death as walking one side of me,
And the thought of death close-walking the other side of me,

And I in the middle as with companions, and as holding the
hands of companions,
I fled forth to the hiding receiving night that talks not,
Down to the shores of the water, the path by the swamp in the
dimness,
To the solemn shadowy cedars and ghostly pines so still.

The "crape-veil'd women" singing their dirges through the night for Lincoln are hardly to be distinguished from Eliot's "murmur of maternal lamen-
tation," and Whitman's "tolling tolling bells' perpetual clang" goes on tolling
reminiscent bells in *The Waste Land,* as it does in "The Dry Salvages." Yet all
this is only a first-level working of the influence process, of interest mostly as
a return of the repressed. Deeper, almost beyond analytical modes as yet available to criticism, is Eliot's troubled introjection of his nation's greatest and
inescapable elegiac poet. "Lilacs" has little to do with the death of Lincoln
but everything to do with Whitman's ultimate poetic crisis, beyond which his
strongest poetry will cease. *The Waste Land* has little to do with neo-Christian
polemics concerning the decline of Western culture and everything to do
with a poetic crisis that Eliot could not quite surmount, in my judgment,
since I do not believe that time will confirm the estimate that most contemporary critics have made of *Four Quartets.*

The decisive moment or negative epiphany of Whitman's elegy centers
on his giving up of the tally, the sprig of lilac that is the synecdoche for his
image of poetic voice, which he yields up to death and to the hermit thrush's
song of death. Eliot's parallel surrender in "What the Thunder Said" is to ask
"what have we given?" where the implicit answer is "a moment's surrender,"
a negative moment in which the image of poetic voice is achieved only as
one of Whitman's "retrievements out of the night." In his essay on Pascal,
Eliot says of Montaigne, a little resentfully but with full accuracy, that "he
succeeded in giving expression to the skepticism of *every* human being," presumably including Pascal, and Shakespeare, and even T.S. Eliot. What did
Whitman succeed in expressing with equal universality? Division between
"myself" and "the real me" is surely the answer:

Looks with its sidecurved head curious what will come next,
Both in and out of the game, and watching and wondering at it.

Thomas Stearns Eliot, looking with side-curved head, both in and
out of the game, has little in common with Walt Whitman, one of the
roughs, an American, yet almost can be identified with that American
"Me myself."

The line of descent from Shelley and Keats through Browning and Tennyson to Pound and Eliot would be direct, were it not for the intervention
of the genius of the shores of America, the poet of *Leaves of Grass*. Whitman
enforces on Pound and Eliot the American difference, which he had inherited from Emerson, the fountain of our eloquence and of our pragmatism.
Most reductively defined, the American poetic difference ensues from a sense
of acute isolation, both from an overwhelming space of natural reality and
from an oppressive temporal conviction of belatedness, of having arrived after
the event. The inevitable defense against nature is the Gnostic conviction
that one is no part of the creation, that one's freedom is invested in the primal abyss. Against belatedness, defense involves an immersion in allusiveness,
hardly for its own sake but in order to reverse the priority of the cultural, pre-
American past. American poets from Whitman and Dickinson onward are
more like Milton than Milton is, and so necessarily they are more profoundly
Miltonic than even Keats or Tennyson was compelled to be.

What has wasted the land of Eliot's elegiac poem is neither the malady
of the Fisher King nor the decline of Christianity, and Eliot's own psychosex-
ual sorrows are not very relevant either. The precursors' strength is the illness
of *The Waste Land*; Eliot, after all, can promise to show us "fear in a handful
of dust" only because the monologist of Tennyson's *Maud* already has cried
out: "Dead, long dead, / Long dead! / And my heart is a handful of dust."
Even more poignantly, Eliot is able to sum up all of Whitman's extraordinary
"As I Ebb'd with the Ocean of Life" in the single line: "These fragments I
have shored against my ruins," where the fragments are not only the verse
paragraphs that constitute the text of *The Waste Land* but crucially are also
Whitman's floating sea drift:

Me and mine, loose windrows, little corpses,
Froth, snowy white, and bubbles,
(See, from my dead lips the ooze exuding at last,
See, the prismatic colors glistening and rolling,)
Tufts of straw, sands, fragments,
Buoy'd hither from many moods, one contradicting another.
From the storm, the long calm, the darkness, the swell,
Musing, pondering, a breath, a briny tear, a dab of liquid or soil,
Up just as much out of fathomless workings fermented and
thrown,
A limp blossom or two, torn, just as much over waves floating,
drifted at random,
Just as much for us that sobbing dirge of Nature,
Just as much whence we come that blare of the cloud—trumpets,

We, capricious, brought hither we know not whence, spread out
before you,
You up there walking or sitting,
Whoever you are, we too lie in drifts at your feet.

"Tufts of straw, sands, fragments" are literally "shored" against Whitman's
ruins, as he wends "the shores I know," the shores of America to which,
Whitman said, Emerson had led all of us, Eliot included. Emerson's essays,
Eliot pugnaciously remarked, "are already an encumbrance," and so they
were, and are, and evermore must be for an American writer, but inescapable encumbrances are also stimuli, as Pascal learned in regard to the overwhelming Montaigne.

Elizabeth Bishop

In her early poem "The Unbeliever," Elizabeth Bishop juxtaposed three
poets (as I allegorize it) or else kinds of poets, in the figures of cloud,
seagull, and unbeliever. The cloud is introspective or even solipsistic: a William Wordsworth or a Wallace Stevens. The gull is a visionary in a tower: a
Shelley or a Hart Crane. The unbeliever, dreaming catastrophe, is an Emily
Dickinson or an Elizabeth Bishop. Where Stevens or Crane asserts the
power of the poet's mind over the sea or universe of death, Bishop observes
the sea accurately in her dream:

which was, "I must not fall.
The spangled sea below wants me to fall.
It is hard as diamonds; it wants to destroy us all."

Though she stemmed from Wordsworth and Stevens as well as from
Dickinson and Marianne Moore, Elizabeth Bishop shied away from celebrating the powers of poetry, which she judged sublimely "useless." One sus-
pects she meant "useless" as Oscar Wilde meant it: to be free of moralizing
purposes.

Bishop is one of the major American poets, the peer of Whitman and
Dickinson, Frost and Stevens, Eliot and Hart Crane. She is so meticulous and
so original that she tends to be both underread and rather weakly misread.
Most frequently she is praised for her "eye," as though she were a master of
optics. But her actual achievement is to see what cannot quite be seen and to
say what cannot quite be said.

The influence of Wallace Stevens on her work rendered Bishop rather
uneasy, and she would like to have been considered a disciple of Marianne
Moore, her friend and mentor. But poets are chosen *by* their precursors: They

do not choose. Stevens's greatest poetry gives us what he called "the hum of thoughts evaded in the mind," and so does Bishop's. Moore, endlessly curious about *things*, created a mosaic of impressions, brilliantly vivid. With Stevens and Bishop, we are in a cosmos of imagined things, things taken up into the mind. Stevens's massive aesthetic broodings are scaled down and somewhat ironized in Bishop, but her mode of reflection essentially is his. And her sense of the poet's predicament is also his: that we live in a place that is not our own and, much more, not ourselves.

"At the Fishhouses" is Bishop at her most memorable, no longer an unbeliever but "a believer in total immersion." Like Wordsworth returning to Tintern Abbey, there to exchange experiential loss for imaginative gain, Bishop goes back to Nova Scotia, where she had lived for a time in childhood, with her maternal grandparents. The long, first verse paragraph is held together by an imagery of gloaming: "All is silver." An "apparent translucence" is enhanced by the iridescence of the remnants of fish, the sequinlike fish scales that adhere to the old fisherman, a friend of Bishop's late grandfather.

A brief, six-line transitional section takes us from "thin silver / tree trunks" to the gray stones in the water. In the long third verse-paragraph, we move from the "all is silver" vision to the grayness of stone and icy water. If the silver is the emblem of experiential loss, then the gray ambivalently suggests an imaginative gain that is dangerous and potentially hurtful. Water and stones burn with "a dark gray flame":

> It is like what we imagine knowledge to be:
> dark, salt, clear, moving, utterly free,
> drawn from the cold hard mouth
> of the world, derived from the rocky breasts
> forever, flowing and drawn, and since
> our knowledge is historical, flowing, and flown.

Translucence is lost, and no present knowing is gained in its place. Yet the utter freedom of that "flowing, and flown" has to be an imaginative value, an achievement of a fully articulated poem.

"The End of March," which I think is Bishop's supreme poem, culminates on a wonderful trope of "the lion sun," Stevensian but turned against Stevens's figure of thought. In Stevens, the lion is emblematic of poetry as a destructive force or again of the poet imposing the power of his mind over the universe of death. The great culmination of this figure is in *An Ordinary Evening in New Haven*:

Say of each lion of the spirit
It is a cat if a sleek transparency
That shines with a nocturnal shine alone.
The great cat must stand potent in the sun.

That lion sun is Whitmanian: It represents an American sublime. Affectionately, Bishop answers Stevens with a playful difference, more like Dickinson or Moore than like Whitman:

They could have been teasing the lion sun,
except that now he was behind them
a sun who'd walked the beach the last low tide,
making those big, majestic paw-prints,
who perhaps had batted a kite out of the sky to play with.

This lion sun is poetry as a playful force and not a destructive one. Bishop's wit, never more playful, is never more luminous. To the stark shore odes of Whitman and of Stevens she has added a postlude, as memorable in its mode as Whitman and Stevens were in theirs.

PETER SCHMIDT

Paterson *and Epic Tradition*

At times there is no other way to assert the truth than by stating our
failure to achieve it.

—William Carlos Williams

Epic poems are like the cities of Rome and New York: all roads lead to
them. Similarly, for a reader of Williams' work, all roads lead to *Paterson*, or
away from it. It is impossible not to treat Williams' earlier work in prose and
in poetry, despite its diversity, as a prelude to the epic poem that occupied so
much of Williams' energy in the 1940s and 1950s. The reader cannot help
but see the earlier work as a trying out of various ways of writing that would
be rolled up into a sum in *Paterson*. And it is hard not to treat Williams' later
work as a response to *Paterson*, even if a few of the poems he published in the
1950s were absorbed in the last installment of *Paterson* in 1958.

Like several of his Modernist contemporaries, in the later decades of
his life Williams dreamed of a collection of poems that would form one long
poem, "The Complete Collected Exercises Toward A Possible Poem," as he
called it.[1] And *Paterson* seems like a (large) scale model that Williams used
to work out the possibilities of synthesis. His use of the infinitive tense in
setting his goal in the poem's preface ("To make a start, / out of particulars /
and make them general, rolling / up the sum, by defective means—" [*P*, 3])
suggests not only the epic immensity of his task but the fact that this credo

From *William Carlos Williams, the Arts, and Literary Tradition*, pp. 173–205. Copyright ©
1988 by Louisiana State University Press.

does not apply to *Paterson* alone. The challenge of the poem's unity would also be the challenge of the unity of all Williams' work; if, like Sisyphus' attempt to roll a boulder up a hill, the task proved impossible, far more than just the failure of one long poem would be implied. Williams' faith in the coherence of his entire enterprise would be jeopardized.

This chapter approaches the site of *Paterson* from several directions, on the principle that such diversity will give a better sense of the lay of the land. . . . Williams' mixture of art and literary traditions is emphasized, on the principle that like the "city" and the "man" in *Paterson*, the poem itself is an "interpenetration, both ways" (*P*, 3). Crucial influences of Dada on the poem are examined first, from the notorious library-burning episode in Book Three and the grotesque mock-pastoral poetry of Book Four, where Dadaist influences surface most dramatically, to other episodes where Dada's subversive pressure is largely hidden underground. The evolving role of Dada's influence for the overall plan of the epic is considered next, with emphasis on how during the course of composition Williams gave the poem two thoroughly different endings, first with Book Four in 1951 and then with Book Five in 1958, thus radically altering our sense of the "plot" of the poem and of its relation to epic tradition. The chapter concludes with a meditation on the meaning of the collage form as Williams uses it in *Paterson*—both the contradictions between Cubist and Dadaist versions of the form and the larger, ideological implications of choosing such a form for an epic about an American industrial city.

*   *   *

In the fall of 1936 a translation of a Dadaist diary appeared in *transition*, one of William Carlos Williams' favorite periodicals at the time, that may have influenced two of the most famous passages in *Paterson*, the flood and the fire episodes in Book Three. The work was excerpted from writings of Hugo Ball published in Germany in 1927 that dated from 1916 and 1917, when Ball and Tristan Tzara were two of the founding members of Zurich Dada. Entitled "Dada Fragments," the *transition* pieces were selected and translated by the editor of the magazine, Eugene Jolas, who had turned his publication into an American port of entry for the French Surrealists, James Joyce, and other European avant-garde writers. Jolas also thought of *transition* as a museum and exhibition gallery for documents relating to the then-defunct European Dada movement. By the 1930s, those manuscripts needed protection: Dada's obstreperous demonstrations had faded from the European scene as suddenly as if they had marched down one of the narrow streets of Paris, Cologne, or Zurich and then vanished around a corner.

The excerpts from Ball's diary that Jolas published in 1936 are not particularly original Dadaisms, for they all lack the telegraphic urgency that was Dada's most arresting feature. Ball's entries read more like private, lapidary epigrams, and one wonders whether he didn't polish them up a bit before publishing them. Several of Ball's statements in *transition*, nonetheless, are of particular interest for the reader of Williams' work. They provide us with a succinct example not only of how Dadaist ideas influenced *Paterson* but also of how Williams struggled to integrate the legacy of his Dadaist work with that of his other writing styles, particularly the reassessment of traditional literary forms that characterized his work in Precisionist and Cubist veins.

Echoing Dada's general determination to scramble all logically ordered syntax, Ball wrote in his June 18, 1916, entry that "We have developed the plasticity of the word to a point which can hardly be surpassed. This result was achieved at the price of the logically constructed, rational sentence. . . . People may smile, if they want to; language will thank us for our zeal. . . . We have charged the word with forces and energies which made it possible for us to rediscover the evangelical concept of the 'word' (logos) as a magical complex of images."[2] This call to disrupt rational sentences ought to have reminded Williams of "Dada Soulève Tout" in *The Little Review*. That tract had also called for the derangement of syntax, but unlike Ball's it practiced the heresies that it preached. Such works served as precedents for Williams a decade later, when he composed the jumble of broken sentences in *Paterson*, Book Three, to represent the debris of dead clichés that blocked his search for a living language. . . . Williams calls this page "a sort of muck, a detritus, / in this case—a pustular scum, a decay, a choking / lifelessness" (*P*, 140). This excerpt from *Paterson*, Ball's diary entry, the *Little Review* announcement, Tzara's 1918 manifesto, and other similar Dada pieces all have the same motive for disordering syntax and linear reading: they spit out a flood of things once known and believed but now thrown up in disgust and despair.

A later entry of Ball's in *transition* bears even more directly on *Paterson*, particularly the library-burning episode in Book Three. At that point in the poem, the local Paterson library is an Inferno packed with dead thoughts, "books / that is, men in hell" who "reign over the living." To overthrow their rule he proposes to fight their deadly hellfire with a fire of his own, writing that will obliterate the past in a great firestorm: "The writing / should be a relief, // relief from the conditions / which as we advance become—a fire, // a destroying fire." The spark that will start the conflagration is laughter: "A drunkenness of flames . . . a multiformity of laughter." The past is mocked and then cremated, thus clearing space for the myriad new examples of beauty:

                                      Papers
(consumed) scattered to the winds. Black.
The ink burned white, metal white. So be it.
. . . .
Hell's fire. Fire. Sit your horny ass
down. What's your game? Beat you
at your own game, Fire. Outlast you:
Poet Beats Fire at Its Own Game! The bottle!
the bottle! the bottle! the bottle! I
give you the bottle!
      (*P*, 113–18)

The birth of spring in *Spring and All* (1923) was similarly preceded by a drunken, violent upheaval: "The imagination, intoxicated by prohibitions, rises to drunken heights to destroy the world. Let it rage, let it kill" (*CP1*, 179).

The following excerpts from Ball's diary in *transition* may have inspired Williams to make the library in Book Three a synecdoche for the vaguer world of *Spring and All* and to shift his symbolic liberating action from murder to arson: "*January 9, 1917*—We should burn all libraries and allow to remain only that which every one knows by heart. A beautiful age of the legend would then begin . . . *March 30, 1917*—The new art is sympathetic because in an age of total disruption it has conserved the will-to-the-image; because it is inclined to force the image."[3] Admittedly, in *Paterson* Williams does not advocate a return to oral formulaic literature and innocent audiences, as Ball does; he stresses what Ball calls the "will-to-the-image," the difficult necessity of inventing or seeking out new forms of the Beautiful Thing, the "radiant gist that / resists the final crystallization" (*P*, 109). But other assumptions in the Williams and Ball passages seem similar, most notably the premise that no search can be begun until the ground is violently cleared. Moreover, the use of a library by both writers to represent decadent traditional culture is a striking parallel, because the usual examples of such decadence for the Dadaist were public monuments, art museums, churches, government buildings, and the marketplace, not libraries.

When precedents for Williams' symbolic destruction of the library in *Paterson* have been discussed, the Dada movement has been mentioned casually, if at all, and then usually in reference to Antonin Artaud, who came to Paris in 1920, followed Dada street theater, and joined the Surrealists in 1924, publishing articles in *La Revolution Surréaliste* and making a living as a stage and film actor.[4] The Artaud connection is stressed because Williams mentions him in *Paterson* during the flood scene and its Dadaist jumble of textual fragments. Williams praised Artaud for the purity of his Dadaist principles;

like Ball, Artaud had demanded that masterpieces be "broken apart" and "destroyed" to allow literature to become more "plastic" so that it could take on the imprint of contemporary life: "Masterpieces of the past are good for the past: they are not good for us.... We must get rid of our superstitious valuations of texts and written poetry. Written poetry is worth reading once, and then should be destroyed. Let the dead poets make way for others. Then we might even come to see that it is our veneration for what has already been created, however beautiful and valid it may be, that petrifies us, deadens our responses, and prevents us from making contact with that underlying power, call it thought-energy, the life force." Elsewhere, Artaud had written, "The library at Alexandria can be burnt down. There are forces above and beyond papyrus: we may temporarily be deprived of our ability to discover these forces, but their energy will not be suppressed.... [A] culture without space or time, restrained only by the capacity of our own nerves, will reappear with all the more energy."[5] Striking as these passages are for their parallels with Williams' thought (Artaud's ideal of "contact," for example, must have been particularly intriguing for Williams), the importance of Artaud's influence on *Paterson* is easy to overstate, given the fact that the above passages were published in 1938 and that Williams had had much earlier contact with these same Dadaist principles through *291, 391, The Little Review, transition*, and other magazines. Artaud did not give Williams new ideas so much as eloquently recall old ones.

Williams acknowledged his debt to the founders of Dada throughout Books Three and Four of *Paterson*, though always in a more oblique way than his citation of Artaud. Of the destroying fire in Book Three, for example, he says that it gives "relief" from the oppressive past that the library represents (*P*, 113). This recalls the definition of Dada that Williams improvised in *The Great American Novel* in 1923: "It is the apotheosis of relief. Dadaism in one of its prettiest modes: *rien rien rien*" (*I*, 173). That definition was in turn inspired by Francis Picabia, who published a tract in *391* in 1920 declaring that all Dadaists desire to know "*rien rien rien*" so that their art will be truly spontaneous; it was quoted in *New York Dada* in 1921.[6]

What may be another buried tribute to Picabia and the early Dadaists in *Paterson* Three alludes to a little piece Picabia brought out in André Breton's proto-Surrealist magazine *Littérature* in 1923. "What I like," Picabia boasted, "is to invent, to imagine, to make myself a new man every moment, then forget him, forget everything. We should be equipped with a special eraser, gradually effacing our works and the memory of them."[7] Similarly, in *Paterson*, Book Three, Section III, Williams hoped that the flood would destroy the past and allow him to begin afresh: "how to begin to find a shape—to begin to begin again, / ... / ... The leaf torn from / the calendar. All forgot" (*P*, 140). This description may seem like a general paraphrase of Dada's belief that memory should be obliterated, but mixed in with Williams' Dadaist praise of amnesia is what may be a specific reference to Picabia's analogy of erasure: "It is dangerous to leave written that which is badly written. A chance word, upon paper, may destroy the world. Watch carefully and erase, while the power is still yours, I say to myself, for all that is put down, once it escapes, may rot its way into a thousand minds, the corn become a black smut, and all libraries, of necessity, be burned to the ground as a consequence" (*P*, 129). At first it may seem that only the badly written is to be erased, but when Williams' fire storm appeared in Book Three it consumed the library's treasure and trash alike.

Most deeply buried of all the allusions to Dada in *Paterson*, however, is perhaps the most personal of all the sources of inspiration for Williams. In 1916 three American poets, Marjorie Allen Sieffert, Harold Witter Bynner, and Arthur Davison Ficke, were involved in a quintessentially Dadaist literary hoax, when under the pseudonyms of "Emanuel Morgan" and "Anne Knish" they published a parodic volume of avant-garde verse called *Spectra: A Book of Poetic Experiments* and then, a year later, participated in a special issue of the little magazine *Others*, edited by Williams and Alfred Kreymborg. Williams became a correspondent with Sieffert, who used "Elijah Hay" as a pseudonym, and when in 1918 the Spectric hoax was exposed, Williams greatly enjoyed the joke, even though it had partly been at his own expense. One of the Spectric manifestos in *Others* is particularly relevant to *Paterson*; it is the single most important source for Williams' library-burning episode:

Prism on the Present State of Poetry

Knish:—
   Out of a cradling has there come a sunset?
   Oh for the fellowship when once in Alexandria
   The world of learning burned!
Morgan:—
   Laughter, dear friends, will do for kindling;
   And we shall wear ridiculous beads of flame
   To tinkle toward the corners of the world.
   Slapping with light the faces of old fools.[8]

Not only does this passage connect laughter and fire, as *Paterson* does, but it also raises the issue of violence, an attempt to disrupt the decline of all ideas in time, from the promise of their "cradling" to the decadence of "old fools."

The American sources for the poem's satire become much more strongly emphasized in Book Four, Section I, which presents a mock pastoral (complete with attempted homosexual seduction) staged by Dr. Paterson's alter ego, the lesbian poetaster Corydon. Several critics, especially Paul Mariani and Jay Grover-Rogoff, have noted the many allusions to Hart Crane's epic *The Bridge* in this section, as if Williams were simultaneously paying homage to an earlier attempt to render Manhattan in epic poetry and stressing that rival's decadence and failure.[9] Just as relevant for a reading of this section, however, is the parodic machine art of Picabia and Duchamp, particularly its emphasis on sterility, greed, and meaningless repetition:

> While in the tall
> buildings (sliding up and down) is where
> the money's made
> up and down
>   directed missiles
> in the greased shafts of the tall buildings
> They stand torpid in cages, in violent motion
> unmoved
> but alert!
>   predatory minds, un-
> affected
>   UNINCONVENIENCED
>   unsexed, up
> and down (without wing motion) This is how
> the money's made . . . using such plugs.
>   (*P*, 165)

Passages such as this one overlay allusions to Crane (especially the "Proem" in *The Bridge*) with references to Picabia's and Duchamp's work, most notably Duchamp's *The Large Glass* and Picabia's *Prostitution universelle* and *Portrait d'une jeune fille americaine*, the latter two satiric portraits of Americans as a spark plug and various kinds of pistons. . . . Voices upon voices from Williams' contacts with the Dadaists in the 1920s and 1930s echo in Books Three and Four, with the most important influence, New York Dada, being the most thoroughly disguised, and the most recent influence, Artaud, given more prominence.

* * *

Excavating such buried allusions within *Paterson* should not become an exercise in critical treasure hunting but should be undertaken because it allows us to pose the following crucial question: granted Dada's pervasive presence underneath the surface of the poem, especially in the third and fourth books, to what degree can it help us better understand the structure of the epic as a whole? By recalling Dada's most colorful slogans, of course, Williams involves himself in an inextricable paradox: he shows that he can't forget Dada's ideal of forgetfulness. Furthermore, Williams' very act of attempting an epic is a profound reenactment of literary tradition, an affirmation of the past's enduring power. Hence Williams' allusions to Dada in *Paterson* not only raise the question of what role Dadaist ideas could play in the overall organization of his poem, particularly its use of collage; they also require us to consider how Williams' long poem remembers epic tradition even though it may also give the illusion of erasing or repressing it.

In the traditional epic, the action begins *in medias res*, with the hero and his companions farthest from their goal. The narrative approaches its end as the hero approaches his home: Odysseus' reformed Ithaca, mankind's Christian paradise regained, William Wordsworth's mature retrospection, Whitman's transference of his quest for the union of body and soul to the reader. Conventionally, epic narrative also has two points of view. One is prospective and dramatic, recreating the past adventures of the book's hero. The other is retrospective and (relatively) static, magisterially framing the action to let us know not only that its events have previously occurred but also that their meaning and their part in the larger story of the hero's race have already been defined. This retrospective point of view can be said to operate even in epics like Vergil's *Aeneid* or John Milton's *Paradise Lost*, which seem at first glance to end still in the middle of their stories. In both cases, the endings allude by their self-conscious incompleteness to the larger story of which they are a part. For Vergil, this story is the rise of Augustan Rome, which had already occurred when he composed the *Aeneid*; for Milton, it is God's judgment of man, which will occur at the end of time. From Augustus Caesar's point of view in history or God's point of view above history, the epics are retrospective. In the romantic period, the epic's prospective and retrospective points of view began to dissolve into one, creating an epic without a frame in which the poet's developing consciousness became the one subject in romantic art that had the nobility and universality traditional epic narratives required. Some indication of this redefinition of epic retrospection by romanticism can be seen in Wordsworth, who planned a four-part epic describing his growth as a poet but was able to finish only its prelude. As the opening lines of *The Prelude* make clear, however, the poem is narrated retrospectively, from the vantage point of the poet's mature consciousness. It is English romanticism's version of the retrospective epic. American romanticism was more radical. Whitman's egotistically sublime "Song of Myself" is also a poem about the poet's developing consciousness, but unlike Wordsworth's it is brazenly ahistorical and open-ended and thus carries to an extreme the process of conflating the twin points of view that had been begun by Wordsworth. Whitman's poet-protagonist does not have a past and a present identity so much as two selves perpetually in flux, the natural "Me myself" and the artificial (or social) "the other I am." And as is well known, the last sentence of the poem in the 1855 edition did not end with a period. This was because Whitman's quest itself could not end; it was *periodic*, to be continued by each reader who takes Whitman up on his challenge to make himself the hero of his own life. Twentieth-century epics, most notably Pound's, have now generally made these unfinished and unfinishable histories of the growth of the poet's mind the norm for the epic, so that any firm separation between retrospective and prospective points of view becomes impossible. Eliot's *Four Quartets* and James Merrill's *The Changing Light at Sandover* are calculated exceptions to this generalization; they both pointedly try to reestablish the extratemporal perspective and formal closure of Dante's long poem as a model.

Recently several critics have tied *Paterson* firmly to romantic epic tradition by stressing that the protagonist, Dr. Paterson, gradually matures during the course of the poem. In their account, Dr. Paterson possesses an idealized, mythic vision of the Beautiful Thing at the opening of the poem, but he loses it and then slowly learns to search instead for a humbler, more time-bound vision that concedes that in modern Paterson beauty will necessarily be imperfect and impermanent. James Breslin in particular has drawn our attention to the implications of the scene involving Dr. Paterson and a poor black woman that follows the fire storm in Book Three. Dr. Paterson encounters the woman in a basement and suddenly recognizes in her all the primal power that the library lacked—power for which he has been searching since the beginning of the poem. The woman becomes a battered Kora or Persephone figure, imperfect and even filthy but carrying within her all of nature's powers of renewal. "I can't be half gentle enough, / half tender enough / toward you," he says, humbled and awed, and then sings, "BRIGHTEN / the cor / ner / where you are!" (*P*, 128). ("Corner" is split by a line break here to emphasize the parallel with "core" and "Kora.") As Breslin has shown, Dr. Paterson in this scene has changed markedly since the previous section of Book Three. When he encountered the same woman then, he first turned her into a virgin in a "white lace dress," and then when she did not conform to his idealized fantasy self-righteously treated her as if she were a whore:

(Then, my anger rising) TAKE OFF YOUR
CLOTHES! I didn't ask you
to take off your skin . . . I said your
clothes, your clothes. You smell
like a whore. I ask you to bathe in my

opinions, the astonishing virtue of your
lost body (I said)
    (*P*, 104–105)

Williams here unflinchingly records Dr. Paterson's brutal treatment of the
woman but also includes key phrases in parentheses that separate Williams
the narrator from Dr. Paterson the protagonist, therefore encouraging us to
criticize Dr. Paterson's actions and rhetoric. Such ironic asides in parentheses are absent from the later lyric rhapsody sung by the contrite Dr. Paterson
to the woman (*P*, 128) and help to portray Dr. Paterson's partial regenera-
tion, his new willingness to find beauty in this world, not an ideal one of his
own making. Much of the drama of *Paterson* can therefore be uncovered if
we attend to Dr. Paterson's own struggle to change and the many successes
and reversals he undergoes.[10]

Despite many instances of Dr. Paterson's growing self-knowledge, however, the examples of anger, despair, and divorce that surround Dr. Paterson
at the start of the poem become dominant in Books Three and Four, thereby
changing the overall mood of Books One through Four from celebratory to
satiric. Book One began in prehistory, with Dr. Paterson witnessing the male
and female principles of the poem interpenetrating perfectly.

Paterson lies in the valley under the Passaic Falls
its spent waters forming the outline of his back. He
lies on his right side, head near the thunder
of the waters filling his dreams!
. . . .
And there, against him, stretches the low mountain.
The Park's her head, carved, above the Falls, by the quiet
river; Colored crystals the secret of those rocks
    (*P*, 6, 8)

This mythic and timeless union is immediately counterpointed by a vision
of modern spiritual, sexual, and intellectual dysfunction, as represented by
"automatons" living in the cities,

    Who because they
neither know their sources nor the sills of their
disappointments walk outside their bodies aimlessly
    for the most part,
locked and forgot in their desires—unroused.
    (*P*, 6)

At the start of *Paterson*, the theme of marriage predominates, and the passages introducing the poem's examples of divorce are kept clearly subordinate. The later books shift their focus downstream from the Falls (first to the park by the Falls, then to the areas of Paterson below the Falls such as the library, then to New York City and the Atlantic Ocean), and examples of spiritual and physical divorce play an increasingly prominent part in the poem. The economy is shown to be more usurious, the language more corrupt, the communication between people—especially between lovers—more sterile. In Book Four, Section II, admittedly, Madame Curie emerges as a heroine, and as such represents an advance beyond the grim frustration of the lesbian Corydon in the poem's previous section. But viewing Madame Curie in the context of all of Book Four, we see that she is surrounded by figures representing self-destruction rather than self-discovery: Corydon, the murderer Jack Johnson, the "blood-red" Atlantic, and the shark that snaps at his own guts (*P*, 200), among others. Even Curie's own important discovery of how to split the uranium atom and release energy (*P*, 175–78) is parodied in the same section of the poem by another kind of splitting, in which a corrupt evangelist accepts "27 Grand" for his efforts to divide striking Paterson mill workers by "calling them to God" instead (*P*, 172–73). Book Four, Section II, in other words, is not a "visionary" answer to Corydon's mock pastoral in the first section; its hopeful vision glows strongly at times, but most often in this particular section and in Book Four as a whole we feel the leaden oppressiveness of history.[11] In general, Book Four reads like a long mock pastoral with few truly pastoral or visionary interludes. It is dominated by figures in historical and modern Paterson who distort pastoral's traditional celebration of love, fertility, labor, and honor, and by beasts like the shark, which eats its own guts and thus is a grotesque parody of the interpenetrating River and Mountain at the beginning of Book One.

Book Four also represents the sharpest reversal in the poem of Dr. Paterson's epic quest to discover the Beautiful Thing. At the end of Book Three, he was hoping to make a fresh start. And, indeed, the homage he paid to the black Kora figure had suggested that he might succeed. But by the opening of Book Four, Dr. Paterson seems as far as he has ever been from his goals of reforming society, language, and himself. The liberating clearing of the ground accomplished by the flood and the fire in Book Three has been lost; Book Four is set in the most congested locale of the entire poem, the shores and the mouth of the polluted Passaic River as it enters the Hudson and then the Atlantic. As Corydon says at the start of the book, the three guano-stained rocks in the East River that she sees out of her window are "all that's left of the elemental, the primitive / in this environment" (*P*, 152). Even

Dr. Paterson himself is apparently not immune from this corruption. At one point the poem's narrative comments sardonically,

> Oh Paterson! Oh married man!
> He is the city of cheap hotels and private
> entrances . . . of taxis at the door, the car
> standing in the rain . . .
> . . . .
> Goodbye, dear. I had a wonderful time.
> Wait! There's something . . . but I've forgotten.
>   (*P*, 154)

"He is the city": Dr. Paterson as a sleazy city is much closer to the "automatons" in Book One or to the exhausted Tiresias of *The Waste Land* who imitated the clichés of conversation ("Goodnight ladies, goodnight, sweet ladies") than he is to the mythic giant Paterson in the poem's opening pages or to the humble but resolute poet at the end of Book Three. Moreover, despite Dr. Paterson's discovery of Madame Curie, Social Credit, and so on, in the later episodes of Book Four, he is largely reduced to satirizing stale literary conventions rather than finding ways to make those conventions new: like Corydon, his alter ego, he writes a long mock-pastoral poem. Compared with his deliriously successful obliteration of tradition in Book Three, this attack on tradition in Four seems labored and ineffectual. The "white-hot man" (*P*, 123) of Book Three reshapes and invents; the exhausted man of Book Four largely resigns himself to parody, documentary, and nostalgia.

Dr. Paterson's tragic descent seems consistent both with the topography of the Passaic River valley, which descends toward the sea, and with certain general principles of Dada that appear to have influenced the structure of *Paterson*. The Dadaists believed that art and ideas petrify and therefore have to be discarded soon after they are invented. This is why they urged artists to forget everything they learned; the memory of what they and others have done would impede their efforts to do new things. Dada thus made artists martyrs to the impossible ideal of perpetual self-renewal. As J. Hillis Miller has noted, Williams consistently discriminated between creative shaping energy and the passive forms created by that force and then left to congeal as the force passes on.[12] In Book Four of *Paterson*, Williams calls this shaping force "the radiant gist," while the stale forms of beauty that congeal after the creative force passes on are called both "the final crystallization" and "lead" (*P*, 109, 178). In Williams' earlier volume *Kora in Hell*, he imagined creativity and decadence as a wheel cycling between upturn and downturn: "When the wheel's just at the up turn it glimpses horizon, zenith, all in a burst, the pull of the earth shaken off, a scatter of fragments, significance in a burst of water striking up from the base of a fountain. Then at the sickening turn toward death the pieces are joined into a pretty thing, a bouquet frozen in an icecake" (*I*, 71). The beginning of *Paterson* draws on this passage from *Kora in Hell* to represent the buoyant creativity of the Falls. Its waterdrops, Williams shows us, are suspended against gravity and against time: "fall, fall in air! as if / floating, relieved of their weight" (*P*, 8). But this energy gradually succumbs to its natural fate, to gravity and time; *Paterson* becomes dominated by references to blockage, divorce, decay, murder, and "pretty things" such as the stale literary parody used by Corydon in her *Corydon, a Pastoral* (*P*, 159–62). The shift in the epic's overall tone from sweet to sour is thus emphatic. All we need do is compare the first few pages of Books One and Four to see that the pure, spontaneous energy of the Falls has run its course. The free water of the Falls is now, Williams puns, "sea-bound" (*P*, 200).

At the conclusion of Book Four, Dr. Paterson awakens from this suicidal nightmare of modern history: "Waken from a dream, this dream of / the whole poem . . . sea-bound" (*P*, 200). If the descent of Dr. Paterson imitates the fate of creativity in time (inevitably declining into decadence, parody, death), at the very end of Book Four Williams' hero eludes such a fate by refusing to be either sea-bound or tradition-bound. He audaciously stands the traditional conclusion of the epic on its head:

> I say to you, Put wax rather in your
> ears against the hungry sea
>   it is not our home!
>   draws us in to drown, of losses
> and regrets
>   (*P*, 201)

Books One through Four do not conclude as a traditional epic does, when the hero arrives home, but when the hero realizes that he is *farthest* from home, from the Passaic Falls and their unending creative power. And when Williams wittily alludes to Odysseus' blocking his sailors' ears from the Sirens' song, he reminds us that as the wily pilot of his own epic craft he hears the beautiful music of epic precedent, the temptation to follow the "correct" way of ending an epic, but refuses to give in to it.

For Dr. Paterson, discovering how far he is from home is the first step toward a successful Odyssean escape from the forces that entrap him. During the very last pages of Book Four images of cleanliness and fertility dominate the poem once more. After swimming in the sea, Dr. Paterson is greeted joyfully by his dog (one of his alter egos throughout the epic), spits the seed from a beach plum out onto the dunes, and then heads inland with the "steady roar, as of a distant / waterfall" on his mind (*P*, 203). In doing so, he reverses the direction of the entire poem and begins a new quest to recover the creative powers he has gradually lost. Williams, of course, originally planned to have his epic be only four books long. He thus intended to conclude the poem at the moment that his hero, after a pause, renews his quest. Such an ending is a prospective or "open" one, despite Williams' references to "the eternal close" and "the end" on the book's last page. We leave Dr. Paterson as he stands on the dunes contemplating an endless series of other Odyssean descents into history—and, consequently, an endless series of further losses and self-defeats. Williams emphasizes this pessimistic, Dadaist truth by interrupting Dr. Paterson's lyrical meditation on rebirth with a reference to the eternal violence of history: "John Johnson, from Liverpool, England, was convicted after 20 minutes conference by the Jury. On April 30th, 1850, he was hung in full view of thousands who had gathered on Garrett Mountain and adjacent house tops to witness the spectacle" (*P*, 203). This juxtaposition of a rebirth and an execution contains in miniature the entire descent of Books One through Four.

When Book Four was published in 1951, Williams thought he was done. But after recovering from several strokes, he conceived and wrote Book Five, inspired by his harrowing of death. By adding it to the first four books of *Paterson* in 1958, he makes us read the ending of Book Four differently from how we read it when considering Books One through Four alone. The ending of Book Four implies that a sequel to the epic does not need to be written because any further adventures of Dr. Paterson would inevitably be other descents made up of gradually increasing despairs and diminishing awakenings. But if Books One through Five are taken as a unit, it seems that when Dr. Paterson walks on the dunes at the end of Book Four he meditates not just on another descent but on Book Five, which thoroughly revises the role played by descent in Williams' poem.

In Book Five the destructive and creative principles that had been at war throughout the previous books are wrested at last into equilibrium, so that each creative "upturn" and the decadent "downturn" are fiercely held in balance. If the mythical nature-goddess the Mountain dominated the opening of Book One and the decadent Corydon the opening of Book Four, in Book Five Williams introduces a paired or doubled image of women: "The moral // proclaimed by the whorehouse / could not be better proclaimed / by the virgin" (*P*, 208). This doubling continues throughout the book as Williams counterpoints references to powerful women (including Mary in Brueghel's Nativity painting, the Virgin in the Unicorn tapestries, Sappho, and the anonymous passerby on pages 219–20 to whom Williams impulsively dedicates all his poems) with those to barren or self-destructive women (such as the whores in Gilbert Sorrentino's letters on pages 214–15, or the poignant old woman on the penultimate page of the poem who wore "a china doorknob / in her vagina to hold her womb up"). Similarly, if Dr. Paterson migrates in Books One through Four from expressing the comic realm of mythic creative power free from time (the Falls and the Mountain) to the tragic, degenerative fate of all that is born into history (Paterson the city), in Book Five fallen history and the eternal world of art are interwoven into a harmonious, tragicomic design. The descent motif no longer controls the poem: its powers are continually counteracted by motifs of ascent and recovery.

In Book Five, moreover, Williams gives Dr. Paterson the homecoming denied him in Book Four:

> Paterson, from the air
>   above the low range of its hills
>   across the river
> on a rock-ridge
>   has returned to the old scenes
>   to witness
> What has happened
>   since Soupault gave him the novel
>   the Dadaist novel
> to translate—
> *The Last Nights of Paris.*
>   "What has happened to Paris
> since that time?
> and to myself?"
>   A WORLD OF ART
>   THAT THROUGH THE YEARS HAS
>   *SURVIVED!*
>   (*P*, 209)

Dada's principles guided Dr. Paterson during his descent into decadence in Books One through Four. But in Book Five Williams puts Dada in its place, satirizing it and carefully restricting its destructive energy. The movement that was to end all art has survived, as have the works it meant to destroy. The apocalyptic Surrealist novel *Last Nights of Paris* (written in 1929 by Philippe Soupault, who coauthored *Les Champs magnétiques* with André Breton) has been translated into another language, and Paris itself has survived two European wars. Dada's pessimistic view of the fate of art is now counterpointed by a faith that creative power is perpetually able to escape from the forces that try to destroy it. As Williams caustically says near the very end of Book Five, alluding to Duchamp's celebrated announcement (which later proved untrue) that he was rejecting art for chess: "Equally laughable / is to assume to know nothing, a / chess game" (*P*, 239). Book Five of *Paterson* thus restores the traditional epic conclusion that Williams excluded from his earlier ending for the poem. That is, if we take Books One through Four as a unit, we find that the epic ends with the hero realizing that he is farthest from home. But if we consider Books One through Five together, the poem ends classically, with the hero symbolically returning to the Falls, to a world where the eternal and the time-bound, the creative and the decadent, may be held in balance.

Williams acknowledges in the last lines of *Paterson* that this balancing act characterizes Book Five as it does no other book in the poem. The lines describe a satyr's dance. The "tragic" beat of the satyr's foot represents history as a tragedy in which creativity is lost and the artist is inevitably reduced to Dadaist satire and erasure ("We know nothing" [*P*, 239]). Because the satyr is half-man, half-goat, he can be seen as an emblem of a grotesque degeneration from the norm of what man should be, and is thus connected etymologically for Williams with satire, the mode of literature, including Dada, that criticizes such deviations. As Williams had said at the end of Book One, quoting J. A. Symonds, "The Greeks displayed their acute aesthetic sense of propriety, recognizing the harmony which subsists between crabbed verses and the distorted subjects with which they dealt—the vices and perversions of humanity—as well as their agreement with the snarling spirit of the satirist. Deformed verse was suited to deformed morality" (*P*, 40). But throughout Book Five Williams also syncopates this tragic, "deformed" beat with what he calls a "pre-tragic" or comic one.[13] It, too, is associated with the satyr, but in this case the satyr represents man's sexual and spiritual potency, his ability to create.

> the Satyrs, a
> pre-tragic play,
> a satyric play!
>   All plays
> were satyric when they were most devout.
>   Ribald as a Satyr!
> Satyrs dance!
>   all the deformities take wing
>   (*P*, 221)

The complementary meanings of Williams' references to satyrs thus contain in miniature the contrapuntal, tragicomic structure of Book Five itself.

We know that in the late 1950s Williams decided that *Paterson* was to have been an open-ended epic, for drafts for a sixth book survive. As the poem now stands (or dances, rather), it is an epic documenting the history of a locality, Paterson, New Jersey, in which its hero, Dr. Paterson, succeeds when he discovers that local history is both his proper home and his place of exile. He must journey downriver and face the failures of his city and his self—he must, in his own words, look "death / in the eye" (*P*, 106). But by the end of Book Four he is also freed to somersault upstream, aware that his decline into satire, Dadaist disgust, and violence is merely part of an inexorable creative dance that will soon counter its own rhythms. If the first four books of Williams' epic seem to descend from their early poetic heights (as most contemporary critics, comparing the poem to the other epics they knew, saw and protested), Williams would perhaps answer that that is the way time, rivers, and modern epic poems naturally flow. But Book Five countered Dadaist pessimism by describing the fate of art and the body in time without despairing of the mind's ability to rediscover its creative heights. Books Four and Five thus construct two endings for *Paterson*. The first is an open ending, with the poet beginning a new journey. The second is a truly closed ending in which the poet concludes an old journey: as Williams says near the end of Book Five, "The (self) direction has been changed / the serpent / its tail in its mouth / 'the river has returned to its beginnings'" (*P*, 233). In creating two endings for his long poem, Williams fashioned an agitated equilibrium between the impulses toward closure and exposure, retrospection and progression, that have informed epics from the *Iliad* on.

* * *

Is *Paterson* a Dadaist or Cubist collage of texts? What does reading a collage of texts in fact entail? Williams critics have only just begun to consider these questions.[14] If we glance at the architecture of Books One through Four and then Books One through Five, it seems at first as if they are both Cubist. After all, their use of heterogeneous materials is carefully selected and composed, as can be seen from the following note on his collage techniques that Williams wrote to himself while working on *Paterson*:

> There are to be completely worked up parts in *each* section—as completely formal as possible: in each part well displayed.
> . . . But—juxtaposed to them are unfinished pieces—put in without fuss—for their very immediacy of expression—as they have been written under LACK of a satisfactory form.
> —or for their need to be just there, the information.[15]

Paterson uses "found" materials as Williams' Cubist odes did, except that in his epic Williams greatly increases the variety and length of found materials that he includes in comparison with, say, "Overture to a Dance of Loco-motives" or "Rapid Transit." And *Paterson* also combines both improvised sections written quickly with the "mistakes" left in (akin to "The Rose" or Williams' Improvisations) *and* "completely worked up parts" as carefully composed as any of Williams' Precisionist lyrics or dramatic monologues. Further, the many texts in *Paterson* recurrently cluster around central themes and symbols—especially natural versus urban, female versus male, demo-cratic versus totalitarian, among others. Finally, Williams' procedures in *Paterson* require that he select, detach, and order as carefully as his Cubist poems do. As Williams says in his preface, he is rolling up a "sum" of mate-rials to make an ordered aggregate.

Yet Williams' confidence that he can compose such an "identity" for his collage-epic is also seriously undercut. Problems first surface in the preface, in which Williams laments "the defective means" available to him and warns against letting his craft be "subverted by thought," "no more than the writing of stale poems" (*P*, 3, 4). These are early warnings of the Dadaist frustration with being "blocked" (*P*, 72) and forced to write "under LACK of a satisfactory form" that appears more and more frequently as the poem develops. This fail-ure emphasizes not the Cubist coherence of *Paterson* but its Dadaist decom-position: Dr. Paterson is increasingly forced to resort to defective means such as parody or mere vandalism. He becomes less and less a composer in the Cubist sense. Book Five, however, appears to reverse this trend and restore Dr. Paterson's ability to create an "identity" out of history's fragments.

In order to be useful, such a distinction between the Cubist and Dadaist energies of Williams' collage method ought to be applicable to *any* section of the poem, not merely as a way to describe the poem's "closed" and "open" end-ings. As a test case, we may consider, say, Book Two, Section II. If the poem indeed chronicles a kind of epic combat between generation and decay, then such a conflict ought to be dramatically present in each section of the poem, with either "composition" or "decomposition" gaining the upper hand (so to speak), depending on that section's place within the overall plot of the poem. Such a close reading of Williams' use of collage in a particular section also makes it possible to ask whether Williams managed to integrate all the differ-ent styles of his earlier writing, particularly those influenced by Precisionism, Cubism, and Dada, or whether Williams was forced to concede that there were inveterate contradictions among those styles.

In Book Two, Section II, we indeed find that Dr. Paterson plays the two roles of composer and decomposer. One is that of Faitoute (*P*, 62), French for "to make everything." The other role (to coin a name) is that of Faitrien, a Dadaist poet of decomposition, irony, and despair. The title of Williams' epic gives us another possible set of names for these two roles: Dr. Paterson plays both the role of a *pater*, an authority figure creating an order, and a *son*, a recreant perpetually dismantling that order and searching for a new one. The section has a representative mix of texts, from raw prose taken from newspapers, history books, a sermon preached in a park, and personal letters to Williams, to poetry both high and low—a bitter satiric ballad, Faitoute's own narration and interior monologues, and three examples of carefully finished, high poetry ("Is this the only beauty here?," "The gentle Christ," and "If there is subtlety," [*P*, 71, 72, 74–75]).

The prose texts are selected, edited, and rearranged according to Cubist principles: they are treated as found objects removed from their original context with enough clues left of that context to allow a complex dialectic to emerge between their original context and the new one that is created for them. One way to think of these found passages is to consider them as offspring or "sons" faithful to their parental texts; through them, many of the original meanings of their parental texts may be reconstituted. Once those found passages are also allied with the text of *Paterson*, however, they may act as both submissive and subversive sons: they may be contained within the new structure that Faitoute their foster father has built, but they may also destabilize and revise that structure.

Williams' poetic texts work in a similar way to his found ones, especially to the degree that they allow him to criticize monopolies of all kinds in private and public history. Yet since the poems are invented rather than found texts, they may do what found texts usually do not—function as self-questioning meditations on the methods of *Paterson* itself, its successes and failures. In Section II, the poem that most clearly performs this inquisitorial function is the lyric that comes at the very end, "If there is subtlety" (*P*, 74–75).

The most prominent event in Section II is Williams' transcription of and reactions to a sermon on the mount (Mount Garrett) informally preached in the park by the Passaic Falls by a born-again German immigrant named Klaus Ehrens. The sermon's topic is a familiar one: having come to America to pursue the American Dream, Ehrens finds that the true pursuit of happiness can only be a pursuit of spiritual, not material, wealth. But Williams' short introduction to the section gives us an outline of the context in which he will place Ehrens' confession. This section of *Paterson* is to be a history of failures to find spiritual wealth in America by religious, economic, artistic, and political figures. The general principle guiding Williams' diagnosis is clear: all monopolies that attempt to control the means of production and distribution are dangerous, whether they involve the tangible goods of politics and economics or the intangible "good" of religion and art. In their place, Williams

argues for what he claims is a more "natural" form of organization—*many*
sources of production and no control of the rights of distribution. Thus the
action of the section properly opens with Faitoute's exemplary "wandering"
through the park. Dr. Paterson's freedom to see and think as he chooses (and
to organize this section of the poem around what he discovers) is placed in
pointed opposition to all forms of restriction and control.

Ehrens' sermon provides an example of how to rebel against monopolies: it is improvised, evangelically Protestant, and spiritualist, as opposed to
ritualistic, institutionally sanctioned, and materialist. It is frequently interrupted, however, as Williams combines a series of examples of monopolistic
behavior from American history and (ironically) Williams' own private life.
The most obvious of these examples is a series of texts on the economic and
ideological importance of the city of Paterson in colonial and nineteenth-
century American history. Paterson was named in honor of the governor of
New Jersey, who signed the charter granting Alexander Hamilton's Society
for Useful Manufactures the right to sell capital stock and create the colonies'
first industrial city, and it had America's first textile mills and manufactured
its first locomotives and Colt revolvers.[16] In the texts Williams chooses, Alexander Hamilton emerges as the first in a long line of industrialist tycoons. He
is for Williams a sort of American Antichrist, a figure who under the guise
of rebelling against Britain's political and economic monopolies would have
set up new monopolies in America to take their place. Williams focuses on
Hamilton's authoritarian Federalism, which envisioned the creation of various systems for the control of the manufacture and distribution of material
goods, money, and political power.

> The Federal Reserve System is a private enterprise . . . a private
> monopoly . . . (with power) . . . given to it by a spineless Congress
> . . . to issue and regulate all our money. . . .
>
> Witnessing the [Passaic] Falls Hamilton was impressed by
> this show of what in those times was overwhelming power . . .
> planned a stone aqueduct following a proposed boulevard, as the
> crow flies, to Newark with outlets every mile or two along the
> river for groups of factories: The Society for Useful Manufac-
> tures: SUM, they called it.
>
> The newspapers of the day spoke in enthusiastic terms of the
> fine prospects of the "National Manufactory" where they fondly
> believed would be produced all cotton, cassimeres, wall papers,
> books, felt and straw hats, shoes, carriages, pottery, bricks, pots,
> pans and buttons needed in the United States. (*P*, 73–74)

An earlier quotation from a history of Paterson stresses the irony of these plans: Hamilton protested against English political and economic policy, but the means with which he chose to make America economically and politically independent *subverted* his dream (in Williams' view, at least) and merely reproduced the oppressive features of English corporate capitalism in the New World.

> The new world had been looked on as a producer of precious metals, pelts and raw materials to be turned over to the mother country for manufactured articles which the colonists had no choice but to buy at advanced prices. They were prevented from making woolen, cotton or linen cloth for sale. Nor were they allowed to build furnaces to convert the native iron into steel.
>
> Even during the Revolution Hamilton had been impressed by the site of the Great Falls of the Passaic. His fertile imagination envisioned a great manufacturing center, a great Federal City, to supply the needs of the country. Here was water-power to turn the mill wheels and the navigable river to carry manufactured goods to the market centers: a national manufactury. (*P*, 69)

In Williams' analysis, Hamilton's dream of independence was endangered by the monopolistic forms with which that independence was declared: American workers would become as dependent on the Federal manufactury as they once were on the British system; the means of production and distribution were still to be highly centralized and thus monopolistic. Moreover, since Hamilton defined the American Dream in primarily material rather than spiritual terms, his failure was all the more ignoble. By juxtaposing Hamilton's dream with Ehrens' sermon, Williams helps us see the self-defeating principles of Hamilton's thought more clearly than we could if we read the passages on Hamilton alone.

Other texts interrupting the sermon are similar examples of self-defeat. One is an angry parody of "America the Beautiful" inspired by Hamilton's monopolistic Federalism. Another is an account of the American eagle being forced back into its egg. The most startling of these examples, however, are taken from Williams' private life—two letters from Marcia Nardi, a woman who as an aspiring artist imagined herself to be controlled and blocked by Williams. Her letters emphasize the very things that Williams criticized Hamilton for doing. They accuse him of paternalistic authoritarianism— of unconsciously controlling another person's right to speak and act independently, and of refusing to admit that such an unfair situation exists. We cannot judge the truth of Nardi's accusations, of course, nor are we meant to. But by including her letters in *Paterson* Williams inevitably challenges his own authority as an interpreter and a maker of history: he may not practice what he preaches.[17]

Williams' collage techniques in Book Two, Section II (as in others), are Cubist insofar as they force the various meanings of his texts to converge around central principles such as the evils of monopoly in all its forms. They are Dadaist insofar as they subvert these organizing principles, ironically revealing contradictions between his ends and means. Williams criticizes Hamilton for creating the monopolistic Society for Useful Manufactures, for example, but in the same section of the poem is accused of wanting to monopolize another poet's life. Furthermore, Hamilton's "SUM" project is reminiscent of Williams' attempts throughout *Paterson* to make an epic *summa* of his own: "To make a start, / out of particulars / and make them general, rolling / up the sum" (*P*, 3).

This is not to argue that the book's Cubist methods are monopolistic while its Dadaist ones are heroically subversive. Williams' Cubist collage techniques themselves create a play of various meanings throughout the texts that they use, never a single meaning. By placing the passages on Hamilton within the context of Ehrens' sermon, for example, Williams sets up a rich interaction between Hamilton's vision of independence (which Ehrens and Williams would certainly praise) and his failure to realize that vision. The passage can hardly be read "monopolistically," as signifying merely one thing. This is even more clearly seen when we widen its context still further, including in our analysis not only the sermon but, say, the following fragment, which follows immediately after the first passage about the Society for Useful Manufactures quoted above:

> Washington at his first inaugural
> . . . . . wore
> a coat of Crow-black homespun woven
> in Paterson. . . . .
>   (*P*, 74)

After reading the passages on Hamilton, we must note the irony of Washington's coat being called "homespun," for Hamilton's Society for Useful Manufactures was an organized effort to supplant the cottage weaving industry with modern mass production financed by selling capital stock. Yet the above passage also celebrates American independence, signified by Washington and by his American-made coat, and recalls the many links that were drawn in the late eighteenth and early nineteenth centuries between the rise of American manufacturing and the survival of the republic.[18] In its own way, the passage is as much about spiritual values as Ehrens' sermon. Thus by juxtaposing fragments of three texts (the sermon, the discussion of Hamilton, and the above lines) Williams has created an interlocking system of cross-references and various possible interpretations. It does not merely condemn manufacturing and praise Ehrens' spirituality. And there are many more texts within this part of Book Two, Section II; my discussion has inevitably reduced the Cubist multiplicity of possible readings that Williams has constructed. Their number increases each time the context is broadened and a new fragment introduced into the collage for consideration.

As with Williams' Cubist lyrics, however, the variety of possible readings produced by such a collage in *Paterson* is neither infinite nor self-destructive and wholly indeterminate. The readings suggested by each text check and balance the readings created by the other texts. The result is a reinforcement of our faith in the profundity and authority of the collage method itself. Its creator, Faitoute, is an exemplary master who selects, edits, supplements, and juxtaposes his materials in ways that *celebrate* his ability to create a new order, a rich sum of readings that does justice to the complexity of his materials, enforcing his point about the evils of monopolies and yet also depicting how Paterson played an important role in the birth of an independent American economy.

Dadaist collage techniques, on the other hand, subtract and divide rather than create sums; they destabilize the Cubist play of meaning and question the authority of the composer himself. More than any other piece of material in Book Two, Section II, the Nardi letters perform this Dadaist function. Indeed, they impugn Williams' authority as an interpreter: if he is accused of being mechanical and impersonal in his private life, then why does he claim the right to criticize those qualities in public life? The letters thus upset the Cubist balance of meanings that I have paraphrased; they cannot be as easily assimilated into the structure's play of meanings as, say, the passage about Washington's homespun coat could be. At the start of his epic, Williams said that his goal was to make particulars "general"—that is, to use his collage techniques to interpret the meaning of his particular pieces of data. But fragments such as the letters, or the poem "If there is subtlety," do little to support the general readings that Williams is elsewhere trying to create. Instead, they assert the independence and idiosyncracy of all "particulars" in the poem and disrupt the authority of all interpreters to make them signify "general" truths. Dada is an energy of fission, as Cubism (ultimately) is that of fusion. Together they are as contentious and interdependent in *Paterson* as *pater* and *son*—or (in view of Nardi's importance) as *pater* and *daughter*.

As Books One through Four evolve, Williams' authority as an interpreter is increasingly undercut, as is the integrity of the materials he works
with. This loss is the burden of the superb lyric "If there is subtlety." It is
addressed to the Beautiful Thing, the object of Williams' epic quest through
history's fragments:

> how futile would be the search
> for you in the multiplicity of
> your debacle.
> . . . . . .
>   in your
> composition and decomposition
> I find my . . .
>   despair!
> (*P,* 75)

In Book Five, in contrast, Dr. Paterson's compositions are not so violently
decomposed; his Cubist will to order masters the Dadaist demon of irony.
Despite the frequent play of irony throughout the book (as in the placement
of the rather inarticulate interview with Mike Wallace at the end of Section
II), that play is always subordinated to Williams' faith that his quest repeatedly succeeds.

Hence it is possible to argue that in the sequence of Books One through
Four each episode aspires to be a Cubist collage but inevitably degenerates
into a Dadaist one, with that failure becoming more obvious and violent as
we progress through the books. In the sequence of Books One through Five,
on the other hand, Williams tries to reshape the poem into a stable (not
static) Cubist construction in which the play of composition and decomposition is rigorously held in balance. Such critical indeterminacy is necessary
on the reader's part, I think, to appreciate a poem whose twin endings aspire
simultaneously to closed and open forms. *Paterson* is an epic gathering of the
multiple and contradictory poetics that Williams developed since he came
into contact with Precisionism, Cubism, and Dada many years before.

* * *

To what degree was such a vision of the modern epic primarily Williams',
and to what degree was it shared with his contemporaries and his romantic predecessors? A key to handling this question comes from a surprising
source—William Wordsworth. *The Prelude* of course is the venerable pro-
genitor of all modern epics that present themselves as honorable failures,

unfinishable histories of the growth of the poet's mind whose gaps and contradictions are as important as its continuities. Wordsworth was profoundly troubled by the specter of such lacunae, however, as if he realized that they would be the high price paid for the romantic era's discovery of the egotistical sublime as it unfolds in time. One scene in *The Prelude* is particularly memorable for its dramatization of Wordsworth's fear that all modern epic quests must be fragmented and unfinished: the famous dream of the Arab, the stone, and the shell in Book Five, lines 50–191. This episode holds parallels with the drama of *Paterson* that are especially worth exploring.

Reading *Don Quixote* by the seashore, Wordsworth falls asleep and dreams that a Quixote-like Arab approaches him in a desert carrying a stone and a seashell "Of a surpassing brightness." The former symbolizes Euclid's *Elements*, the Arab tells him; the latter, not a particular book so much as the power of speech itself, for it

> Had voices more than all the winds, with power
> To exhilarate the spirit, and to soothe,
> Through every clime, the heart of human kind.

Yet when Wordsworth puts the shell to his ear, he hears sounds that are distinctly unsoothing:

> in an unknown tongue,
> which yet I understood, articulate sounds,
> a loud prophetic blast of harmony;
> An Ode, in passion uttered, which foretold
> Destruction to the children of the earth
> By deluge, now at hand.

The Arab tells Wordsworth that he is going to bury the two "books" to save them from the coming flood, and as soon as he says this Wordsworth looks behind him and sees

> over half the wilderness diffused,
> A bed of glittering light: I asked the cause:
> "It is," said he, "the waters of the deep
> Gathering upon us."[19]

There are many reasons to pair *The Prelude* and *Paterson*, not least among them the fact that they have the two most powerful flood scenes in all of modern poetry. Wordsworth's Book Five and Williams' Book Three are primarily

about the destruction of books—both the epic poet's guilty participation in
such a scene and his deep fears about what such fantasies mean. As J. Hillis Miller, one of Wordsworth's most astute readers, has pointed out, Wordsworth's dream in Book Five centers on his profound ambivalence toward
books. They seemed to him both to entomb his living voice and to be the only
way that that voice could *escape* permanent entombment. Miller mentions
several negative references to printed books in *The Prelude*, especially in some
lines in Book Three that could serve as the credo for that same book in *Paterson*: Wordsworth describes all the books he did *not* read while in the library
of Cambridge University as "those long vistas, sacred catacombs, / Where
mighty minds lie visibly entombed."[20] Yet books also seem to be the only safe
bearers of the living voice. When Wordsworth in his dream places the Arab's
shell next to his ear, the passage stresses the oral rather than the textual life
of the words: it is as if Wordsworth is listening to the archetypal sound of
human speech itself, an "unknown" tongue that is the tongue of tongues, their
primal source. (This reading is strengthened by the fact that in a seashell, of
course, one hears the sound of one's own blood circulating, primal noise—like
the sea's—antecedent to all articulate speech.) Wordsworth is so anxious to
help the Arab bury his two "books" not (or not *only*) because they seem dead
to him but because they seem so alive, so worthy of being preserved from
impending destruction.

In *Paterson* Williams is equally ambivalent about books; they represent
both the death or "sleep" of living speech and (using imagery identical to
Wordsworth's) speech at its most fluid and alive. Yet, as in *The Prelude*, in
Paterson that very fluidity makes what the poet hears frightening as well; it
seems a deluge:

> with the roar of the river
> forever in our ears (arrears)
> inducing sleep and silence, the roar
> of eternal sleep . . . challenging
> our waking—
>   (*P* 18)

> The past above, the future below
> and the present pouring down: the roar,
> the roar of the present, a speech—
> is, of necessity, my sole concern . . .
> . . . .
>   I must
> find my meaning and lay it, white,

        beside the sliding water: myself—
    comb out the language—or succumb
        (*P*, 144–45)

If texts seem to fix the poet's living voice, water represents a danger of
another kind: speech that is *too* fluid, that drowns individual articulation,
the poet's ability to order.

Ultimately, both Wordsworth and Williams seek texts that mysteriously
are neither too fixed nor too fluid. Wordsworth wants to bury the shell so
that it may survive the deluge and meditates on the frailty of books and their
precious cargo:

    Oh! why hath not the Mind
    Some element to stamp her image on
    In nature somewhat nearer to her own?
    Why, gifted with such powers to send abroad
    Her spirit, must it lodge in shrines [that is, books] so frail?

Williams, similarly, sees the "roar" as "challenging" his waking and fights to
"comb out the language" into lines on the page so that his particular voice
won't be lost. For him as for Wordsworth the flood of the "real language of
men" is as frightening a source as it is indispensable; he fears the submer-
gence of his own voice within it, like a spectator at the Passaic Falls drawn
toward the brink, or Odysseus tempted by the music of the Sirens.[21]

The fact that Wordsworth was reading *Don Quixote* before his dream in
The Prelude also has significance for the reader of *Paterson*. For *Don Quixote*
stands for Wordsworth as an example of an epic quest narrative that may be
in fragments but nevertheless accomplishes its two most challenging tasks: it
vanquishes the dead language of the past and records its own living cadences
for posterity. In Miller's words, *Don Quixote* was "supposed to be reproduced
from an incomplete manuscript, its lacunae testifying to the fact that it has
survived a catastrophe, perhaps like the one which awaits those books the
Arab hurries to bury in Wordsworth's dream. An episode of book burning in
Don Quixote demonstrates that Cervantes, like Wordsworth, was concerned
not only for the power to induce madness possessed by books, but also for
their impermanence."[22] A flood and a fire: for Wordsworth as for Williams
imagining catastrophe forces the poet to explore the dangers of his commitment to living speech and to speech recollected and fixed on the page.
Yet the marks of such a catastrophe—the lacunae and fissures in the poet's
text—then become its badges of honor, its sign of having been immersed
in flood and flame and endured. Wordsworth's dream in Book Five of *The*

Prelude at first glance may seem the *opposite* of Books Three and Four of *Paterson* (Wordsworth is, after all, openly reverential toward books and fearful of their destruction), but there is a fundamental agreement among these epics in their imagination of disaster and in their strategies for surviving it. Williams' collage text, rebellious Modernist son though it is, here shows itself to have been sired by romanticism. Its contradictions and lacunae are the identifying marks, the Odyssean scars, of the modern epic form. And if the form of *Paterson* seems even more scored and broken than that of *The Prelude*, it is the result, Williams would no doubt argue, of a deeper plunge into more dangerous waters. Yet both texts emerge from the waters like the Arab's seashell, "Of a surpassing brightness."

NOTES

1. Wallace, *A Bibliography*, xix.

2. Hugo Ball, "Dada Fragments," *transition*, XXV (Fall, 1936). Republished in Motherwell (ed.), *The Dada Painters and Poets*, 52.

3. Motherwell (ed.), *The Dada Painters and Poets*, 53.

4. See especially Margaret Glynne Lloyd, William Carlos Williams' *"Paterson": A Critical Reappraisal* (Cranbury N.J., 1980), 254; Miller, *Poets of Reality*, 338–39; and Anne Janowitz, "Paterson: An American Contraption," in Carroll F. Terrell (ed.), *William Carlos Williams: Man and Poet* (Orono, Maine, 1983), 317. Mike Weaver, in *William Carlos Williams: The American Background*, does mention Artaud and other Surrealists in the context of *Paterson*, but his handling of Artaud's relevance to the poem is rather oblique (he doesn't discuss *The Theatre and Its Double* or the flood episode, for example), and he gives little background on Williams' earlier contact with Dada.

5. Antonin Artaud, *The Theatre and Its Double*, trans. Mary Caroline Richards (New York, 1958), 74, 78, 10. The book was originally published in Paris by Gallimard in 1938. See also Lloyd, *William Carlos Williams' "Paterson,"* 254. Mariani, in *William Carlos Williams: A New World Naked*, 574, notes that Williams later denied Artaud's relevance to *Paterson*, implying that he included the quotation from *The Theatre and Its Double* in the flood episode because he thought it was merely a cliché. In view of what happens in *Paterson*, Book Three, however, I am not sure that we can take Williams at his word.

6. Picabia quoted in Lippard ed., *Dadas on Art*, 166.

7. Picabia quoted in Lippard ed., *Dadas on Art*, 171.

8. For more on the Spectric hoax and Williams' friendship with Sieffert, see Barbara Herb Wright (ed.), "Fourteen Unpublished Letters by William Carlos Williams," *William Carlos Williams Review* XII (Spring, 1986), 22–38. This quotation is from page 24.

9. Mariani, *William Carlos Williams: A New World Naked*, 615–18; Jay Grover-Rogoff, "Hart Crane's Presence in *Paterson*," *William Carlos Williams Review*, XI (Spring, 1985), 20–29.

10. James Breslin, *William Carlos Williams: An American Artist*, 192–95; for a more general discussion of the significance of "reversal" in the poem, see 178–82. Mariani first pointed out the core/Kore pun in *William Carlos Williams: A New World*

Naked, 581–82. Other critics besides Breslin who stress that *Paterson* is an ironic epic in which the hero continually has to redefine what he is searching for include Walter Sutton, "Dr. Williams' *Paterson* and the Quest for Form," *Criticism*, II (Summer, 1960), 242–59; Guimond, *The Art of William Carlos Williams*, 153–200; Todd M. Lieber, *Endless Experiments: Essays on the Heroic Experience in American Romanticism* (Columbus, Ohio, 1973), 191–241; Joseph Riddel, *The Inverted Bell: Modernism and the Counterpoetics of William Carlos Williams* (Baton Rouge, La., 1974), especially 255–301; Paul Bové, "The World and Earth of William Carlos Williams: *Paterson* as a 'Long Poem,'" *Genre*, XI (Winter, 1978), 575–96; James E. Miller, *The American Quest for a Supreme Fiction* (Chicago, 1979), 126–60; Lloyd, *William Carlos Williams's "Paterson"*; and Tapscott, *American Beauty: William Carlos Williams and the Modernist Whitman*, 177–225. None of these critics, however, explores the role played by Dada in the poem. A reading that dissents from the critics who stress the "descent" of *Paterson* is M. L. Rosenthal and Sally M. Gall, *The Modern Poetic Sequence: The Genius of Modern Poetry* (New York, 1983), 233–68.

11. Breslin, *William Carlos Williams: An American Artist*, 201.

12. Miller, *Poets of Reality*, 328–44.

13. See also Lloyd, *William Carlos Williams's "Paterson,"* 267–71.

14. The best discussion of *Paterson* as a collage is by Henry Sayre, in *The Visual Text of William Carlos Williams*, 93–117. Sayre does not make a distinction between Cubist and Dadaist collage principles, but he does argue that beginning with Book II, *Paterson* begins to deny its own dream of synthesis. Readers interested in Williams' use of collage should also consult Perloff, *The Poetics of Indeterminacy*, 109–54; Perloff, "The Invention of Collage"; and Margaret L. Bollard, "The Interlace Element in *Paterson*," *Twentieth Century Literature*, XXI (1975), 288–304.

15. These phrases are from a note to himself that Williams wrote while working on *Paterson*. The note is cited by Joel Conarroe, *William Carlos Williams's "Paterson": Language and Landscape* (Philadelphia, 1970), 26. Conarroe's is the best book-length study of Williams' epic published to date.

16. See Weaver, *William Carlos Williams: The American Background*, 118–19; and Conarroe, *William Carlos Williams's "Paterson,"* 155–56 n. 30, on the important sources for Williams' knowledge of Paterson's history: William Nelson and Charles A. Shriner, *History of the City of Paterson and the County of Passaic New Jersey* (Paterson, N.J., 1901); Nelson and Shriner, *Records of the Township of Paterson, N.J., 1831–1851* (Paterson, N.J., 1895); John W. Barber and Henry Howe, *Historical Collections of the State of New Jersey* (New York, 1894); and Herbert A. Fisher's unpublished manuscript "Legends of the Passaic." The best brief summary of Paterson's history is in Conarroe, 49–51. The following secondary sources ought to be essential reading for anyone concerned with the historical importance of Paterson and Alexander Hamilton's views on Federalism, banking, and corporate capitalism: Federal Writers Project, *New Jersey: A Guide to Its Present and Past* (New York, 1939); Louis M. Hacker, *Alexander Hamilton in the American Tradition* (New York, 1957), 127–90; Broadus Mitchell, *Alexander Hamilton: The National Adventure, 1788–1804* (New York, 1962), 181–98; Jacob Ernest Cooke, *Alexander Hamilton* (New York, 1982), 58–108; Nancy F. Cott, *The Bonds of Womanhood: "Woman's Sphere" in New England, 1780–1835* (New Haven, Conn., 1977), 19–62, on the transition of New England textile making from cottage-industry homespun to mass production between 1790 and 1830; and Herbert G. Gutman, *Work, Culture, and Society in Industrializing America* (New York, 1976), 211–60.

17. Compare the ground-breaking readings of the Nardi material in *Paterson* by Theodora R. Graham, "'Her Heigh Compleynte': The Cress Letters of William Carlos Williams' *Paterson*," in Daniel Hoffman (ed.), *Ezra Pound and William Carlos Williams: The University of Pennsylvania Conference Papers* (Philadelphia, 1983), 164–93; and Sandra M. Gilbert, "Purloined Letters: William Carlos Williams and 'Cress,'" *William Carlos Williams Review*, XI (Fall, 1985), 5–15.

18. The best discussion of this topic is by Kasson, *Civilizing the Machine*, 3–135.

19. William Wordsworth, *The Prelude*, Book Five, 107–109, 93–98, 128–31.

20. *Ibid.*, Book Three, 341–42.

21. *Ibid.*, Book Five, 45–49.

22. Miller, *The Linguistic Moment From Wordsworth to Stevens*, 92. Miller's two chapters on Wordsworth and Williams are relevant (59–113 and 349–89, respectively), but with Williams he focuses on the lyrics, not *Paterson*. On the general topic of textual fragments, see Eugenio Donato, "The Ruins of Memory: Archeological Fragments and Textual Artifacts," *Modern Language Notes*, XCIII (May, 1978), 575–96.

JEROME J. MCGANN

The Cantos of Ezra Pound, the Truth in Contradiction

Repression does not . . . abolish the existence of the repressed element
which continues as a contradiction, often invisible, in the social fact. As
such, it continues to wage the class struggle of consciousness. The history of Anglo-American literature under capitalism is the history of this
struggle.

—Ron Silliman, 'Disappearance of the Word,
Appearance of the World'

Byron's life became a scandal in his own age, and remained so for many
people for a long time afterwards. The scandal of his *work*, on the other
hand, began in earnest only towards the end of his career. Thence it flour-
ished through the age of Victoria as well as that equally high-toned aftermath we call Modernism. That his *life* was not *truly* scandalous we know
because it never ceased to fascinate—never ceased to build its huge library of
biographical studies. But his poetry was generally shunned by those two fas-
tidious cultures which succeeded the Regency. Pious imaginations, whether
moral or poetic, prefer to read what they think is good for them.

The case of Blake is somewhat different, for his work was a scandal
in his own time. Though we call it the Romantic period, 1789–1824 was a
worldly age. Indeed, Romanticism fed upon and grew fat in that worldliness.
Yet Blake was its most scandalous figure, for not even the saints of the time,

From *Towards a Literature of Knowledge*, pp. 96–128. Published by the University of Chicago
Press. Copyright © 1989 by Jerome J. McGann.

Southey and Coleridge for example, could take seriously the imaginations of
a man who saw angels, and who claimed that to be inspired, to write from the
dictation of beings who lived in eternity, was a 'literal' truth, and not metaphor or poetic convention.

As for Rossetti, his work is still a scandal. The Fleshly School contro-
versy which erupted around him was never in itself very serious. Rossetti
went mad, but Buchanan did not drive him to it. He went mad from having
looked too long into the heart of vacancy—his own and that of his age. He
put down what he saw in *The House of Life*, a vision of hell which English and
American readers have learnt to avoid. Hell is more easily observed across a
channel, in any other country where, perhaps, flowers of evil may be taken for
things of beauty.

But the scandals surrounding the work of these men are as nothing
compared to the scandal of Ezra Pound's *Cantos*. We are amused to think that
anyone ever felt Byron might have been mad, bad, and dangerous to know.
We are not amused by the *Cantos*. Like Pound's letters and so much of his
prose, the *Cantos* is difficult to like or enjoy. It is a paradigm of poetic obscurity because its often cryptic style is married to materials which are abstruse,
learned, even pedantic. The poem also makes a mockery of poetic form; and
then there are those vulgar and bathetic sinkings which it repeatedly indulges
through its macaronic turns of voice.

All that is scandalous, but the worst has not been said. For the *Cantos*
is a fascist epic in a precise historical sense.[1] Its racism and anti-Semitism
are conceived and pursued in social and political terms at a particular point
in time and with reference to certain state policies. Those policies led to a
holocaust for which the murder of six million Jews would be the ultimate
exponent. That is truly scandalous.

For anyone convinced that works of imagination are important to
human life, however, the scandal takes a last, cruel twist. Pound's *magnum
opus* is one of the greatest achievements of Modern poetry in any language.
That is more a shocking than a controversial idea. It shocks because it is outrageous to think so; but it is in fact a commonplace judgement passed on the
poem by nearly every major writer and poet of this century. The greatness of
the *Cantos* was as apparent to Pound's contemporaries as it has been to his
inheritors, to his enemies as to his friends, to those who have sympathized
with Pound's ideas and to those who have fought against them.

The problem of the *Cantos* locates a more general problem about works
of imagination which clerical minds do not like to face. It was exposed for
our modern world most trenchantly by Hazlitt in 1816 when he was lecturing
on *Coriolanus*.

The language of poetry naturally falls in with the language of power. The imagination is an exaggerating and exclusive faculty: it takes from one thing to add to another: it accumulates circumstances to give the greatest possible effect . . . The understanding is a dividing and measuring faculty: it judges of things not according to their immediate impression on the mind, but according to their relations to one another. The one is a monopolising faculty . . . the other is a distributive faculty. . . . The one is an aristocratical and the other a republican faculty. The principle of poetry is a very anti-levelling principle. It aims at effect. . . . It has its altars and its victims, sacrifices, human sacrifices. . . . 'Carnage is its daughter'.[2]

This statement is an implicit plea for a literature of knowledge rather than a literature of power—or rather, a plea that the literature of power, poetry, find a way of accommodating itself to the demands of justice and consciousness. Hazlitt here is subjecting the entire ground of his work—specifically, his judgement that Wordsworth is the most important poet of the age—to a critical revolution. The inquiry will not lead him to an apostasy from Wordsworth. It will lead him to develop critical ideas which we now usually associate with Keats and the concept of 'negative capability'.

Some of the best work on Pound has been done in recent years by readers who do not shrink from the carnage which his work embodies.[3] The concept of negative capability has been specifically invoked as a vehicle for exposing the structures of contradiction which abound in the *Cantos*.[4] But this Keatsian principle, even in its Hazlittian (that is to say, in its socially conscious) salient, will finally prove too fragile for a work like Pound's. For at the back of Wordsworth's idea that the carnage of war is the daughter of a just God are those struggles of France, ultimately Napoleonic France, with England and her monarchical allies. Those circumstances encouraged a negative capability toward the parties involved. The equivocal contests in Europe between 1789 and 1815 discovered those equivocal responses which have been preserved in the living memory of Romantic art.

The same is not the case with Pound's *Cantos*. Sympathizing, as I think one can and should, with so much in the poem's indictment of the Europe (and America) of 1914–38, ultimately one's powers of sympathy—one's negative capabilities—come to a halt. The poem has entered, we soon discover, a world of evil that is too terrible for a Romantic sympathy or imagination. Yeats's father, that exemplary aesthete and Romantic, glimpsed this truth about the *Cantos* very early and tried to warn his son away from becoming too deeply involved with the demonic Pound:

The poets loved of Ezra Pound are tired of Beauty, since they have met it so often. . . . I am tired of Beauty my wife, says the poet, but here is that enchanting mistress Ugliness. With her I will live, and what a riot we shall have. Not a day shall pass without a fresh horror. Prometheus leaves his rock to cohabit with the Furies.[5]

This is extraordinarily prescient, and wonderfully expressed. But what Yeats's father saw in 1918 as Ugliness would eventually reveal itself in more frightful—in unspeakable—guises. Having, against his father's judgement, put himself to school to Pound, Yeats began to cultivate poetical relations with that mistress whom Jack Butler Yeats saw as the young American's wicked new beloved. 'A terrible beauty is born', Yeats declared as he began to explore his own visions of Prometheus cohabiting with the Furies. But his words—his experience—fall far short of the realities which Pound was bent upon pursuing. That elegant oxymoron of 'A terrible beauty' is a Romantic phrase embodying a Romantic judgment; as such, it is wholly inadequate to the contradictions which are brought forth through Pound's *Cantos*.

II

Let us approach those contradictions cautiously. We begin by recalling Pound's famous (1927) letter to *his* father in which he gave Homer Pound the 'outline of main scheme—or whatever it is' which would structure the long poem he had embarked upon:

> 1. Rather like, or unlike subject and response and counter subject in fugue.
> A. A. Live man goes down into world of Dead
> C. B. The 'repeat in history'
> B. C. The 'magic moment' or moment of metamorphosis, bust thru from quotidien into 'divine or permanent world.' Gods, etc.[6]

This is essentially the same 'scheme' which he outlined about two years later at Rapallo for Yeats, who reported as follows:

> it will, when the hundredth Canto is finished, display a structure like that of a Bach Fugue. There will be no plot, no chronicle of events, no logic of discourse, but two themes, the descent into Hades from Homer, a metamorphosis from Ovid, and mixed with these mediaeval or modern historical characters.[7]

Yeats was interested in this 'scheme' because in his reading of the first twenty-seven cantos he had been troubled and confused. 'I have often found there some scene of distinguished beauty but have never discovered why all the suits could not be dealt out in some quite different order' (*Packet*, 2). Yeats was never entirely persuaded by Pound's schema, and he even confessed that he agreed 'philosophically' (*L* 739) with Wyndham Lewis's critique of the new art of Joyce and Pound, that 'If we reject . . . the forms and categories of intellect there is nothing left but sensation, "eternal flux"' (*Packet*, 2n). But his 'philosophical' sense was not able to resist entirely what Joyce and Pound were doing in their work and he determined to try to sympathize with the *Cantos*:

> It is almost impossible to understand the art of a generation younger than one's own. I was wrong about 'Ulysses' when I had read but some first few fragments, and I do not want to be wrong again—above all in judging verse. Perhaps when the sudden Italian spring has come I may have discovered what will seem all the more [in the *Cantos*], because the opposite of all that I have attempted, unique and unforgetable. (*Packet*, 4)

Yeats's uncertainty about the *Cantos* was, as we know, matched by Pound's. 'The whole damn poem is rather obscure, especially in fragments' was how he opened the 'fugue' letter to his father, and his descriptive 'scheme' likewise begins on a hesitant note: the poem is 'Rather like, or unlike' the form of a fugue. As the years passed and the work accumulated, Pound swung back and forth in his confidence about its ultimate form. In the end he decided it was a failure, and he lapsed into the stony silence of the final years. The Poem finished as it had begun in 1915–27, before Pound had formulated the first of his 'grand schemes' of the work, in a nervous swirl of fragmentary pieces.[8]

But Pound was as deceived about the *Cantos* at the end as much as he was at the beginning. The poem had not failed, though it *was* a record of failure and self-deception. The fugal scheme is not strictly applicable, as Pound's vacillation in his use of it suggests; and all those other schemes he formulated were at worst mere blustering, at best shots in the dark.

Take those 'two themes' which he singled out, the descent into hell and the Ovidian metamorphosis. These do in fact appear, not merely at the outset as Cantos I and II respectively, but recurrently through the poem as Pound's 'repeat in history'. The poem plunges into Hades with Odysseus in Canto I, and the descent is explicitly a figure of a quest for knowledge, a mission to consult with Tiresias, the man 'Who even dead, yet hath his mind entire'

(XLVII. 236).[9] His message is: 'Odysseus / Shalt return through spiteful Neptune, over dark seas, / Lose all companions' (I. 4–5)

The words are well known, a supreme text in western culture; but what do they actually mean here in Pound's poem, what do they signify in this latest 'Repeat in history'? Pound was, like his friend Yeats, uncertain. The words themselves, if we consider them merely as a linguistic event, and set aside their historical relevance, send out a cryptic and equivocal message, for they seem to promise both comfort (the 'return' home) and loneliness ('Lose all companions'). Even that reading hangs fire, however, especially when we remember the deceptiveness of the source: an uncertain oracle (is it Tiresias, Homer's *Odyssey*, or Pound's Canto I?) whose pronouncements are subject to many constructions, including misconstructions. Beginning from an oracle is not propitious.

While such an ominous note is not clearly struck in Canto I, it is difficult to miss, if it is still only half sounded, in Canto XLVII when the same Homeric text is recalled, this time through the figure of Circe:

> This sound came in the dark
> First must thou go the road
>   to hell
> And to the bower of Ceres' daughter Proserpine,
> Through overhanging dark, to see Tiresias,
> Eyeless that was, a shade, that is in hell
> So full of knowing that the beefy men know less than he,
> Ere thou come to thy road's end.
> Knowledge the shade of a shade
> Yet must thou sail after knowledge
> Knowing less than drugged beasts. (XLVII. 236)

Circe's message is even more ominous than Tiresias'; and when we recall the hell into which the *Cantos* make their descent, the contradictoriness of the work becomes especially clear.

Cantos XIV–XVI were to represent the rottenness of the British Empire, 'the foetor of England' where 'evil [is] without dignity and without tragedy' (*L* 247–8). The cantos move via Dante into a place where all light is muted, and where a series of obscene and fragmented images stagger along. Pound's narrative in these 'Hell Cantos' recall plates 17–20 of *The Marriage* of *Heaven and Hell* and various parts of *The [First] Book of Urizen*, and they were to have a powerful influence on such later works as Ginsberg's *Howl*.[10]

But Eliot's critical comments on these visions, which he published in *After Strange Gods* (1934), point toward something important and even more troubling in this poetry: 'Mr. Pound's Hell ... is a perfectly comfortable

one for the modern mind to contemplate, and disturbing to no one's com-
placency: it is a Hell for the *other* people, the people we read about in the
newspapers, not for oneself and one's friends'.[11] The descent into hell is associated in Pound's work with knowledge, and he certainly thought these cantos contained a revelation of truths which most people would not face or did
not know. But so far as Pound's project is concerned, Eliot touched a crucial
problem: the hell of the *Cantos* does not appear to yield up an unknown
world, and the poem does not go there to acquire knowledge. It goes there
to preach. 'I am perhaps didactic,' Pound said of these cantos, but he brushed
the criticism aside:

> It is all rubbish to pretend that art isn't didactic. A revelation is
> always didactic. Only the aesthetes since 1880 have pretended the
> contrary. (*L* 248)

Pound is correct—in principle. Unfortunately, his remarks call attention to
the contradictions in his understanding of what a descent into hell means
for a poem which is itself questing after knowledge. Perhaps, as we shall see,
there is a revelation in the 'Hell Cantos' which Pound and his poem were
unable to realize in 1922.

  If we consider Pound's use of Ovidian metamorphosis—the second of
his work's two major 'themes'—a similar set of problems arises. According to
Pound, metamorphosis was to come as a magical moment of transition 'from
quotidien into "divine or permanent world"'. Metamorphosis was his poem's
explicit paradisal figure, brilliantly and perhaps most famously exemplified at
the opening of Canto III, where the text recalls Pound in a quotidian Venice
of 1907:

> For the gondolas cost too much, that year,
> And there were not 'those girls', there was one face,
> And the Buccentoro twenty yards off, howling 'Stretti'
>   (III. 11)

But gradually this scene changes, and a set of romantic images rises up:

>   Gods float in the azure air,
> Bright gods and Tuscan, back before dew was shed.

The passage unfolds to one of those 'scenes of distinguished beauty' which
so struck Yeats, and which have been the focus of interest for many readers
of the *Cantos*. Here, however, it itself undergoes a metamorphosis when the

text abruptly shifts to the vicious world of medieval Spain via the *Cantar de myo cid*, a world of 'drear waste', 'silk tatters', and 'Ignez da Castro murdered'.

Metamorphosis in the *Cantos* appears indeed, like the descent into hell, as a 'repeat in history', but in all cases the experience of metamorphosis carries with it images of threat and destruction. In Canto II, where the theme of metamorphosis is first explicitly announced, the figure of ultimate beauty appears in a dissolving series of fearful and inspiring faces:

> Sleek head, daughter of Lir,
>   eyes of Picasso
> Under black fur-hood, lithe daughter of Ocean;
> And the wave runs in the beach-groove:
> Eleanor, ἑλέυαυς and ἑλέπτολις
> And poor old Homer blind, blind, as a bat,
> Ear, ear for the sea-surge, murmur of old men's voices:
> Let her go back to the ships,
> Back among Grecian faces, lest evil come on our own,
> Evil and further evil, and a curse cursed on our children,
> Moves, yes she moves like a goddess
> And has the face of a god
>   and the voice of Schoeney's daughters,
> And doom goes with her in walking. (II. 6)

We do not have to translate or register all the allusions and word-plays in this dense passage to recognize its antithetical structure. Here is metamorphosis with, quite literally, a vengeance—a structure of metamorphosis like nothing so much as the cruel story of Actaeon, which Pound recurs to throughout the *Cantos*.

To the degree that Pound's work sets out to redefine, for the twentieth century, an order of permanent or foundational civilization, it does not merely fail, it engenders the plot of its own failure. Pound began and ended with the intention of writing such an earthly paradise. But he found his intentions constantly frustrated. 'It is difficult to write a paradiso', he told Donald Hall in 1960, 'when all the superficial indications are that you ought to write an apocalypse'.[12] But even in 1960 he wanted to call the adversative elements 'superficial', for he still had in view that 'order of ascension' in his poem which would conclude in a Paradiso.

The order of ascension was the act of writing to date (and as it turned out the date did not matter since it was endlessly repeated) in which he was 'writing to resist the view that Europe and civilisation are going to Hell' (DH 48). That formulation of the project is extremely interesting since Pound saw the passage to hell as an essential experience, and hardly one to be resisted. Thus we see how ambivalent the image of hell is for Pound, torn as his work was between the demands of Homer on one hand and Dante on the other. Indeed, hell in the *Cantos* is itself a metamorphic figure.

Pound's (poetic) quest for Total Form, like his (cultural) quest for the earthly paradise, survives only in its own contradictions. These are not simply metaphors, however, like Yeats's 'terrible beauty', they are ugly and furious, as Yeats's father knew. In what Pound named 'the fight for light versus subconsciousness', he saw that the struggle 'demands obscurities and penumbras', or what he sometimes called 'my muddles' (DH 48). These sentimental formulations scarcely touch the edge of the whole truth, however. 'A lot of contemporary writing avoids inconvenient areas of the subject', Pound said, and he determined to try not to avoid those inconveniences in the *Cantos* (DH 48). That determination made him seek for a form 'elastic enough to take the necessary material. It had to be a form *that wouldn't exclude something merely because it didn't fit*' (DH 23, my italics).

That is a startling, a paradoxical idea, yet it only repeats, in a more direct way, what he had said of the *Cantos* around 1915, in one of his earliest drafts for the work: 'Let in your quirks and tweeks, and say the thing's an artform, / . . . the modern world / Needs such a rag-bag to stuff all its thoughts in'.[13] At that point Pound thought *Sordello* would be his model, but had he listened to the *tone* of his early efforts he might have realized that Byron and *Don Juan* would be even more powerful presences in his work.

III

The contradictions in the *Cantos* were finally (1936) judged by Yeats, who tried to sympathize with them, to have been 'carried beyond reason', a work of 'more deliberate nobility and the means to convey it' than any other contemporary poem, but one which is 'constantly interrupted, broken, twisted into nothing by its direct opposite, nervous obsession, nightmare, stammering confusion'. Working in this way Pound has not 'got all the wine into the bowl', for to Yeats poetic 'form must be full, sphere-like, single'.[14] The charge would have struck home because Pound had always embraced the idea that '"Good Writing" is perfect control'.[15]

And yet how odd does Yeats's critique now seem coming from that great inheritor of Blake! Had the antinomian Romantic annotated the passage, he would have subjected it to the same abuse he heaped upon Bishop Watson's 'Apology for the Bible' and Wordsworth's *Excursion*. If Pound in the *Cantos* had been 'carried beyond reason', Blake would have applauded his condition, and if his wine spilt from or overflowed his chalice, that too would have received Blake's applause. Only men like Sir Joshua Reynolds, men who knew nothing of inspiration, imagined that the soul of art was an orderly one. 'Bring out number weight & measure in a year of dearth'; 'The cistern contains, the fountain overflows'.[16] Blake's work, as we have seen, is itself notably fractured and unstable—'You shall not bring me down to believe such fitting & fitted'—and he would have sympathized with Pound's desire to put into the *Cantos* whatever could not be made to fit.

Whether he would have also recognized the sheer physical similarities between his 'composite art' and Pound's ideogrammatical texts is not so clear. None the less, the congruities are quite plain. Any page of the *Cantos* immediately strikes one with its material weight and physique. This quality is most pronounced in the later cantos (from LII to the end), at least in the texts that most readers know. But even on pages that have no ideograms the effect is unmistakable. Letters, words, and phrasal units are treated as material things, so that we encounter the page both as configuration and as discourse. The effect is produced partly by the optical appearance of a free verse form, partly by the different type-founts required when so many languages are being used, and partly by the recovery of various kinds of 'found' materials. None of these pages deploy Chinese ideograms; nevertheless, they are all 'ideogrammatical' texts.

The page itself in Pound thus becomes one of his most prominent figures of permanence. Nothing illustrates this so well as the first editions of the first two installments of the *Cantos*, those two badly neglected books privately printed as *A Draft of XVI Cantos* (1925) and *A Draft of the Cantos XVII–XXVII* (1928). These texts, oversize quartos printed on laid paper, distinctly recall—as Pound well knew[17]—the work of William Morris and the whole tradition of decorated book production which was revived in the late nineteenth century. The very title of Pound's first instalment of cantos seems to be a deliberate echo of the first instalment of Dante Gabriel Rossetti's *The House of Life* sequence. The borders and decorated capitals in Pound's texts were done by Henry Strater and Gladys Hynes, but these two artists were not allowed to work on Pound's texts as free agents. We know from their correspondence that they followed Pound's specific and detailed instructions.[18]

But while the face of these texts says one thing, their converse says something very different. They offer, initially, an appearance of finishedness and monumentality, but of course their titles move in the opposite direction. In each case we are dealing with 'A Draft of' something, or sets of texts which are in process—both on their way towards some future conclusion, and (presumably) in a present condition of intrinsic tentativeness. These early editions come to the reader in figures of immensity and permanence, yet they are both among the most transient of Pound's works. Few readers have ever seen them, and in the many reprintings of the *Cantos* these initial incarnations have been completely forgotten. The third book instalment of Pound's work, *A Draft of XXX Cantos* (1930), was also privately printed, but its format is small octavo and the splendid coloured designs in the first two books are no longer present.

There will be 'a repeat in' this early history throughout the later printing career of Pound's work.[19] For example, unless you had copies of the first installments of Pound's poem, each new part would come to you on its own, fragmented from the whole. Cantos XXXI–XLI were published in 1934, Cantos XLII–LI in 1937, Cantos LII–LXXI in 1940, and Cantos LXXIV–LXXXIV in 1948. Only at that point (1948) did a 'collected' edition of the *Cantos* appear, and when it did the contradictory impression of monumentality and instability was once again apparent. It is a massive book, of course, but censored passages appear from time to time (these kinds of publisher's interventions began in 1940), and—most startling of all—the sequence is interrupted by the complete absence of Cantos LXXII–LXXIII.

When the sections *Rock Drill* and *Thrones* were added to the work in 1955 and 1959, the *Cantos* gestured toward the achievement of some massive synthesis. But once again that gesture would prove an illusion, and its illusory nature would be exposed with the appearance, in 1970, of the final book-section, *Drafts and Fragments*. In this culminant period of the work's publishing history during Pound's lifetime, to trace the development of the many reprintings of the 'collected' editions is profoundly instructive. As each new instalment appeared after 1954, both New Directions and Faber and Faber would add it to their collected editions of the *Cantos* whenever a reprinting was called for. In addition, local changes in these texts were made from time to time, but in the most random and idiosyncratic ways, and independently by each publisher. The text kept changing before one's eyes, and the process did not stop with Pound's death. New reprintings brought the addition of yet further pieces of text, which were then added at the end of the book—or in certain instances, deleted from the book, as opinion changed about the authenticity of the texts.

The poem's incompletion thus seems duplicated and reduplicated even as it also seems unable to cease its pursuit of that illusive sense of an ending. The most recent (the tenth) reprinting (1986) by New Directions represents what Pound might well have called 'an apocalypse' of his text, for it tacks on new material at the beginning and the ending alike: a title and half-title said (in a 'Publisher's Note') to have been authorized by Pound, a concluding set of gratulant verses to Olga Rudge, and—at last—the missing Cantos LXXII–LXXIII. These cantos were first printed in Italy in 1944–5 in ephemeral fascist periodicals—they are written in Italian—and they were later reprinted in a private edition in 1983, also in Italy.[20] The text in the New Directions collected *Cantos* follows the text of 1983, but that is very different indeed from the texts of 1944–5. Furthermore, there are other texts of these cantos—typescripts—which have never been published.

The text of the *Cantos* thus turns out to be as nervous and unbalanced in its posthumous existence as it ever was during Pound's lifetime of working at it. He didn't want to 'exclude something [from it] merely because it didn't fit', and as he kept avoiding such exclusions himself, so his inheritors have followed after him. It is a poem, as Yeats saw, in which there must be 'nothing to check the flow' (YO, p. xxiv), a poem directed toward a form and order which will only be possible through what Yeats was dismayed to call Pound's 'loss of self-control' (YO, p. xxv).

The *Cantos* thereby moves into its forbidden and forbidding territories, seeks its 'sympathy for the devil'. This is no play of mask and anti-mask, however, no marriage of heaven and hell. The *Cantos* is so resolute in its will to include everything that it goes to the limit of the known—which is to say our idea of the civilized or moral—world. Fascism is our word for that limit, but it is only a word, a critical abstraction. Not everything in the *Cantos* is fascist, of course, any more than every part of Eichmann's life was absorbed in his activities for the Third Reich. But when the work is fascist there is no mistaking the fact: for example in Canto CIV, when he presents Hitler as a Blakean figure, 'furious from perception' (CIV 741) because he has grasped the international Jewish conspiracy of bankers and usurocrats; or at the opening of the first of the Pisan Cantos, in Pound's elegiac lines for the dead Mussolini; or throughout Canto XLI's presentation of Mussolini's economic programmes; or, perhaps most dramatically, in the suppressed Italian Cantos, which are an extended poetic tribute to the tradition of Italian fascist ideology and personal character.

The poem finds the local habitations and the names for what it signifies to be fascist. It is particular on these matters, as it should be; for being particular is what poetry does, is what poetry is supposed to do. Thus the particularity of Pound's fascism is matched by the particularities of his anti-Semitism throughout the *Cantos*, as numerous passages could be adduced to show. Whether the poem should have dared these particularities, whether it should have entered such worlds in the first place, are other questions, questions which Yeats, for example—who more than sympathized with Pound's actual views—decided in the negative. But to Pound, Yeats's decision could only be one which avoided what Yeats' found to be 'inconvenient areas of the subject'.

Pound did not think that fascism was an inconvenient area of his subject. On the contrary, Mussolini was central. But as the 'poem including history' went on, it accumulated an array of 'heteroclite elements' (DH 48), and if they did not easily fit together, they were none the less, for Pound, indispensable—Homer, Frobenius, Coke and the *Institutes*, Sigismundo Malatesta, Confucius, Jefferson and Adams, the Sienese bank Monte dei Paschi, and so forth. The pursuit of paradisal knowledge became in the *Cantos* a mutant—an empiricist—reconstruction of the myth of Faust. The poem is itself a continuous descent into hell, an unending consultation with sources of truth. In the event, a metamorphosis of the entire poem also takes place. The *Cantos* turns on Pound, like Actaeon's dogs; the poem unfolds its nightmares.[21]

This great metamorphosis affects every text in the work. The prophecy of Tiresias in Canto I appears, in the context of the entire poem, an ironic forecast indeed. The Hell Cantos, so full of hate, jar against the work's later attempts to ground the poem in an ideal of love. More than that, however, those cantos turn out not to be a vision of hell at all—as Eliot had so shrewdly discerned. Or rather, they become a vision of hell in a sense utterly transformed from what the text, and Pound, had originally intended. Pound did not imagine them as a 'repeat' of the consultation with Tiresias, though they turn out to be, in part, precisely that, only the knowledge they deliver emerges in contradiction as the text turns back on itself:

> bog of stupidities,
> malevolent stupidities, and stupidities,
> the soil living pus, full of vermin . . .
>   pandars to authority,
> pets-de-loup, sitting on piles of stone books,
> obscuring the texts with philology . . .
> the air without refuge of silence,
>   the drift of lice, teething,
> and above it the mouthing of orators,
> the arse-belching of preachers . . . (XIV. 63)

The lines give back to us fore-echoes of his post-war commentaries, both in and out of the *Cantos*, on his own life's work. Indeed, Canto XIV preaches down 'the betrayers of language' in the language of that betrayal, and the text thereby betrays itself, as Pound himself would later show. This is not a hell for other people, as Eliot thought, it is a hell for anyone, and for Pound as well. No names are assigned to the damned here, as they were in Dante, only pieces of names—cryptic letters dangling at the end of ellipses:

> . . . . e and . . . . . n, their wrists bound to
>   their ankles . . .
> And with them . . . . r. (XIV. 61)

Pound thought this style appropriate since the damned were both inhuman and legion.[22] But it is an invidious style which leaves no one safe, least of all the man whose name is informed with his own infernal letters, *ezra pound*. The text, seemingly so confident of what it knows and sees, stands blind and unconscious of itself. The conclusion of Canto XV is therefore particularly striking:

Ἡέλιου τ᾽ Ἡέλιου
    blind with the sunlight,
Swollen-eyed, rested,
      lids sinking, darkness unconscious. (XV. 67)

The poem emerges from its understanding of Malebolge into a language prophetic with contradictory meanings, 'blind with the sunlight' in an entirely ironic sense.

    Pound's text is thus 'carried beyond reason', beyond his own Modernist reason as well as the Romantic reason of his friend Yeats. Pound wishes to exclude nothing, and the poem fulfils his wish. It descends into hells and undergoes metamorphoses, but the experiences are born along by shadowy counter-currents. We tend to comprehend the demonic elements under the name fascism, but that is only a name, and to most Anglo-Americans very much a hell for other people. If the *Cantos* could speak, however, part of what it would say is 'I myself am hell'; and if it could be read, its readers would have to find ways of repeating those words.

    Poetry must have sympathy for the devil, nor can that demon be a beast for other people. Poems come to show the human face of what we would rather imagine as inhuman. The *Cantos* are not vitiated or ruined by their fascism—that is merely a sentimental way of reading them, a way of allowing us to preserve our own confidence in the possession of their truth. The fascism of the poem is the work's ultimate experience of metamorphosis—for Pound, obviously, but for us his readers as well. The poem forces us to the brink of an ultimate spiritual catastrophe that corresponds exactly to what we associate with Pound. The experience tells us that evil is what human beings bring into the world, that evil is what we do (though it is not the only thing we do). Fascism, like Ezra Pound, occupied the human world, and occupied it in a powerful, even a dominant, way. Human beings have extraordinary capacities for evil. Fascism is one way human beings decided to be human in the twentieth century, and the *Cantos* shows us how this was, how this might have been, true. Though the name for this way has gone out of fashion, it is not a way that has yet been abandoned, or that can be forgotten. It is our touchstone for reading the *Cantos*.

IV

We should like to think, perhaps, that in its quest for knowledge the poem moved in a tragic rhythm to some final anagnorisis, a culminant revelation of the error and evil to which it had been committed. The Pisan Cantos are commonly read in this way because of their subject-matter and the circumstances of their composition. Written while he was imprisoned for treason in the Disciplinary Training Center at Pisa after the defeat of the Axis powers, these cantos ruminate the disaster which had overtaken Pound's life and his most cherished ideals. They are full of nostalgia, regret, self-recrimination. One of their most attractive qualities is their loving attention to small details—personal memories and pictures from the gone world of years before, and a kind of Thoreau-like attention to immediate particularities. He will observe with great care the way a wasp builds her nest or the behaviour of a colony of ants, and he will then cast the experiences—tiny though they be—into the most splendid, and apposite, poetic forms:

As a lone ant from a broken ant-hill
from the wreckage of Europe, ego scriptor. (LXVVI. 458)

But we must not be deceived by these 'scenes of distinguished beauty'. The catastrophe of the *Cantos* remains, like the hell uncovered in Canto XIV, if not entirely without dignity, then certainly without tragedy. To imagine hell as tragic forms the structure of Romantic satire when it turns to face the hypocrisy of the middle classes. That is Byron's and Blake's way of imagining, but it is neither Rossetti's nor Pound's.

When we think to read the Pisan Cantos as Pound's tragic recognition—for that matter, when we think to read the *Drafts and Fragments* that way—we might pause to remember how much remained unrecognized, to the end, by Pound. Obviously he had met with some terrible disaster, but the event left his commitments to fascism almost completely intact. During the years at St Elizabeth's Hospital he remained in close communication with American Nazis and other fascist sympathizers, whose activities and ideas he encouraged.[23] Academics like to emphasize his contacts during that period with sympathetic figures like Charles Olson, or his later interviews with Donald Hall and Allen Ginsberg. Important as these events were, there is another, bleaker truth to the matter of Pound's post-war years. Olson finally stopped going to see Pound because he could no longer bear to listen to his anti-Semitic and racist talk.

We know that Pound ultimately repudiated his anti-Semitism, but we have not been so attentive to the way that repudiation was expressed. It came during his interview with Ginsberg in 1967, when Pound surfaced briefly from the suffocating muteness of the last ten years. As Ginsberg praised the old man's achievement in the *Cantos*, Pound flinched away, called it all 'A mess ... My writing—stupidity and ignorance all the way through', and he went on to declare that 'The intention was bad':

> That's the trouble—anything I've done has been an accident—any good has been spoiled by my intentions—the preoccupation with irrelevant and stupid things.... But my worst mistake was the stupid, suburban prejudice of anti-Semitism, all along, that spoiled everything.[24]

We shall return to consider the question of intentional as opposed to accidental achievements. Here one must note the appalling inadequacy of Pound's reference to his anti-Semitism as a 'stupid, suburban prejudice'. Had it been a prejudice he cultivated as a small suburban shamefulness, this formulation might have sufficed. But Pound was a public figure, and he broadcast his 'prejudice' as part of an entire vision of an ideal human culture; and he placed that vision in practical service to fascist Italy, and linked it to fascist Germany; and he did this in the *Cantos* as well as in his unspeakable radio broadcasts. To confess all this as a 'stupid, suburban prejudice' is not merely to misuse words, it is to have mistaken the issues entirely. Pound's final bitter silence, his inarticulate sense of some kind of utter failure, is far more eloquent, far more truthful.

In such a context, one ought no longer to be mistaking the way contradiction functions in Pound's *Cantos*. Perhaps the most famous text in the Pisan section, the conclusion of Canto LXXXI, is a good case in point. The incantation against 'vanity', for example, is commonly read as Pound's charge against himself, and while this reading is not merely possible but necessary, it runs parallel (or counter) to another that may have been even more to Pound's purposes:

> The ant's a centaur in his dragon world.
> Pull down thy vanity, it is not man
> Made courage or made order or made grace ...
>   Pull down thy vanity
> Thou art a beaten dog beneath the hail,
> A swollen magpie in a fitful sun,
> Half black half white
> Nor knowst'ou wing from tail
> Pull down thy vanity
>   How mean thy hates

Fostered in falsity,
>   Pull down thy vanity,
> Rathe to destroy, niggard in charity,
> Pull down thy vanity,
>   I say pull down. (LXXXI. 521)

Pound here is talking about the 'Half black half white' American army who, having won the war, parade their courage, grace, and order.[25] He is talking as well about what such an army has done to Italy ('Rathe to destroy'), but most of all he is thinking of the privations to which he has been personally subjected. Hatred has been a recurrent subject in Canto LXXXI and this passage means to oppose that meanness with a positive ideal which Pound associates with active love. The generosity of the black American soldier who made Pound a table from a packing case is a figure of such love presented early in the canto, but Pound delivers the *figura* so as to emphasize that the act had to be performed surreptitiously lest the soldier be reprimanded by his superiors ('doan yu tell no one I made it', 519). Unlike that single black soldier, the American army is 'niggard in charity', the text declares, thus making an aural (and, incidentally, a racist) word-play back to the charitable soldier.

The touchstone for that soldier's charity is the vision that enters Pound's tent at the end of the canto, and that introduces the 'vanity' passage. It is a vision of eyes that show no anger or hatred, 'the full Ειδως' of how Pound had first and last conceived his own work:

>   To have gathered from the air a live tradition
> Or from a fine old eye the unconquered flame,
> This is not vanity. (522)

The eye here is explicitly that of Wilfred Scawen Blunt, but it is figuratively Pound's as well; for it is Pound who attributed to the coarse and self-important Blunt such splendid virtues, and it is Pound who made his life's work that project of preserving cultural greatness.[26]

Here and to the end of his poem Pound would confess to the vanity of his negligence, his failures to act ('error is all in the not done'). He would never inquire into, let alone penetrate, the evil in his loves:

What thou lovest well remains,
>   the rest is dross
> What thou lov'st well shall not be reft from thee
> What thou lov'st well is thy true heritage

Whose world, or mine or theirs
              or is it of none?
First came the seen, then thus the palpable
    Elysium, though it were in the halls of hell,
    What thou lovest well is thy true heritage
What thou lov'st well shall not be reft from thee (521)

There is a sentimental way of reading these great lines, a way that agrees to
be moved by their devotion to some ideal of love. Nor is that way entirely
wrong. But it is mistaken, for in truth this is a frightening passage, and it
will appear as such so long as we keep our minds clear about what it is,
exactly, that Pound and his poem have loved so long and well. 'The full
Ειδως' is an 'Elysium', but its roots strike down to 'the halls of hell', nor is
that hell a mere metaphor. Is it a comfort or a catastrophe that what this
poem loves, what Pound loves, shall 'not be reft' away—in a word, that its
fascism will stay with it for ever, as an essential part of its 'true heritage'?
Surely we must see how this is a catastrophe, and we do Pound's work a
profound disservice if we do not also call it that holocaust in which, like
Paolo and Francesca, his work will turn for ever. What Pound loves so well
'remains' and its 'heritage' may and should be traced in its full Ειδως, to the
end. The rest, the illusion that his poetry—that any poetry?—is a matter of
unadulterated beauty, is mere dross. Pound's text speaks a fuller truth than
his mind was able to grasp, and one may well recall, in this Poundian hymn
to love, the sobering alternative truths that Swinburne had earlier put into
the mouth of Althaea:

Love is one thing, an evil thing, and turns
Choice words and wisdom into fire and air.
And in the end shall no joy come, but grief,
Sharp words and soul's division and fresh tears.[27]

V

These words from Swinburne's great poem bring us back to the problem of
truth in poetry and—just as important—of how the reader is to deal with
it. What Althaea says here about love is, in a sense Swinburne wants to
make very clear, obviously *not* true. Love in *Atalanta in Calydon* is not at
all 'one thing', though it is 'an evil thing'—whatever else it may be besides
(including a good thing). In an abstract sense, therefore, the passage seems
to say something about Love which is untrue. But the lines are cunning. In
emphasizing the partiality of Althaea's view, as well as its blindness, Swinburne makes her speak so that we shall sympathize with that view but, at

the same time, understand its limitedness. Love is many things in *Atalanta in Calydon*, some of them are evil, some of them are not.

The poem knows more than the character in the poem, and one structure of poetic truth is founded in that distinction. But because poems are also agents in the field of themselves,[28] they do not represent truth, or embody knowledge, in a formally self-completed way. That idea is what Arnold, for certain historical reasons, wanted to promote—for example in his famous sonnet to Shakespeare, who is Arnold's paradigm of poetic imagination because to be 'Shakespeare' is to be 'Self-school'd, self-scann'd, self-honour'd, self-secure'. Arnold's Shakespeare is Arnold's proof that poetry has the freedom of complete self-integrity.

There are, however, other Shakespeares, some of whom abide our questions, some of whom even nod from time to time. Blake began, for the modern world, a mode of poetic investigation which moved against that view of imagination which Arnold inherited from Kant and Coleridge. Byron and Rossetti represent two related contestatory lines, and the *Cantos* is yet another massive counter-argument, the most sustained to date. But it was not an argument Pound wanted to make. His convictions were all Arnoldian. In *Guide to Kulchur*, which calls itself 'notes for a totalitarian treatise' on art,[29] Pound suggested that there were two kinds of imaginative work: the one, perhaps best exemplified by Dante, he called 'totalitarian' (95) because it appears to make a complete synthesis of its materials; the other he calls 'modern' because it is restless and unfinished, and because it records the struggle for synthesis, but not its achievement. Pound specifically instances the *Cantos* as an example of the latter, a work which exhibits 'the defects inherent in a record of struggle' (135).

The *Cantos* is therefore proof, even on Pound's own showing, that poetry may not be 'totalitarian' even when its ideology is. But the poem develops a more compelling 'proof' by showing in concrete detail how it is that poetry stands beyond anyone's complete possession. Consider again, for example, those much-praised lines from Canto LXXXI: 'Pull down thy vanity, it is not man / Made courage or made order or made grace'. Had Blake read these lines he would have been outraged; and were he asked who made courage and order and grace, he would have said, precisely, 'man', who for Blake made everything—for good and for ill alike. Had one asked Byron who made such things, he would have equivocated: 'If God exists, God made them; but if he doesn't exist, they are the work of Chance.' Rossetti would have attributed them to 'Love' in all its contradictory aspects. For Pound, courage and order and grace are the creations of Nature, or what he calls here 'the green world'.

When Pound, or the *Cantos*, delivers those lines, the form of the discourse insists that they will be read, as it were, beyond themselves. In this case such a freedom, such an openness to questioning and self-questioning, is licensed in the text's shrewd enjambment, which places the word 'man' in two syntaxes—as the complement of the verb 'is', and as the subject of the verb 'made'.[30] One syntax moves to associate, the other to dissociate, the thought of 'man' from the idea of 'vanity', so that a small contradiction is set up. That contradiction is a summons to the reader to intervene, an opening or gap in the poetry which demands some kind of response (initially registered as a choice to be made). In this way the poem sets in motion a dialectical structure of relations which will not be held in check by arbitrary authorities, including the arbitrary authorities of the text itself. Interventions will be as particular as the originary acts of production.

In the recent past critics associated these kinds of poetic structures with the power of metaphor to generate what was often called 'ambiguity'. But Pound, like Blake, was hostile to the metaphoric theory of imagination. Both insisted that poetry was a discourse not of ambiguous but of determinate meanings and forms: a discourse of particulars, of 'bounding lines', of clear distinctions. Pound, quoting the *Odyssey* (XII. 183), invoked a phrase used by Homer to describe the singing of the Sirens, 'Ligur aiode'. When Pound translated it 'keen or sharp singing . . . , song with an edge on it' (*L* 285), he called attention to its antithetical character (a discourse that is both beautiful and dangerous, clear and deceptive). The thought here is to gain a rich texture or poetic surface—and hence to generate significance—by opening the discourse not to 'levels of interpretation' but to multiplicities of response.

Such an imagination of imagination inclines to a metonymic rather than a metaphoric engineering. It can take many forms—Blake's, Byron's, Rossetti's, and Pound's work are all inclined to metonymic forms, though in other respects these poets could scarcely be more different. Poetry in this mode—allegory and satire are its greatest genres—will always tend to the accumulative and the ornamental, just as it will always tend to clarify the distance that separates itself from its audiences. This larger rhetorical structure mirrors the events which develop in the more local ways we have observed. The *Cantos* will seek the most precise expression, or what Pound idealized as the exactitude of prose: the ideogram and the image are the exponents of what he had in mind to do.

The paradoxical result of this pursuit of precision and limitedness is what one registers in the face of a sculptured form. The form's definition opens the field of itself, or—as art commentators like to say—creates the space within which it stands or moves. Wallace Stevens's 'Anecdote of a Jar' is one of the clearest statements of this kind of beauty, which Stevens called 'the beauty of inflections' (as opposed to 'the beauty of innuendoes'). The determinateness of the image sets up a gravitational field towards which everything which is not the image inclines to move; and when those othernesses move into the field, they do not implode into the initial image, but preserve their distinctness.

Such a form of poetry is always, consequently, unequal to itself, is radically self-contradicted. As image succeeds to image, the discourse accumulates a structure that grows increasingly overdetermined. Every part becomes open to invasion from every other part, nor are those 'parts' always what we think they are. The *Cantos* runs to many hundreds of pages, but it also runs to many decades of time; and histories which did not even exist when the first canto was produced come to impinge upon it later, and to force it to be seen, and read, in other terms and contexts.

The paranoia which some critics have noticed in the poem—the stylistic screed we saw in the Hell Cantos, the theme of the universal conspiracy of bankers and Jews—is a reflex of those contradictions. Such passages, particularly when they involve explicit presentations of Pound's anti-Semitism and fascism, come in for the heaviest kind of censure, or contempt, from most readers now. The following lines from Canto L, for example, are simply dismissed by John Lauber:

> And Ferdinando Habsburg . . .
> got back a state free of debt
>   coffers empty
> but the state without debt
> England and Austria were for despots without commerce
> considered
>   put back the Pope but
> reset not republics: Venice, Genova, Lucca
> and split up Poland in their soul was usura
> and in their hand bloody oppression
> and that son of a dog, Rospigliosi,
> came into Tuscany to make serfs of old Tuscans.
> S. .t. on the throne of England, s. .t. on the Austrian sofa
> In their soul was usura and in their minds darkness
> and blankness, greased fat were four Georges
> Pus was in Spain, Wellington was a jew's pimp
> and lacked mind to know what he effected.
> 'Leave the Duke, Go for Gold!'
> In their souls was usura and in their hearts cowardice
> In their minds was stink and corruption
> Two sores ran together, Talleyrand stank with shanker
> and hell pissed up Metternich (L 248)

I have quoted somewhat more of the passage than Lauber because it is important to see what the lines are about in literal fact: that is, they develop a commentary on the restoration of the European thrones and dominions in the aftermath of the French Revolutionary and Napoleonic Wars.[31] One might add, in passing, that what Pounds says here is approximately what one will find in Byron's and Shelley's various commentaries on the European settlement engineered by England after the Napoleonic Wars.[32]

That said, one must observe as well that Lauber has not *read* the passage, he has simply reacted to—recoiled from—Pound's offensive rhetoric. Are we to think that a writer of Pound's skill was not *aware* of what he was doing, that he simply *missed* a shot at the beautiful here and lapsed into his anti-Semitic invective? Surely not, and when readers dismiss writing of this kind they are often merely exposing their own failures of intelligence—specifically, their failure to read, and to think through their reading.

Pound's anti-Semitism and fascism are important, in this context, because they can serve readers of the *Cantos* as convenient excuses not to read and not to think, and to believe that Pound—when he writes as an anti-Sem-ite and a fascist—is unthinking as well. This is a great and a typical mistake among readers of the *Cantos*. The passage from Canto L, for example, uses its offensive rhetoric precisely as part of its strategy to challenge and call out the reader. If we lapse away by imagining (for example) that an absence of beauty here is a sign of bad writing, we shall merely have exposed our own habits of bad reading.

Beauty is not the issue here, any more than pleasure or beauty must be the criteria by which we measure the presence of poetry. Any careful reading of Rossetti, for instance, will reveal how a good writer may use the beautiful as an instrument of terror, or may expose the nightmare of pleasure and even happiness. Such writing is typical of the late nineteenth century, and of course Pound is a direct inheritor of that kind of writing.

Pound's writing is not devoted primarily to beauty, it is devoted to intel-ligence (and this frequently in its own despite). Beauty is one of the devices of intelligence in his work—and ugliness is another. Pound made this very clear very early, as we see in his essay 'The Serious Artist'. There he makes an important distinction between what he called 'the art of diagnosis and the art of cure' (45). The one he associated with 'ugliness' and the other with 'beauty', and he went on to observe: 'The cult of beauty and the delineation of ugli-ness are not in mutual opposition' so far as art is concerned. 'If the poets don't make certain horrors appear horrible who will?', Pound asked Felix Schelling. 'All values ultimately come from our judicial sentences. (This arrogance is not mine but Shelley's, and it is absolutely true....)' (L 249).

Pound's writing has its failures, to be sure, but we should not be too quick in judging when and where these failures occur. Many of the *Cantos*'s self-contradictions, as we have seen, are anything but signs of weak writing. In the present instance, moreover, we confront a passage which fairly *announces* its call upon the intelligence of the reader. I am not thinking merely of the line 'and lacked mind to know what he effected'—with all that it must imply in context. Observe as well the beginning of the passage, and especially the fall of the word 'considered'. The spatial management of the text is excellent in that it directs our attention to the acts of mind with which 'England and Austria' were engaged in the immediate aftermath of the wars with Napoleon. The word also comes as a challenge to readers, to think in their turn about those events, to imagine *how* those events might be judged, and *why* anyone in 1937 might 'consider' such a re-consideration important.

From *our* point of view, here in 1988, we likewise have some thinking to do. If we attend to the style of the passage, for example, we will see how the whole movement pivots around the verse 'and split up Poland in their soul was usura'. This line releases a burst of energy by refusing to insert the stop after 'Poland' which the prose syntax calls for. The text refuses even a caesura and the consequence is an extraordinary leap in pace and tone.

So far as the sense of the passage is concerned, the line is equally crucial in that it centralizes 'Poland' as a figure of international political and economic manipulation. Pound is asking us to think back to the years 1817–22 and to the restoration of the European thrones under the leadership of England. The text recalls in particular the settlement of Poland, which involved, among other things, England's callous breach of the promises she had made to Polish patriots who were seeking freedom from Russian control. Tossing Poland to Russia was part of the European 'settlement', as were various other moves—Pound alludes to some of them—to ensure that hereditary and church power would be secured against the growing surge throughout Europe for nationalist autonomy.

The poetic effect here is all the more powerful because the lines are stylistically 'objectivist'. The deployment of this style, however, produced consequences for the poem that Pound—in trying to control his work—certainly did not foresee. First-person authority is a useful device for supplying poetry with an (illusory) resort from ideology, a stylistic 'place' which is imagined to be non-ideological. An objectivist procedure removes that particular resort, and the consequence is what has sometimes been called 'naked poetry', that is, a poetry whose illusion is that no part of the poetry will be set aside in a position of privilege—in this case, that no part of the poetry will be imagined as free of ideology.

Pound's satire on the crass politics of the restoration is one part of the ugliness in this passage, but the lines, once again, turn back on themselves and set off in pursuit of other forms of ugliness. 'Pus was in Spain, Wellington was a jew's pimp' is more than an incredibly clever (and incredibly offensive) satire on the suppression of the newly fledged Spanish patriotic revolution, more than an attack on the economic hegemony England was establishing for herself in Europe. The style of the line is that of the Hell Cantos, and the phrase 'A jew's pimp'—in the context of the poem—establishes (and re-establishes) many connections besides the immediate one to Baron Rothschild.

'Jew's pimp' is not just 'anti-Semitic', it is anti-Semitic in a context of great complexity and concreteness. The phrase cannot be 'controlled' in the way that Pound, and Yeats, imagined that poetry could and should be controlled. As a consequence, the passage yields to its internal contradictions and over-determined pressures. The attack upon the European settlement does not here specifically mention Napoleon, though he is a major figure throughout Canto L (and elsewhere in the *Cantos*), where his energy is presented to contrast with his monarchical enemies: 'the Austrian sofa . . . greased fat [of the] four Georges'. But the *Cantos* cannot control the figure of Napoleon, any more than Napoleon—genius that he was—could control the world, or even his own destiny. There is a 'minds darkness' that goes beyond the darkness of monarchical wickedness or English political cynicism and that sweeps up Napoleon and all his related poetical *figurae*—Mussolini, Hitler, Sigismundo, Ezra Pound; and it is a darkness set in motion through the objectivism of Pound's work which, as the convict of its own illusions, is forced to place all its particular judgements before the bar of a supervening judgement. That supervening judgement is not a set of precepts or ideas, it is rather the law of this work's poetic style.[33]

The demon and the hero—the Jew (or Wellington) on one hand, and Napoleon on the other—are the text's ideological figures of ugliness and beauty, but their over-determined relations with other figures and texts in the *Cantos* cuts them loose from a fixed law and order. Consequently, what is horrible in these lines will appear as one thing to Pound while it will seem quite another to John Lauber, or to me, or—I dare say—to my readers. The lines make 'certain horrors appear horrible', and they do it in the way that poetry always does, by opening to critical thought those ideologies to which the poetry has committed itself.

And we must say 'ideologies', in the plural, because the commitments are as various as all those who will have ever been engaged with the poetry. Pound's objectivism collapses the distinction between 'writer' and 'reader'. We see this most clearly when we remember that Pound is writing this canto in the context of 1936–7. At that time the Polish Question once again was a crucial focus of European political interests; indeed, in 1936–7, if one took the Polish point of view, England's soul was indeed 'consumed with usura', and equally indifferent to Poland's political fate with respect to Russia and Germany. We forget that in the years immediately before the war England was anything but a friend to Poland, and that Poland regarded English policy with the deepest suspicion.

The general point, however, is that this text calls upon us to read with accuracy and intelligence, and in particular to consider the 'repeat in history' which it is imagining. Equally important to see, however, is that reading with intelligence does not necessarily entail agreeing (or disagreeing) with some or all or any of the judgements set forth in Pound's text. Those judgements, having been committed to the poem, have thereby submitted themselves to judgement in their turn.

In this way Pound's texts, like Byron's, enter a dialogue with their readers; this is what Pound, like Byron before him, wanted. Our text from Canto L calls out for reciprocal acts of thought from its readers. Such judgements often, as we have seen, work to expose the contradictions which the Poundian texts generate, and these antithetical readings are no more than what the poem expects from us.

But what of our failures to read, the lapses of intelligence to be discovered in those who look at Pound's poem? Does the work expect from its readers that seeing they may not see, and hearing they may not hear? In an important sense I think it does. Pound's texts make serious demands upon those who take them up, and the incredible arrogance of his work often functions, stylistically, as a cunning temptation to the reader's weakness. The poem has many resources for exposing critical thoughtlessness; one of its most effective may be located exactly in those passages where readers feel—out of their horror or out of their sympathy—that they have no difficulty in understanding. Here it is that Pound's work will commonly catch us at our worst, and expose us as that hypocritical reader known so well to Byron and to Baudelaire.

So we may say that the poem's processes overwhelm, and are overwhelmed by, its own judgements and illusions. The work reads itself in its own despite, and in doing so licenses our critical judgements of the work's fascism. But if we 'later' readers then imagine that the hells are here for 'other' people, for fascists and anti-Semites like Pound, we shall have fallen to the same illusion which led Pound initially to believe he could control and define the significance of his text's satire against England, against Jews, against usurocracy. Poems have hells and heavens for us, and those places are rarely what they seem to us to be.

When Pound was writing the Pisan Cantos, his gaolers became suspicious that he might be producing some kind of coded discourse, perhaps even fascist propaganda. To allay such apprehensions he sent a 'Note to [the] Base Censor' (the pun no doubt intended) in which he gave assurances that the new cantos 'contain nothing seditious', and 'nothing in the way of cypher or intended obscurity'.[34] Though he was telling the truth, it was only the truth as he knew it, and by no means the whole truth. If the new Cantos contained 'nothing seditious', they were still wedded to fascist ideology. But the commitment is plain to see and so the cantos were also, to that extent, not written in cipher.

None the less, the poem is (still) being written in a kind of encrypted discourse, because it is still sending messages, making communications, which Pound, the maker of the scripts, cannot master. These are not symbolic scripts, teasing and suggestive, but ideogrammatic ones: bold, expository, completely materialized. Blake would have said that Pound's work was being dictated from eternity in order that the truth, or the many genealogies of good and evil, might be revealed. The *Cantos* is remarkable because when we read it— the whole of it and not simply selected parts—we are prevented from lapsing into transcendental hermeneutics in either of its two predominant forms: the *voluptas* of a pure appreciation ('Gods float in the azure air'), or the *superbia* of final judgements ('malevolent stupidities and stupidities'). We are forestalled from these positions because the *Cantos* has been there, in each case, before us, and has displayed the consequences.

VI

Yeats's efforts to understand the *Cantos* were not, finally, successful. He misread the work because he wanted the *Cantos* to be something other than what it is. This misreading was first set out in the small book we glanced at earlier, *A Packet for Ezra Pound*, where Yeats sent his younger friend an appropriate, if highly equivocal, gift. The 'packet' is in three parts: an opening section where Yeats makes a brief representation of the *Cantos* against the background of Pound's life at Rapallo; the central part—the gift proper—which is titled 'Introduction to the Great Wheel' and which contains a kind of synopsis of the growth and key features of *A Vision*; and finally a concluding (rather than a covering) letter 'To Ezra Pound'.

Yeats associates his own work on *A Vision* with the *Cantos* for very specific reasons. In the first place, he sees an analogy between this chaotic project of Pound's and the 'scattered sentences' (12) of his wife's automatic writing. Secondly, he judges that *A Vision* represents a triumph over the randomness of immediate experience and circumstance, and hence that it may provide Pound with a model, or norm, for a work like the *Cantos*, where Pound was being 'carried beyond reason'. Yeats gives Pound a glimpse of the Great

Wheel, the totalized body of fate within which all reality may find its appropriate place.

The figure presiding over the Great Wheel, according to Yeats, is an image 'from Homer's age', a primitive form removed 'from Plato's Athens, from all that talk of the Good and the One, from all that cabinet of perfection' (35). The figure is Oedipus:

> When it was already certain that Oedipus would bring himself under his own curse he still questioned, and when answered as the Sphinx had been answered, stricken with that horror which is in 'Gulliver' and in the 'Fleurs du Mal', he tore out his own eyes. . . . He knew nothing but his own mind, & yet because he spoke that mind fate possessed it and kingdoms changed according to his blessing & his cursing. . . . I think that he lacked compassion seeing that it must be compassion for himself. (35–6)

Yeats deplored Pound's passion for politics and social reform—'all that cabinet of perfection'—and urged him, with this powerful imagining of Oedipus, to separate his art from his materials of art. The poet must represent, not be, Oedipus, just as the poem must rise above the horrors it takes up. But Pound was bent on exploring precisely those relations which Yeats, by a kind of categorical imperative, refused to consider. To imagine the poet as Oedipus—which is precisely what Pound did—was too cruel an imagination for Yeats. Better to imagine him as Homer, whose blindness is not linked to confusion but to a clarified and fulfilling insight.

That is the poetic imagining which Pound too wanted, but in the event he reached a different conclusion. The passionate endurance of his quest for a 'totalitarian' form, and its rooted mistakenness, have their analogues in Yeats and in that figure of Oedipus. The *Cantos* expresses the pursuit of totality, as Yeats guessed, but it turns the screw on Yeats's representation. In Pound, only the work has 'Total Form', there is no primal vision or ultimate knowledge. As a consequence, the work is equal to itself in a sense that neither Pound nor Yeats had thought: every part of the work, productive and reproductive, stylistic and contextual—every synchronic aspect and every diachronic phase—impinges on every other. Coming in judgement, the work thereby sets in motion a series of second comings by which it finds itself made subject to continuous judgement.

The effect reminds me of the message, and in certain cases the medium, of many Pre-Raphaelite poems. Rossetti's work we have already examined in such a perspective, but I am thinking now of Swinburne's 'Hertha' and, perhaps even more, of that impressive conclusion to 'A Forsaken Garden':

> As a god self-slain on his own strange altar,
>   Death lies dead.

In the *Cantos* Pound used the Blakean phrase 'furious from perception' to describe both himself and Adolf Hitler (Cantos XC and CIV). It was a phrase he meant to associate with a certain form of the 'minds darkness', a kind of error which he wanted his text to judge *as* error, but not as fundamental error. It was an error, in other words, that he was prepared to forgive (in himself and in others). 'But there is a blindness that comes from inside' (CIV. 741), the text adds, thereby gesturing towards a more fundamental error which will not be forgiven, a kind of sin against the light.

Pound meant to except Hitler and himself from an accusation of that sin, but the *Cantos* will not permit it. The blindness that comes from inside is no more exceptional than are those favoured and furious perceptions. Yeats's pitiless figure, hovering above the text, drains it of all its compassionate illusions. This is why the *Cantos* is not, finally, a tragic work.[35] It would be something far worse—something cruel, and utterly void of pity and compassion—were it not simply something different, something which, like the lives we know, turns alternately through pity and indifference, evil and beauty. Submitting itself to those same contradictions, the work embodies a disturbing mode of truth: equivocal authority, uncertain knowledge—a fascist, and not a Daniel, come to judgement. For the documents of civilization—the writings of the great poets, the readings of the high-minded critics—are all of them, as Benjamin said, equally and at the same time documents of barbarism.

Notes

1. See John Lauber, 'Pound's *Cantos*: A Fascist Epic', *The Journal of American Studies*, 12 (1978), 3–21; Victor C. Ferkiss, 'Ezra Pound and American Fascism', *The Journal of Politics*, 17 (1955), 173–97. The most comprehensive exploration of this subject appeared too late for me to profit from it in this writing; I mean Robert Casillo, *The Genealogy of Demons: Anti-Semitism, Fascism, and the Myths of Ezra Pound* (Evanston, 1988).

2. *Complete Works of William Hazlitt*, ed. P. P. Howe (London, 1930–4) iv. 214–15.

3. See Michael A. Bernstein, *The Tale of the Tribe: Ezra Pound and the Modern Verse Epic* (Princeton, 1980); Ian F. A. Bell (ed.), *Ezra Pound: Tactics for Reading* (London, 1982), especially the essays by Peter Brooker, David Murray, and H. N. Schneidau; Martin Kayman, *The Modernism of Ezra Pound* (London, 1986); Jean Michel Rabate, *Language, Sexuality, and Ideology in Ezra Pound's Cantos* (Albany, NY, 1986); Andrew Parker, 'Ezra Pound and the Economy of Anti-Semitism', in Jonathan Arac (ed.), *Postmodernism and Politics* (Minneapolis, 1986), 70–90; Richard Sieburth, 'In Pound We Trust: The Economy of Poetry/The Poetry of Economics', *Critical Inquiry*, 14 (Autumn 1987), 142–72.

4. Alan Durant, *Ezra Pound: Identity in Crisis* (Brighton, 1981).

5. Letter from J. B. Yeats to his son, 12 Mar. 1918, cited in Richard Ellman, 'Ez and Old Billyum', in Eva Hesse (ed.), *New Approaches to Ezra Pound* (London, 1969), 60.

6. *The Letters of Ezra Pound 1907–1941*, ed. D. D. Paige (London, 1951), 285 (hereafter cited in the text as *L*).

7. *A Packet for Ezra Pound* (Cuala Press, 1929), 2 (hereafter cited in text as *Packet*).

8. See R. Peter Stoicheff, 'The Composition and Publication History of Ezra Pound's *Drafts and Fragments*', *Twentieth Century Literature*, 32 (1986), 78–94.

9. The text of the *Cantos* used throughout is the latest reprinting from Faber/New Directions (the 10th, 1986), which contains some new material, and especially texts of the 'forbidden cantos', LXXII and LXXIII.

10. Pound specifically alludes to Blake at the outset of Canto XVI; Carroll F. Terrell in his indispensable *Companion to the Cantos of Ezra Pound* (Berkeley, 1980, 1984), i. 69, gives only a vague general citation here. Pound's text shows that he is thinking specifically about certain plates in *The [First] Book of Urizen* and *The Marriage of Heaven and Hell*. For Pound's later influence see the work of Marjorie Perloff, especially *The Poetics of Indeterminacy: Rimbaud to Cage* (Princeton, 1981) and *The Dance of Intellect: Studies in the Poetry of the Pound Tradition* (Cambridge, 1985).

11. *After Strange Gods* (London, 1934), 43.

12. See Donald Hall, 'Ezra Pound: An Interview', *Paris Review*, 28 (1962), 47 (hereafter cited in the text as *DH*).

13. The text is reproduced in Ronald Bush, *The Genesis of Ezra Pound's Cantos* (Princeton, 1976); see p. 53.

14. 'Introduction', *The Oxford Book of Modern Verse 1892–1935* (Oxford, 1936), pp. xxiv–xxvi (hereafter cited in the text as *YO*).

15. 'The Serious Artist', in *Literary Essays of Ezra Pound*, ed. T. S. Eliot (London, 1954), 49.

16. William Blake, *The Marriage of Heaven and Hell*, plate 7.

17. See Pound's letter of 1924 to William Bird, and particularly his comment to Wyndham Lewis in a letter of 3 Dec. 1924 (*L* 262).

18. Lawrence Rainey demonstrates this beyond any doubt in his forthcoming essay on Pound, 'Desperate Love'.

19. See Barbara C. Eastman, *Ezra Pound's Cantos: The Story of the Text 1948–1975* (Orono, 1975), and Peter Makin, *Pound's Cantos* (London, 1985), ch. 16.

20. See Massimo Bacigalupo, 'The Poet at War: Ezra Pound's Suppressed Italian Cantos', *The South Atlantic Quarterly*, 83 (1984), 69–79.

21. Hugh Kenner has an excellent discussion of the 'arrayed' structure of the poem (*The Pound Era*, London, 1975, 360–1), which he links to Buckminster Fuller's concept of synergy, or 'the behaviour of whole systems, unpredicted by the knowledge of component parts' (360). Kenner does not use these ideas to show how the *Cantos* might be fated, as it were, to undermine itself at all points by the employment of such modes. In effect, that is what I am trying to do here. For an analogous, but wholly theoretical, discussion of Pound's self-contradictions see Andrew Parker (above, n. 3).

22. See *L* 293, where Pound discusses these matters in a letter to John Lackey Brown.

23. See especially the powerful recent study of E. Fuller Torrey, *The Roots of Treason: Ezra Pound and the Secrets of St. Elizabeth's* (London, 1984).

24. 'Encounters with Ezra Pound', in Allen Ginsberg, *Composed on the Tongue* (Bolinas, Calif., 1980), 7, 8. Ginsberg says that the wording attributed to Pound is 'almost exact'.

25. See Peter D'Epiro, 'Whose Vanity Must Be Pulled Down?', *Paideuma*, 13/2 (Fall, 1984), 247–52.

26. Terrell in the *Companion* (ii. 454) simply accepts Pound's evaluation of the colourful Blunt.

27. *Atalanta in Calydon* (London, 1865), 11.

28. The phrase is adapted from a line in John Hollander's *Reflections on Espionage* (New York, 1976), 15, where he writes (in reference to poets figured as spies): 'Each is an agent in the field of himself.'

29. (New York, 1952), 27. Two further citations below are given in the text.

30. Elizabeth Helsinger suggests to me that the passage may involve a third reading (with the enjambment working to create the adjective 'man-made'). And Leofranc Holford-Strevens suggests that 'one might take "made" as a passive participle agreeing with "man" and having "courage" etc, for complement (the pattern of "Jesus Christ was God made man")'.

31. For annotations see Terrell, *Companion*, i. 194–5. But Terrell believes Pound is only thinking of the Congress of Vienna (181) whereas he in fact has in mind the arrangements made there as well as the later rearrangements made at the Congress of Verona (182).

32. See especially Byron's mordant late satire *The Age of Bronze* (1823).

33. See Kenner, *The Pound Era*, 444: 'Pound sought to outwit connoisseurship by devising a style inseparable from what it delivered'. And he succeeded, thereby creating a style which made his own poem subject to its own structures of judgement.

34. C. David Heymann, *Ezra Pound: The Last Rower* (London, 1976), 172.

35. Pound's final remark in his interview with Donald Hall points toward the 'tragic' reading of the *Cantos*: 'Somebody said that I am the last American living the tragedy of Europe' (DH 51). This seems to me a sentimental, and finally a pathetic, observation coming from Pound.

ROBERT PINSKY

Marianne Moore: Idiom and Idiosyncrasy

Marianne Moore's poems have a social presence, you might even say a sociable presence. That presence is distinct from Moore's tiresome public caricature as a genteel, fey, impishly brilliant old lady in a peculiar hat—and yet gentility and idiosyncrasy are unquestionably part of the true social presence in the poems. Like many stereotypes, this is one we can neither quite feel comfortable with, nor altogether reject. In Moore's best work, the outer force of manners penetrates beyond a charming or complacent gentility, to become a profound moral force, as in the great novelists; and the inner force of idiosyncrasy becomes the sign of a passionate, obdurate selfhood. I think that to understand the peculiar strengths or limitations of this poet, we have to look at her work in the light of such matters as the relation of language and poetry to social life and even to social class. These matters seem all the more important because Moore was a Modernist, one of the generation of poets that raised new questions about the kind of poetry that might be suitable for an American and democratic culture.

Partly because of our own social habits and predispositions, we readers often respond to Moore's work in social terms: people dote on her poems, or find them annoying, a little as if responding directly to a person and her remarks. Here is a very slight but relevant early poem that presents itself explicitly as a social action. The poem (omitted from the *Complete Poems* of

From *Marianne Moore: The Art of a Modernist*, edited by Joseph Parisi, pp. 13–24. Published by UMI Research Press. Copyright © 1990 by Joseph Parisi.

1967) has the pleasing title "To Be Liked by You Would Be a Calamity." It begins with a quotation from Thomas Hardy:

> "Attack is more piquant than concord," but when
>> You tell me frankly that you would like to feel
>>> My flesh beneath your feet,
>>>> I'm all abroad, I can but put my weapon up, and
>>>>> Bow you out.
> Gesticulation—it is half the language.
>> Let unsheathed gesticulation be the steel
>>> Your courtesy must meet,
>>>> Since in your hearing words are mute, which to my senses
>>>>> Are a shout.[1]

One thing this little epigram demonstrates is that Moore can write in the mode of colloquy without writing colloquially. That is, address and something like exchange take place, but not vocally, and not in words much like any conversational language of twentieth-century America: the words "I can but put my weapon up, and / Bow you out" represent part of an exchange, but an exchange imagined in the terms of another century. Like the deliberately period metaphor of swordplay, the "steel" that is "unsheathed" and "put up," this period voice is a defensive and offensive weapon, a way to keep anger and hatred at some distance while striking at them. Even "My flesh beneath your feet," because of "flesh," is a bit stagy and unreal. The most spare, "natural" language and the most memorable phrase coincide on the phrase "Gesticulation—it is half the language." And that moment in the poem is the most clearly inward: self-addressed, not directed toward the imagined interlocutor at all. The poem is indeed about conversation that does not take place, words that are withheld, language as a social weapon that goes unused except in Moore's powerful imagination.

    The artificiality, in other words, is the point. We can picture the actual gesture with which Moore politely and hostilely bowed someone out of her office—personally, I believe such a moment did actually happen—but the address is not only highly, but pointedly, artificial, an invention that represents its underlying true action of silence or reserve. She creates an artificial dialogue to dramatize, and to protect, her inward poise. The poem attains a feeling of social superiority through artifice and the weapon of refusal, the submerged sharklike intelligence that conceives both the unsheathed steel of gesticulation and the "put up" weapon of actual speech. The poem is, in short, an elaborate way of saying "I am not speaking to you"—or, more accurately, "I am not speaking to that person."

Repeatedly and characteristically, Moore's poems construct an elaborate social presence that contrives to disguise or protect, just as manners sometimes do in life. Moore's ambivalent attraction toward the idea of communal life expresses itself, then teasingly cancels itself, characteristically, in a conversation that is not conversation. Reticence and withdrawal, as in "To Be Liked by You Would Be a Calamity," often underlie apparent engagement. Moore's two most characteristic rhetorical modes, apostrophe and quotation, amount to a kind of parody, or at least a blatantly artificial reconstruction, of discourse between people.

In this mock-colloquy, her quotations invoke the possibility of heeding the voice of another, while the poet contrives to manipulate and assign meanings. And in the other direction, her apostrophes often invoke the possibility of addressing another only to suggest the unreality of such address. In *Observations*, there are poems grammatically addressed to an intramural rat, to a chameleon, to a prize bird who is G. B. Shaw, to the sun, to Disraeli, to military progress, to a steam roller, to a snail, to George Moore, to Molière, to the ibis as statecraft embalmed, to a pedantic literalist, to the son of the author of a history book, to critics and connoisseurs, to one by whom it would be a calamity to be liked, to Ireland, and to roses. In none of these poems does the second-person pronoun have the kind of reality it has in poems like, say, Yeats's "Adam's Curse" or Bishop's "Letter to N.Y."

The unreality of the second person is skillfully exploited in some of these poems, often with comic effect, and often aggressively. In "Critics and Connoisseurs," the polysyllabic, first-person sentences describing the swan are artfully contrasted with an abrupt, monosyllabic turn toward the one addressed; "I have seen you

> I remember a swan under the willows in Oxford,
>   with flamingo-colored, maple-
>   leaflike feet. It reconnoitered like a battle-
>   ship. Disbelief and conscious fastidiousness were
>   ingredients in its
>   disinclination to move. Finally its hardihood was
>   not proof against its
>   proclivity to more fully appraise such bits
>   of food as the stream

> bore counter to it; it made away with what I gave it
>   to eat. I have seen this swan and
>   I have seen you; I have seen ambition without
>   understanding in a variety of forms.[2]

This is very shrewd writing. The sentence "It reconnoitered like a battle-ship," while itself terse and plain, introduces the comically ponderous qual-ity that the next sentences embody, "its hardihood was not proof against its proclivity," and "such bits of food as the stream bore counter to it," and so forth, a deadpan irony of inflation, just a little as if mouthed by Robert Morley. By contrast it gives the cutting social edge to "I have seen this swan and I have seen you."

There are many contrasts at work here: polysyllabic abstract moral terms played against the brilliantly observed, specific feet of the swan; the first person against the second person; sentences like Latin played against sentences like abrupt speech; abrupt compression played against unex-pected flourishes of elaboration. All of these are part of the larger contest between idiom, Moore's acute and rather satirical sense of a communal speech, and idiosyncrasy, her equally sharp sense of language as the weapon of her private self which observes the swan and the ant, the critic and the connoisseur. She addresses herself to these objects of attention, and also addresses them grammatically, in a formal way—but not actually, not socially, or even anything like it. You might call these two poems "mock satires," in that they present personal, inward meditations in the outward form of a social clash.

Idiom is the sameness of the language customarily used by people in a particular place. Idiosyncrasy, with its first half from the same root, is in language the sameness of a particular person's *crasis* or constitution. Consid-ering these two elements as partially opposed is a way to understand the dry, skeptical reservations, the rock-hard mistrusts, that stand behind some of Moore's relatively warm-looking, humanistic passages. The opening stanza of "The Steeple-Jack" (*CP*, 5–6) illustrates the double quality I mean:

> Dürer would have seen a reason for living
> in a town like this, with eight stranded whales
> to look at; with the sweet air coming into your house
> on a fine day, from water etched
> with waves as formal as the scales
> on a fish

The line ending emphasizes the phrase "reason for living" in isolation: a kind of sardonic undertone that emphasizes, not habitation ("living in this town"), but a reason to stay alive. Dürer would have seen a reason for living; do you, or I? Especially in a town like this? That undertone of laconic des-peration is not farfetched, since an ocean turbulence affects both the actual stars and their religious representation:

whirlwind fife-and-drum of the storm bends the salt
    marsh grass, disturbs stars in the sky and the
star on the steeple; it is a privilege to see so
much confusion.

"Confusion" is followed by an extended, hyperbolically long catalogue of
flowers, a profuse list so eclectic and long that it is dizzying, even inchoate,
and becomes bilious, imaginary, "not-right," animal, before it is punctuated
at the end by an apparent apothegm of small-town virtue:

                Disguised by what
      might seem the opposite, the sea-
side flowers and
trees are favored by the fog so that you have
      the tropics at first hand: the trumpet vine,
foxglove, giant snapdragon, a salpiglossis that has
spots and stripes, morning-glories, gourds,
      or moon-vines trained on fishing twine
at the back door:

cattails, flags, blueberries and spiderwort,
      striped grass, lichens, sunflowers, asters, daisies—
yellow and crab-claw ragged sailors with green bracts—toadplant,
petunias, ferns, pink lilies, blue
      ones, tigers; poppies; black sweet-peas.
The climate

is not right for the banyan, frangipani, or
      jack-fruit trees; or for exotic serpent
life. Ring lizard and snakeskin for the foot, if you see fit;
but here they've cats, not cobras, to
      keep down the rats. The diffident
little newt

with white pin-dots on black horizontal spaced-
      out bands lives here; yet there is nothing that
ambition can buy or take away.

This garden is brilliantly disturbed, with its nasty-sounding "salpiglossis
that has / spots and stripes." The bravura gaudiness and excess of lines
like "yellow and crab-claw ragged sailors with green bracts—toad plant"

establish the mood of a centerless, sinister profusion even before a stanza begins with the words "is not right," and the establishment in the homely Eden of a domestic, unspectacular, apparently even innocuous serpent.

But serpent the diffident little newt is, though not "exotic" or tropical. At the apparent climax of an undecipherable abundance, the serpent is there, "yet there is nothing that / ambition can buy or take away." This is the tone and language of a plain, morally stringent provincial sufficiency and calm, but like the opening lines about seeing a reason to live, this Spartan formula has an ironic undertow: the town's garden profusion as rich as the tropics offers nothing that can be used outside of it. Ambition is either enclosed within this place and its terms, or frustrated. Nothing is for export. The student, in the poem's next sentence, sits with his "not-native books" and watches the boats as they progress "white and rigid as if in / a groove."

In this bleached, rigid, self-contained place, economy of gesture governs flux and turbulence, as in a woodcut or engraving. Seagulls rise around the clock or lighthouse without moving their wings—a slight quiver of the body. Even the storm that disturbs the stars in the sky and the star on the steeple does not shake or transform anything; rather, it provides a significant spectacle: "it is a privilege to see so / much confusion." Turbulence without change, abundance without harvest, elegance without bravado, and character without discourse or incident: it is a community, but one in which Moore's characters do not touch or address one another. The president repays the sin-driven senators by not thinking about them, and the college student with his books sees across a long perspective, as in the background of a Dürer woodcut, the central figure of the steeple-jack, who "might be part of a novel," but for us, is not.

The steeple-jack, the title figure in the first poem in Moore's *Complete Poems*, embodies the poet's relation to social or community life. He is not exactly isolated from the town: he serves the town by gilding its paramount symbol, and he also has posted two signs, one in black and white announcing his name and profession, and one in red and white that says "Danger." The steeple-jack is both prominent—he wears scarlet, he has a bold sign, he is high above—and also a small, attenuated figure, letting down his rope as a spider spins a thread. In his remoteness which is a measure of his courage, he resembles other figures, vulnerable and potentially lonely, who have in common their difference from the ambitious and gregarious. The stanza begins with the word "Danger," but the town offers relative safety for those who live with risk and rely on an inward reserve:

This would be a fit haven for
waifs, children, animals, prisoners,

and presidents who have repaid
sin driven

senators by not thinking about them.

Relative safety is a governing ideal in Moore's haven. Those who are as
Moore says "each in his way" at home here—the hero, the student, the
steeple-jack—live familiarly with the risk of failure. They are at home with
that risk, and with countervailing hope, and thus they strive, provisionally.
Manners, compared to morals, are more or less by definition provisional,
and "The Steeple-Jack" is a poem powerfully, subtly contrived to construct
a model of the world of manners, our communal arrangement.

Here, the gap between Moore's personal utterance and the shared language of idiom serves to make the emotion all the stronger. In this secular
world, the poet's voice mediates between the ordinary and the mysterious. It
is a voice sometimes informal, yet never quite demotic; it is nonjudgmental,
yet couched in the grammatical terms of the moralist: what "would be fit" or
"is not right" or "what might seem" or "if you see fit." Her formal inventions
bracket a capitalized "Danger" between stanza break and period, or stretch
over line and stanza a phrase—"the pitch / of the church // spire, not true"—
defining the boundary between secular imperfection and religious hope, or
between the provisional and the absolute:

> Liking an elegance of which
> the source is not bravado, he knows by heart the antique
> sugar-bowl shaped summer-house of
> interlacing slats, and the pitch
> of the church
>
> spire, not true, from which a man in scarlet lets
> down a rope as a spider spins a thread.

Because this figure puts out his danger-signs, "It could not be dangerous
to be living / in a town like this." Up on the untrue spire gilding the solid-
pointed star which on a steeple stands for hope, the steeple-jack is an artist at
home in the town without being precisely in it. He leaves his laconic words
of identification and warning behind, and puts the possibly deceptive gilding on the representation of a possibly justified communal hope. Though
his very name, Poole, denotes a shared aggregate, and though he performs
a communal service in a highly visible manner, he also embodies solitude
and remove.

The aggressive mock-satire of "Critics and Connoisseurs" and "To Be Liked by You Would Be a Calamity" enacts a highly artificial, almost parodic version of social discourse. The poems deal with fury and incomprehension: "ambition without understanding" in the first poem, and, in the second, words which to the person addressed are "mute, [but] which to my senses / Are a shout." The fury in "The Steeple-Jack" has been transformed into "the whirlwind fife-and-drum" of a storm that disturbs, but remains highly localized, though something like repressed anger courses through the ambiguities about reasons to live, the thwarting of ambition, the untrue pitch and the double-edged standing for hope. The incomprehension or distance between people, the motivating force of the earlier colloquy-poems, has become part of Moore's peculiarly allegorized, but enigmatic, town. This brilliant invention, freighted with symbolic meanings but resolutely particular down to its proper names, "Ambrose," "C. J. Poole," supplies a way for the poet to be present and emphatic, yet elusive. It allows her language to be familiar and sociable, yet never bound by the idiomatic. She has imagined a quiet, communal haven for idiosyncrasy, and put it at the beginning of her complete poems.

Marianne Moore touches on the question of idiom in her *Paris Review* interview with Donald Hall. She begins with admiration for a stage play she has seen:

> The accuracy of the vernacular! That's the kind of thing I am interested in, am always taking down little local expressions and accents. I think I should be in some philological operation or enterprise, am really much interested in dialect and intonations. I scarcely think of any that comes into my so-called poems at all.[3]

This is an elaborately complicated response, a maze of false and genuine modesty. However, the description of her poems as reflecting hardly any of the vernacular is basically true. In her next response to the interviewer, Moore talks of taking as an elective at Bryn Mawr a course called, remarkably, Seventeenth-Century Imitative Writing—Fuller, Hooker, Bacon, Bishop Andrewes and Others. One thing that animates the language of *the* "The Steeple-Jack" is the way it takes us into her imagined place without being the language of a place. Moore's language in its full power is not what she calls "the vernacular"—has little to do with the speech of a place, or with that word based on *verna*, a slave born in the master's household; rather, her poetic medium is partly a reflection of the ruminative, capacious discourse of seventeenth-century prose and partly an assertion of the freedom of her own, autocratic *crasis*.

When Moore does reflect the speech of an actual American group or place, it is with an effect of conceivably deliberate distortion, getting things so thoroughly wrong that we wonder nervously if that is the point. That embarrassment is generated, for example, by her poem on the Brooklyn Dodgers, recklessly calling Duke Snider "Round-tripper Duke" or writing of teammates: "Ralph Branca has Preacher Roe's number; recall?" Whether deliberately or not, the mangling of baseball jargon, on one level comical, on another defines the gap between the shared language of the community and the separated, no matter how benign, utterance of the poet, isolated above.

That isolation has many corollaries, and invites speculation. From a viewpoint to do with social class, a strong drama of Moore's work is her effort to accommodate democracy, her egalitarian and patriotic American side, with what seems the unavoidable gentility of her language. This is a matter of manners that shades into politics, but in a complex way. Moore would be incapable of writing as convincingly "spoken" a passage as Bishop's, from "Manuelzinho":

> You paint—heaven knows why—
> the outside of the crown
> and brim of your straw hat.
> Perhaps to reflect the sun?
> Or perhaps when you were small,
> your mother said, "Manuelzinho,
> one thing: be sure you always
> paint your straw hat."[4]

That "one thing" with its colon is not part of Moore's range. Because it is part of Bishop's range, she can write this passage in a poem about a woman and her servant or dependent, a passage and poem that some readers have found condescending and cruel, and that some have found deeply understanding and humane. Either way, Bishop is in a theater of operations, a social place, that Moore does not enter.

From a feminist perspective, Moore's declining to reproduce something like the social art of conversation in her poems, even parodying that art by an autocratic system of apostrophe and quotation, is a way of refusing the realm traditionally or stereotypically assigned to women of intelligence and force: polite conversation, the little room in which Jane Austen's heroines must exercise their wills. There is another sense in which Moore is, in Sandra Gilbert's cogent phrase, a "female female impersonator," exaggerating and exposing expectations related to gender. The refusal of assigned terms characterizes some of her most memorable lines cast in the feminine grammatical gender, from "The Paper Nautilus" (*CP*, 121–22):

> For authorities whose hopes
> are shaped by mercenaries?
>> Writers entrapped by
>> teatime fame and by
> commuters' comforts? Not for these
>> the paper nautilus
>> constructs her thin glass shell.
>
>> Giving her perishable
> souvenir of hope, a dull
>> white outside and smooth-
>> edged inner surface
> glossy as the sea, the watchful
>> maker of it guards it
>> day and night, she scarcely
>
>> eats until the eggs are hatched.
> Buried eight-fold in her eight
>> arms, for she is in
>> a sense a devil
> fish, her glass ram's-horn-cradled freight
>> is hid but is not crushed.

"Hid but . . . not crushed": this treasured, painstakingly insulated "freight" is not merely the kernel of emotion at the center of the poet's art, it seems to be the accomplished burden of her personality itself. What gives emotional power to the images of protection and nurturing, what gives the "souvenir of hope" its dignity, is the way courage is evoked by images of transparency, delicacy, the "dull / white outside." All of these images, because they evoke the nautilus's shell from its outward border, foreshadow the action of the eggs as new life coming out and away from it, to "free it when they are freed." The papery shell is compared to a "fortress," but a fortress less strong itself than the idea of "love," the "only fortress / strong enough to trust to."

This resolution would be sentimental in any poet less fortress-like than Marianne Moore. The amply dramatized isolation and remove, constituted in large part by the idiosyncratic, quasi-archaic, quasi-colloquial turns of word and syntax, all combine to give dignity and penetration to the idea of a shell opening trustfully in love. Depth of protective reserve and the gesture of opening inform the image in the last stanza of "The Paper Nautilus": the white-on-white grooves, "close- // laid Ionic chiton-folds" left in the shell when the eight arms have relaxed their watchful protective embrace.

This is the characteristic action of language and feeling in Moore, and it is a particularly complex or indirect one. Broadly speaking, one can think of poets as having characteristic turns of energy: Dickinson pitting wonder against despair; Yeats fitting together what has been broken; Williams peeling back integuments. The limitations of such quick tags are obvious, and yet it helps me to find the source of feeling in Moore's work if I think of her as constructing, exposing, and disassembling an elaborate fortress. The materials of the fortress are idiosyncrasy and manners, manners of speech, and the social manners they reflect. The town of "The Steeple-Jack," which is referred to as a "haven," does not present actual, kinetic manners between people, but it is depicted in sentences that tease and yearn toward idiomatic speech, then away from it. The town itself is like a newly painted set, ready for the play of social life to commence, with its church columns of stone "made modester by whitewash," and:

> The
> place has a school-house, a post-office in a
> store, fish-houses, hen-houses, a three-masted
> schooner on
> the stocks.

The town, with one figure alone with books on a hillside and another isolated above, is as if poised for the ordinary activities of communal life, below its star which stands for hope—the same quality as in the paper nautilus's "perishable souvenir of hope."

Hope for what? Among other things, hope for the give and take of life, which in both poems is presented as if just about to begin—in the phrase from Henry James that ends Moore's poem on New York, "accessibility to experience." This action of declining a fortress, and welcoming experience, is profoundly moving. The staircase-wit of the mock-satires with which I began consign social experience to a kind of eternal previousness, addressed from behind the walls of idiosyncrasy. In fuller poems like "The Paper Nautilus" and "The Steeple-Jack," a protected and protective shell frees and is freed, a "fit haven" is imagined in a moment of anticipation. Even the poem "Marriage" can be read as a dialectic between the two ideas of that enterprise as a form that contains and as a form that mediates.

The idea of a shell that is first constructed, then disassembled, freeing what was inside and becoming free of it, provides a way of seeing Moore's work. We do not merely identify Marianne Moore by her protective shell of peculiarities, but value her for them. She is not one of those writers about whom we can say she is best when she is least idiosyncratically herself. Utterly to prize idiosyncrasy would be condescension, and yet to suppress or disregard it would reject an essential action of her poetry and the moral energy that drives her work. Overcoming or mastering a social manner that intervenes between the person and "accessibility to experience" provides a central drama in that work.

From one perspective, that drama has to do with a determined, persistent movement toward the demotic and the democratic, cutting against the genteel elements in Moore's idiom. From another, it is the drama of a woman artist alternately refusing and parodying both of the alternate social stereotypes: female charm and male assertion. From the biographical viewpoint, Moore's work reaches outward from the circumstances of her family. The father's insanity and absence from before Moore's birth left a kind of three-person social fortress: the mutual protection of a religious, middle-class family, economically insecure and socially exposed by the absence of the traditional patriarchal head. Dealing with that perpetual deprivation, and that immense embarrassment, gave the truncated family a delicately hardened protective architecture.

The visible forces in Moore's work are peculiarity and generalization, reticence and asseveration, and, in language, the eccentricity of the scholar and the central idiom of the marketplace. These forces bring together what is closed, like a shell or a provincial town, and the open seas of experience. Her evocation of these forces merits, and meets, the standard for art Moore proposes in the concluding line of "When I Buy Pictures":

It must acknowledge the spiritual forces which have made it.

This acknowledgment is exactly parallel to the beautiful ionic grooves, the aftermark of a measured, protective pressure that is relaxed. In language, the line enacts its proposition: to "*acknowledge* the spiritual forces which have made it." The verb "to acknowledge" is subtly and appropriately social; it implies an other: one acknowledges a gift, a compliment, an obligation. That is, social forces acknowledge spiritual forces, in their own terms, and thereby take on spiritual power. What Moore depicts, at her best, is the solitary and laborious approach to that attainment: the trek, you might say, through knowledge to acknowledgment.

The sudden, even unexpected penetrations of emotion in Moore's work flare up from the tireless pressure of the poet negotiating and considering between her own way of talking and our way of talking, between discourse and discourse's imaginary re-making, the suspended life of a town and that life's forever hoped-for resumption. These oppositions embody the shared, socially visible quality of peculiarity underlying the peculiarity of each distinct human soul.

<h1 style="text-align:center">NOTES</h1>

1. Marianne Moore, "To Be Liked by You Would Be a Calamity," in *Observations* (New York: Dial Press, 1925), 37.

2. Marianne Moore, "Critics and Connoisseurs," in *Complete Poems of Marianne Moore* (New York: Macmillan/Viking, 1981), 38–39. Hereafter, poems from this collection will be documented parenthetically within the text with *CP* followed by the pagination of the poem under discussion.

3. Donald Hall, "The Art of Poetry: Marianne Moore," in *Marianne Moore: A Collection of Critical Essays*, ed. Charles Tomlinson (Englewood Cliffs, N.J.: Prentice-Hall, 1969), 23.

4. Elizabeth Bishop, "Manuelzinho," in *The Complete Poems* (New York: Farrar, Straus & Giroux, 1969), 116.

MARK VAN WIENEN

Taming the Socialist: Carl Sandburg's Chicago Poems *and Its Critics*

Carl Sandburg's reputation as the adulatory biographer of Lincoln and as a folksy, silver-haired singer of ballads and reciter of poems has obscured the radically innovative and oppositional character of his earlier poetic work. Set in the context of Sandburg's socialist politics of the teens rather than the moderate populism of his later career, the early poems emerge as protests both against much of conventional American political life and against established literary practice. Most sharply confrontational is *Chicago Poems*, which appeared at a time when Sandburg was active both in socialist politics and in literary circles.[1] These poems reveal that Sandburg was busy propagating American socialism not only in his work as an organizer and a newspaperman, but also in the supposedly apolitical realm of literature. Other materials, particularly reviews of *Chicago Poems* and correspondence between Sandburg, his publisher, and the critics, present another, less visible side to the relationship between politics and poetry: They show the power of literary and publishing establishments to suppress or reinterpret writing that questions their received values. Thus, even though *Chicago Poems* offers significant potential for destabilizing the boundary between literary art and political life, the rhetoric mustered by the critics in response to Sandburg had (and continues to have) great power to reestablish this boundary and thereby blunt the radical critique that Sandburg's work offers.

From *American Literature* 63, no. 1 (March 1991): 89–103. Copyright © 1991 by Duke University Press.

Sandburg was introduced to socialism by Philip Green Wright, one of his Lombard College professors. Sandburg's practical lessons in class politics included occasional unpaid trips by freight train, when he met hoboes who rode illegally out of economic necessity rather than youthful exuberance. While working as a salesman in 1902, Sandburg canvassed parts of Wisconsin and became acquainted with the politics of Robert La Follette, whose brand of progressive populism, he later remarked, made a deep impression.[2] By 1908 he was again traveling Wisconsin, this time serving as a district organizer for the Wisconsin Social Democratic Party, and in 1910 he was appointed private secretary to Mayor Emil Seidel of Milwaukee, the first socialist to preside over a major American city.[3] Sandburg found the Wisconsin party attractive because it was "practical and constructive": "They were 'Opportunists' opposed to the members of the extreme left whom they called 'Impossibilists.'"[4] Indeed, in a recent essay Sally Miller points out that to win the support of middle-class voters outside of their blue-collar, ethnic base, the Milwaukee socialists emphasized "honesty in government more than the class struggle, modernization of city services rather than collectivization, and home rule for the city."[5] Yet while Sandburg's politics were more pragmatic than radical, he was nonetheless committed to the American socialist agenda.[6] Throughout the teens Sandburg worked at various newspapers either directly run by the Socialist Party or sympathetic to socialist aims, serving his longest stints at the Chicago *Day Book*, a tabloid whose editorial policy forbade advertisements and set out "to be the poor man's advocate whether the poor man be right or wrong."[7] The economic inequality on which the *Day Book* focused demonstrated to Sandburg and other socialists that "there is something pitifully wrong, execrably wrong in the main works of our boasted civilization."[8] Basic economic injustice, as well as related inequities of social privilege, legal rights, and political power, became the dominant theme of *Chicago Poems*.

In this collection, Sandburg is consistent not only in speaking out on behalf of laborers and the unemployed but also in blaming the wealthy and the powerful for their predicaments. In "'Boes" he draws from his own experience hitching rides on freight trains, sympathizing with the hoboes whose status is even lower than that of the cattle they accompany: "Well, the cattle are respectable, I thought. / Every steer has its transportation paid for by the farmer sending it to market, / While the hoboes are law-breakers in riding a railroad train without a ticket."[9] "Ready to Kill" presents a speaker who wants to smash a "bronze memorial of a famous general /.... into a pile of junk" (p. 28). He explains that while the general who destroys is memorialized, those who create—"the farmer, the miner, the shop man, the factory hand, the fireman and the teamster"—are forgotten. These are "the real huskies that are doing the work of the world, and feeding people instead of butchering them" (p. 29). Sandburg, however, does not always condemn violence; he can accept it when used for, rather than against, the People. In another poem he writes sympathetically of a radical "Dynamiter": "His name was in many newspapers as an enemy of the nation and few keepers of churches or schools would open their doors to him," and yet, "he laughed and told stories of his wife and children and the cause of labor and the working class. / It was laughter of an unshakable man knowing life to be a rich and red-blooded thing" (p. 21). Sandburg himself is probably not ready to take violent action to advance "the cause of labor," but neither is he ready to condemn the dynamiter for doing so.

Whatever Sandburg's personal politics may have been, in *Chicago Poems* he embraces a wide range of socialist positions. The section titled "War Poems (1914–1915)" adopts the anti-war stand of the American Socialist Party which prompted Sandburg himself to resign membership after the U.S. joined the fighting. The final poem of the section heralds future conflicts fought not on behalf of "kings" but rather for the sake of "men," a vision which implies the traditional Marxist tenets of the class war and the emergence of a classless utopian state:

> In the old wars kings quarreling and thousands of men following.
> In the new wars kings quarreling and millions of men following.
> In the wars to come kings kicked under the dust and millions
> of men
>   following great causes not yet dreamed out in the heads
> of men. (P. 42)

Sandburg does not advocate violence so much as he predicts its inevitability if the problem of economic inequality is not addressed. He puts the matter bluntly in "Choose":

> The single clenched fist lifted and ready,
> Or the open asking hand held out and waiting.
>   Choose:
> For we meet by one or the other. (P. 34)

The persona which Sandburg adopts here is not the disinterested poet but the committed radical who stands alongside and allows himself to be identified with common laborers.

He does this explicitly in "I Am the People, the Mob," one of the last poems of the collection (p. 71). "Do you know that all the great work of the world is done through me?" the speaker asks, then declares, "I am the workingman, the inventor, the maker of the world's food and clothes." But even while Sandburg adopts the voice of the People, he is also a self-conscious observer of their plight; the mob forgets its own strength and is therefore continually vulnerable to exploitation: "I forget. The best of me is sucked out and wasted. I forget. Everything but Death comes to me and makes me work and give up what I have. And I forget." The poem then concludes with this speaker, partly immersed in the mob, partly removed from it, exhorting the People to remember:

> When I, the People, learn to remember, when I, the People, use the
> lessons of yesterday and no longer forget who robbed me last year,
> who played me for a fool—then there will be no speaker in all the
> world say the name: "The People," with any fleck of a sneer in his
> voice or any far-off smile of derision.
> The mob—the crowd—the mass—will arrive then.

Thus Sandburg stands in a relationship both sympathetic to and critical of the common people: his position is much like the one he occupied as a Wisconsin party organizer mobilizing the masses; it is the position, roughly speaking, of the socialist intellectual who discerns and proclaims the spirit of the People.

As critics of Marxism have regularly pointed out, the role of the intellectual speaking on behalf of the People is hardly without complications. These difficulties also apply to Sandburg's poetic persona who knows the popular mind while being distanced from it. In other ways as well, Sandburg's socialist politics are rendered problematic in *Chicago Poems*. "Government," for example, at first sets up a clear opposition between the violence of the state and the just cause of the workers: "I saw militiamen level their rifles at a crowd of workingmen who were trying to get other workingmen to stay away from a shop where there was a strike on. Government in action" (p. 72). By the end of the poem, however, Sandburg appears to undermine his position. Rather than maintaining a clear division between government and the people, he goes on to blur this distinction: "Everywhere I saw that Government is a thing made of men, that Government has blood and bones." Finally, while other poems seem confident about the triumph of the masses, this poem's closing lines appear to offer little hope that government can ever be significantly reformed:

> Government dies as the men who form it die and are laid away in
> their graves and the new Government that comes after is human,
> made of heartbeats of blood, ambitions, lusts, and money running

> through it all, money paid and money taken, and money covered
> up and spoken of with hushed voices.
> A Government is just as secret and mysterious and sensitive as any
> human sinner carrying a load of germs, traditions and corpuscles
> handed down from fathers and mothers away back.

The problem here is bigger than a capitalist system whose "money" inevitably sullies all of political life. Rather, not only the nature of the economic system but also human nature corrupts politics. "Government," which had initially been given a negative charge, and the "people," which had seemed positive, are here equated, so that the opposition which had made for both tension and the possibility of constructive change is neutralized.

Not all the pieces in *Chicago Poems* are overtly political. Roughly one-fifth, distinguished by their attention to a few details of a sharply delineated subject, are clearly in the imagist mode. These poems include the much anthologized "Fog" and a four-line poem, "June," whose imagery ("Two petals of crabapple blossom blow fallen in Paula's hair"[p. 55]) invites comparison to Pound's "In a Station of the Metro." Furthermore, throughout *Chicago Poems* Sandburg exhibits an imagist's bent for describing the bare details of a scene, even in those poems whose enthusiastic and garrulous speakers do not retain the detachment and brevity characteristic of undisputed imagist poems. Fully half of the poems in the collection, though they may even present contemporary scenes, do not diagnose social problems or prescribe socialist ideals.

Given these poems, critics have typically diagnosed a split in Sandburg's poetic personality—the socialist propagandizer versus the lyric poet—and have often proceeded to dismiss Sandburg's political items as propaganda while claiming value only for the imagist poems. Amy Lowell performs this critical alchemy as explicitly as any reader of *Chicago Poems*. In the *Poetry Review*, she discusses Sandburg the socialist for two-thirds of her article, admitting that "the propagandist side of Mr. Sandburg's book . . . challenges us . . . upon many pages."[10] But finally she turns aside Sandburg's challenge: "These are poems," she announces, "and it is as poetry that the work must be judged," a principle which by her interpretation demands ignoring the poems that have held her attention for most of the review and deciding the book's value based on the poems left over. In *Tendencies in Modern American Poetry*, Lowell basically repeats her earlier position, although she also reveals more explicitly her aversion to Sandburg's political interests: "Judged from the standard of pure art, it is a pity that so much of Mr. Sandburg's work concerns itself with entirely ephemeral phenomena. The problems of posterity will be other than those which claim our attention. Art, nature, humanity, are eternal. But the minimum wage will probably matter as little to the twenty-second century as it did to the thirteenth, although for different reasons."[11] In contrast to Sandburg's interest in "the minimum wage," Lowell advocates the higher "standard of pure art." While Sandburg's poetry deals with "ephemeral phenomena," she insists that art connects with the "eternal," expressing the immutable laws of "nature" rather than the vicissitudes of social and political life, and describing universal "humanity" rather than particular groups of people or classes.

Lowell was not alone in distinguishing the lyrical from the political in Sandburg. Writing in the *Dial*, William Aspenwall Bradley contrasts Sandburg the "rather gross, simple-minded, sentimental, sensual man among men"—a "mystical mobocrat"—to Sandburg the "highly sensitized impressionist."[12] He continues: "The first Mr. Sandburg is merely a clever reporter, with a bias for social criticism. The second, within his limits, is a true artist, whose method of concentration, of intense, objective realization, ranges him with those who call themselves 'Imagists.'"[13] Harriet Monroe also promotes this dichotomy. Unlike Lowell and most other reviewers, Monroe claims to appreciate both kinds of poems; yet even her comments tend to read away *Chicago Poems'* contemporary political relevance. Poems of political protest become complaints for the universal pain of human existence, counterpointed by Sandburg's poems celebrating natural beauty:

> This is speech torn out of the heart, because the loveliness of "yellow dust on a bumble-bee's wing," of "worn wayfaring men," of ships at night, of a fog coming "on little cat feet,"—the incommunicable loveliness of the earth, of life—is too keen to be borne; or because the pain of "the poor, patient and toiling," of children behind mill-doors, of soldiers bleeding in the trenches—all the unnecessary human anguish—is too bitter for any human being, poet or not, to endure in silence.[14]

Monroe does call the suffering "unnecessary," yet by putting the reader's response to "the poor, patient and toiling" in roughly the same terms as to "yellow dust on a bumble-bee's wing"—one is "too bitter . . . to endure in silence," the other "too keen to be borne"—she translates any real impulse to eliminate "unnecessary anguish" into an aesthetic experience of angst.

A more keenly political reading of Sandburg's poetry comes from Louis Untermeyer, writing for *The Masses*. In the first place, he recognizes more openly than other critics the political nature both of Sandburg's poetry and of the debate over it; he writes, Sandburg "is a socialist and (or, if the opposition prefers, but) an artist."[15] Untermeyer also suggests that these two characters might be profitably interfused: "Such things as 'Halsted Street Car,' 'Mill-Doors,' 'Masses,' 'Onion Days,' 'Dynamiter,'... could only have been written by one who had the mingled passions of both." This, it seems to me, comes very close to presenting accurately the mixture of political and poetic concerns in *Chicago Poems*. The danger in Untermeyer's reading, however, is similar to the problem in Monroe's: even while he praises Sandburg's politics, Untermeyer risks subsuming them in his depiction of Sandburg's poetic excellence. In his enthusiasm, Untermeyer too suddenly replaces Sandburg the embattled political reformer with Sandburg the poet triumphant, connecting him to the literary tradition of "great writers" like Whitman and apotheosizing him as a "universal man": "It is, at last, an intensely personal volume, and 'who touches this book, touches (in the best sense in which Walt Whitman ever meant it) a man.'"

Untermeyer understands that poetry and politics cannot finally be separated. To filter out Sandburg's socialism, as Lowell and others do, is not just an aesthetic decision; it is itself a political act which dismisses the importance of better working conditions, higher wages, and, consequently, an improved life for working-class people. Yet Untermeyer does not fully recognize the deep rift between the cultural role then (and still) typically allowed to poetry as opposed to that assigned to politics.[16] Politics, which involves disputation over "ephemeral" matters such as the minimum wage, cannot be assimilated to the "eternal" realm of poetry so easily as he believes.[17]

Sandburg resists more successfully the tendency to rewrite political concerns in aesthetic terms; the political is suffused throughout his poetry but not subsumed by it. Thus, for a poem such as "The Harbor," the critical decisions one makes are cast clearly in terms of political choices. The poem first describes the starving people of the city: the speaker passes "doorways where women / Looked from their hunger-deep eyes, / Haunted with shadows of hunger hands" (p. 5). Then, suddenly, the mood shifts; the speaker arrives on the open lakeshore at the city's edge, where he sees, "a fluttering storm of gulls, / Masses of great gray wings / And flying white bellies / Veering and wheeling free in the open." The beginning of the poem sympathizes with the poor of the city; the closing, on the other hand, is more ambiguous. It might suggest, as Untermeyer thinks, "not only ... a view of Whistlerian back yards opening on to the river, but a vision of huddled souls opening out on a sea of freedom"[18]—a kind of Marxist utopian vision. On the other hand, the end of the poem might arguably depict the poet's escape from the world of dismal political reality into a realm of aesthetic delight. One *could* read the poem in either of these or any number of other ways. However, Sandburg's mention of the poor makes their plight an issue; one can choose to read the poem as an escape from responsibility, but such a choice presents implications that are not only literary but inescapably social and political.

Read in conjunction with poems like "The Harbor" that point to contemporary social problems, even seemingly apolitical works take on new political resonances. One such poem is "Lost," which would appear at first to be a straightforward imagist poem:

Desolate and lone
All night long on the lake
Where fog trails and mist creeps,
The whistle of a boat
Calls and cries unendingly,
Like some lost child
In tears and trouble
Hunting the harbor's breast
And the harbor's eyes. (P. 5)

The lost child would seem like only an image of a boat out in the fog, except that in "The Harbor," which immediately follows, the waterfront is bordered by a starving city. Then, in the collection's next poem, the figure of the child is made literal and developed into an explicit accusation against the inequities of Chicago society:

THEY WILL SAY

Of my city the worst that men will ever say is this:
You took little children away from the sun and the dew,
And the glimmers that played in the grass under the great sky,
And the reckless rain; you put them between walls
To work, broken and smothered, for bread and wages,
To eat dust in their throats and die empty-hearted
For a little handful of pay on a few Saturday nights. (Pp. 5–6)

Not only does the poem openly address the political issues of poverty, unhealthy working conditions, and especially child labor, but its polemic readily inflects our perceptions of the surrounding poems. "They Will Say" gives the crying child of "Lost" a concrete referent, thus potentially subverting the apoliticism of the earlier poem: The "desolate" boat not only figuratively reminds us of a lost child but also gestures towards the literal forsaken children of the city. Furthermore, "They Will Say" offers a more complete picture of the unfair economic system which causes the "hunger hands" of "The Harbor."

Throughout *Chicago Poems* we can find juxtapositions of poems such as these three; overtly political work regularly stands side by side with apparently "pure" imagist poetry. That Sandburg had theorized this interplay is doubtful, yet he does seem quite aware of the critical expectations for his poems as well as the decisions he must make to satisfy or deny these. In "Choices" he contrasts the high-poetic subjects of traditional poets with his own subject matter: "They offer you many things," he writes, "I a few" (p. 43). The "many things" include "Moonlight on the play of fountains at night / ... Bare-shouldered, smiling women and talk / ... And a fear of death / and a remembering of regrets"—contemplations of the Beautiful, of elegant society, and of universal human concerns. To these Sandburg offers a harder alternative, one consonant with the realities of working-class life:

> I come with:
> > salt and bread
> > a terrible job of work
> > and tireless war;
> Come and have now:
> > hunger
> > danger
> > and hate.

The contrasting diction in this poem can be seen to represent the duplicity of *Chicago Poems* as a whole. On the one hand, by bringing together into one poem (and into a single collection) both the language of poetic art removed from praxis and the diction of a politically committed poetry, Sandburg closes the distance between the two. Because the "propagandistic" lines and poems are at least as vigorous in rhetoric and imagery as the "poetical" ones, *Chicago Poems* undermines the sharp opposition established by critics between poetry and politics, art and propaganda. On the other hand, Sandburg continues to offer a poetics of socialist activism as a distinct alternative to dominant literary and social practice and inverts the values typically associated with the realms of art and politics. Sandburg portrays conventional art as superficial, whereas his political poems are in touch with the elemental, enduring realities of food, bodily labor, and violent struggle.

What I am suggesting is that Sandburg was a far more political poet—at least in his early work—than we have thought and that one function of criticism has been to "sanitize," to de-politicize him both by encouraging him in his non-political pursuits and by valuing his imagist work more highly than his political. Yet it must also be emphasized that the process of censoring Sandburg was already under way with the manuscript's acceptance at Henry Holt and Company. Alfred Harcourt, then an editor at Holt, had solicited a book of poems from Sandburg; he was to handle the company's correspondence with Sandburg and would see his book through the press.[19] Although sympathetic to Sandburg's socialist commitments, Harcourt suggested pruning the manuscript of *Chicago Poems* in a way that made the book's content less controversial. In a letter Harcourt advises Sandburg, "as to the general principles of selection. For obvious reasons, we think the poems, the subjects of which are living people referred to by name should certainly be omitted." Further, "some of the poems are a little too 'raw'" (20 January 1916).[20]

The "obvious reasons," of course, were threat of libel, which we can assume would be very real considering that the capitalists and politicians whom Sandburg criticizes would be those most able to afford expensive legal proceedings. That Sandburg should have included such poems in those he sent to Harcourt reveals the naiveté of a political journalist confronting the New York publishing establishment. At the same time, it indicates his willingness to attempt the openly political art of lampoon. However expedient Harcourt's advice certainly was, the consequent softening of Sandburg's poetry moves it some distance from political efficacy and towards benign universality.

Sandburg replied to Harcourt's letter with some vigor, revealing a significant commitment to the political stance which his manuscript established. Although he objects to Harcourt's proposed deletions in only one case, and argues with Harcourt's editorial suggestions on just three poems, he defends all four on the basis of their contemporary relevance and political incisiveness. Of "Murmurings in a Field Hospital," which portrays the hallucinations of a dying soldier, Sandburg says, it "has a present time value above that of others."[21] Sandburg also defends "Dynamiter," which, as we have seen, appears to accept the necessity of violent radicalism. He argues that his book's audience properly consists of political progressives, even socialists, rather than more tradition-bound readers: "I believe the backing for this book will come from the younger, aggressive fellows, in the main. Without tying it up to any special schools or doctrines, the intellectual background of it takes color from the modern working class movement rather than old fashioned Jeffersonian democracy."[22] Sandburg's defense of "Buttons," a poem Harcourt objects to because it uses "Christ" as an expletive, makes a similar swipe at conservative readers: "I feel sure all readers with any true streak of religion in them will take this oath as the proper exclamation, a cry not lacking kinship with, 'My God, why hast thou forsaken me?'"[23] Finally, Sandburg pleads at length for inclusion of "To a Contemporary Bunkshooter," then still titled "Billy Sunday."[24] Again, his argument is based on the poem's political significance; Sandburg aims to unveil the chicanery of the well-known evangelist, whom he calls "the most conspicuous single embodiment in this country of the crowd leader or crowd operative who uses jungle methods, stark voodoo stage effects, to play hell with democracy."[25]

Considering that all four of the disputed pieces were included in *Chicago Poems*, we might conclude that Sandburg's attempts to keep politics visible were successful. At the same time, the expletive "Christ" does not appear in the printed version of "Buttons." The title of Sandburg's Billy Sunday lampoon, "To a Contemporary Bunkshooter," changes his personal attack to a more generalized satire of a "typical" evangelist. Harcourt's reply to Sandburg's letter also aims to amend yet another poem whose subject is a "living person referred to by name"; he writes, "The member of our staff who knows north Chicago better than I do wonders if Lublong isn't too much like Budlong, the proprietor of the well known pickle farm. This sort of thing is always more powerful if kept in general terms that would apply to any pickle farm, and also, we do not want a libel suit. I hope you can make this a little less local when you get proof."[26] Could "Budlong" be "Jasper," the character portrayed in Sandburg's "Onion Days," who owns an onion farm and daydreams in church about cutting immigrants' wages to increase profits? (p. 14). Certainly, the condemnation of greedy entrepreneurs "in general" remains clear with a poem like "Onion Days." But neither "Lublong" nor "Budlong" appears anywhere in *Chicago Poems*.

Editorial decisions of this kind had as much to do with tempering the polemical force of *Chicago Poems* as did the reviews which greeted the book. Editors and reviewers perhaps exerted even greater leverage, however, in reshaping Sandburg's very attitudes toward poetry, thereby influencing the composition of books which followed his first collection. As Sandburg gradually accepted a vocation as literary celebrity rather than social activist, his politics became increasingly less radical and the ruptures in his poetry between political and lyric statement grew less pronounced. Criticism of Sandburg likewise came to focus more on his poetic craft (or lack thereof) than on issues of politics. The response of O. W. Firkins to *Cornhuskers* (1918) indicates the tendency of Sandburg's later books and their reviews: "The Vulcan that Mr. Sandburg was, or chose to appear, in *Chicago Poems* is curiously softened in his new book. ... Mr. Sandburg is not quite ready for idylls; his 'Evangeline' is not yet in type: but give him time, prosperity, and another rosy-cheeked little girl or so, and he will write it."[27] Writing in the *Dial*, Untermeyer is not so disposed to give Sandburg over to blissful domesticity; yet he too is forced to admit the softening of Sandburg's voice: His poems "assert themselves with less effort. The war has temporarily harmonized them; they are still rebellious, but somehow resigned."[28] Something is amiss, clearly, if Untermeyer observes, "The chants of revolt are seldom out of tune with Sandburg's purely pictorial pieces."

The active role of the literary establishment in bringing Sandburg's aesthetics and politics to heel is nowhere clearer than in his correspondence with

Amy Lowell. On 23 July 1916, shortly after reading her review of *Chicago Poems*, Sandburg wrote to Lowell, more interested in currying favor than in discussing politics. "That's a pippin," he says of her article, and puts off a rebuttal until later: "I have, of course, a thousand points of defense or counter-offensive against the antagonisms you voice, and I'll get to those sometime with you."[29] When Sandburg gets to this defense, on 10 June 1917, he insists that he does not endorse political activism; rather, he is interested in probing the underlying character of the people, of human beings considered more generally:

> I admit there is some animus of violence in *Chicago Poems* but the aim was rather the presentation of motives and character than the furtherance of I.W.W. theories. Of course, I honestly prefer the theories of the I.W.W. to those of its opponents and some of my honest preferences may have crept into the book, as you suggest, but the aim was to sing, blab, chortle, yodel, like the people, and people in the sense of human beings subtracted from formal doctrines.[30]

Sandburg may admit to sympathizing with socialist and even syndicalist "theories," but he adopts the view that these political ideas should be kept out of his poetry—they "crept" in. In another letter, written later in the same month, Sandburg seems to capitulate even more completely: "Glancing over some old and genuinely propaganda material of mine of ten years ago, I got a sneaking suspicion that maybe you're right and maybe I have struck a propaganda rather than a human note at times."[31] Thus Sandburg not only observes the critical distinction between politics and poetry but also, more crucially, accepts the conventional privileging of poetic art. Consequently he comes to divorce what *Chicago Poems* had bound together: the political and the human.

Notes

1. *Chicago Poems* was Sandburg's last book published while a member of the American Socialist Party. Earlier books were printed exclusively by small presses—four in Galesburg, Illinois, at the Asgard Press (*In Reckless Ecstasy* [1904], *Incidentals* [1907], *The Plaint of the Rose* [1908], *Joseffy: An Appreciation* [1910]), and editions of *You and Your Job* by C. H. Kerr (Chicago, 1908) and by the Socialist Party of Philadelphia (1910). Publication of *Chicago Poems* by Henry Holt and Company thus gave Sandburg a national audience for the first time. In fact, because the book contained poems which had won *Poetry* magazine's Levinson Prize for 1914, it was virtually assured wide critical attention.

2. *Ever the Winds of Chance*, ed. Margaret Sandburg and George Hendrick (Urbana: Univ. of Illinois Press, 1983), pp. 123–24, 136–37.

3. Sally M. Miller, "Casting a Wide Net: The Milwaukee Movement to 1920," in *Socialism in the Heartland: The Midwestern Experience, 1900–1925*, ed. Donald T. Critchlow (Notre Dame: Univ. of Notre Dame Press, 1986), p. 30.

4. *Ever the Winds*, p. 163.

5. "Casting a Wide Net," p. 30.

6. For a survey of Sandburg's socialist commitment during the Wisconsin years, consult not only *The Letters of Carl Sandburg* (New York: Harcourt, Brace, and World, 1989) but also *The Poet and the Dream Girl: The Love Letters of Lilian Steichen and Carl Sandburg*, ed. Margaret Sandburg (Urbana: Univ. of Illinois Press, 1987). Especially helpful in the latter book is the appendix of "Socialist Prose" written from 1907 to 1909.

7. Harry Golden, *Carl Sandburg* (Cleveland: World Publishing, 1961), p. 192.

8. Sandburg, *Ever the Winds*, p. 150.

9. *The Complete Poems of Carl Sandburg* (New York: Harcourt, Brace, Jovanovich, 1969), p. 70. All further citations of poems refer to this volume, and appear parenthetically in the text.

10. "Carl Sandburg," *Poetry Review*, 1, No. 3 (1916), 47.

11. *Tendencies in Modern American Poetry* (New York: Macmillan, 1917), p. 231.

12. "Four American Poets," *Dial*, 61 (14 Dec. 1916), 528–29.

13. "Four American Poets," p. 529. See also O. W. Firkins, "American Verse," *Nation*, 17 Aug. 1916, p. 152.

14. "Chicago Granite," *Poetry: A Magazine of Verse*, 8, No. 2 (1916), 91.

15. "Enter Sandburg," *Masses*, 8 (July 1916), 30.

16. For a later account of the harm that Sandburg's "urge to propagandize" worked on his poetry, see Michael Yatron, *America's Literary Revolt* (New York: Philosophical Library, 1959), p. 134.

17. Leslie Fishbein, *Rebels in Bohemia: The Radicals of* The Masses, *1911–1917* (Chapel Hill: Univ. of North Carolina Press, 1982), p. 184. Fishbein quotes Martha Sonnenberg, who remarked after interviewing Untermeyer, "These artists did not conceive of a synthesis between art and politics, of art as a form of revolutionary activity, or of radical consciousness as a liberated aesthetics."

18. "Enter Sandburg," p. 30.

19. Harcourt would also oversee Holt's publication of Sandburg's next collection of poetry, *Cornhuskers*. Soon thereafter he began his own publishing company, which handled the American publication of all Sandburg's subsequent books.

20. TS letter, 20 January 1916. This and the other Harcourt letter I quote are in the Sandburg Collection of the Rare Book and Special Collections Library, University of Illinois, Urbana-Champaign.

21. *Letters*, p. 107.

22. *Letters*, p. 107.

23. *Letters*, p. 108.

24. Dale Kramer, *Chicago Renaissance: The Literary Life in the Midwest 1900–1930* (New York: Appleton-Century, 1966), p. 283. As Kramer points out, "Billy Sunday" was the poem's title in its earlier appearance in *The Masses*. For *Chicago Poems* Holt and Co. not only changed the title but did not acknowledge this previous publication in the book's credits.

25. *Letters*, p. 108.

26. TS letter, 7 February 1916.
27. "Literature: Pathfinders in America," *Nation*, 4 Jan. 1919, p. 21.
28. "Strong Timber," *Dial*, 65 (5 Oct. 1918), 264.
29. *Letters*, pp. 113–14.
30. *Letters*, pp. 117–18.
31. *Letters*, pp. 119–20.

ROGER MITCHELL

Modernism Comes to American Poetry: 1908–1920

It would be just as misleading to say that the decade 1910 to 1920 was the decade when Modernism reached the United States as it would be to say that it reached here because the two most prominent American poets of the time, Ezra Pound and T. S. Eliot, left the United States and went to London. But the coming of Modernism was the principal literary event of that time (indeed, it is likely to be the principal literary event of the century), and it was Pound and Eliot who were, for a time, its chief advocates and practitioners. William Carlos Williams, H. D., Marianne Moore, Gertrude Stein, and Wallace Stevens all contributed significantly to the development of Modernism in American poetry, but without the examples of Pound and Eliot, it is doubtful that their work would have had the shape and force it did.

Literary history is not an exact science, so it is no surprise that other developments took place at this time. Two of the most notable were the slow rise in reputation of Edwin Arlington Robinson and Robert Frost and the emergence of a school of free-verse Populist poets which included Carl Sandburg, Vachel Lindsay, and Edgar Lee Masters. These poets refined a native strain of verse, largely in the shadow of Walt Whitman, at a time when American poetry suddenly became international. The work of these poets was often grouped with Pound's and Eliot's, but it was almost entirely because

From *A Profile of Twentieth-Century American Poetry*, edited by Jack Myers and David Wojahn, pp. 25–53. Copyright © 1991 by the Board of Trustees, Southern Illinois University.

131

they, too, wrote free verse. It was the "freed verse" that most clearly identified the new poetry to the puzzled reader, but as we know now—and as Pound and Eliot were quick to say then—the new poetry involved a great deal more than the simple abandonment of meter and rhyme. Eliot went so far as to say that the new poetry was not free at all. "No vers is libre," he said, "to the poet who wishes to write well."[1]

Still, this period brought a nonmetrical or irregular verse into being, and its lack of meter and regularity had much to do with the general attempt made at that time throughout the Western world and in all the arts to free aesthetics from premises that thinking people could no longer take seriously. It is because Sandburg, Lindsay, and Masters did not perceive the main intellectual currents of the time or did not grapple significantly with them that their work seems pale today. With Robinson and Frost, it is a different matter. Like Bartleby, they preferred not to—in this case, not to go along with the radical new aesthetics. They listened well, however, and heard what it was saying and in their own sly way spoke to it and to the issues it raised.

Literary history is not neatly divided into decades either, but there is a remarkable knot of energy at precisely this time which might convince the unwary reader that the normal lifespan of literary movements is about ten years. "The heroic era of Modernism in American literature,"[2] to use Eric Homberger's term, might be said to have begun in 1908 when Pound reached London, and ended, to indulge in a Modernist warping of time, in 1920 when Pound left London for France and in 1922 when Eliot published *The Waste Land* in the *Dial*.

"In or about December 1910," wrote Virginia Woolf, "human nature changed. . . . All human relations . . . shifted—those between masters and servants, husbands and wives, parents and children. And when human relations change there is at the same time a change in religion, conduct, politics, and literature."[3] One might argue about the precision of Woolf's reading of history, but there is no mistaking its general accuracy or her urgent sense that something radically new was needed if literature was to keep up with it. The most compelling thing in her statement is the sense it gives of radical social upheaval. The change in literature came not because of internal tinkerings with the machine of literature but because the ground on which all social institutions stood, literature among them, was beginning to tremble. The history of ideas and history itself coincided to produce one of the most volcanic cultural upheavals ever known.

The great disjunction felt at the end of the nineteenth century between art and reality—the condition which precipitated Modernism—is largely attributable to the huge success, if success is measured by wealth and world domination, of the Industrial Revolution. Those qualities which made it possible—hard work, inventiveness, confidence in progress and the future, faith in reason and science, and the almost unchallenged sense that business and industry represented the natural fulfillment of the human race and of God's will—seemed unassailable for a very long time.

Information filtered slowly through the heavy screen of middle-class culture and began suggesting that not all was well or even accurately described. For one thing, the dirt and poverty created by industrialism would not go away. In fact, it spread. Karl Marx, among others, suggested that industry created poverty intentionally for its proper and profitable functioning, a notion that challenged the industrialist's confidence that he was doing the Lord's will. Darwin did further damage, not only by discrediting the version of creation offered by Genesis and therefore the authority of Christianity itself, but also by telling us that we were descended from apes. In a word, we were animals and not some privileged creature halfway to being an angel. Freud's invention and investigations of the subconscious scandalized the Victorian mind by suggesting that if we were civilized—and he raised considerable doubts about that—we were so only because we suppressed our deepest natural desires, which were, at root, selfish and sexual. Freud further threatened the outward calm of Victorian life by suggesting that our real life was an inner and isolated life, not unlike dream, and not that thing we shared or tried to share with other people.

If we add to this picture the strong currents of relativism in philosophy at this time which undermined the validity of absolute truths, Nietzsche's announcement that God was dead, and Einstein's theory that relativity ruled even in the physical world, we can begin to see why people felt that the ground beneath them had begun to shift. The fixed, solid Newtonian world which underlay the culture of the Victorian middle class was breaking up. No poet could dream of announcing, as Browning had in 1841, "God's in his heaven—All's right with the world!"

As a general term, *Modernism* (or *Modernity*) evoked, and still evokes, the culture made by science and technology. Things that are modern are still those that are technologically advanced. But at some time during the first half of the nineteenth century, as Matei Calinescu says, a split occurred between "modernity as a stage in the history of Western civilization—a product of scientific and technological progress, of the industrial revolution ... and modernity as an aesthetic concept. Since then the relations between the two modernities have been irreducibly hostile."[4] Modernism became, in Lionel Trilling's phrase, an "adversary position" to the culture of industrialism and imperial expansion. For this it drew on all earlier complaints, from the faint graceful laments of Goldsmith in "The Deserted Village" to the keening of James Thomson in "The City of Dreadful Night."

The "bourgeois idea of modernity," says Calinescu, coincides with the bourgeois system of values:

> The doctrine of progress, the confidence in the beneficial possibili-
> ties of science and technology, the concern with time (a *measurable*
> time, a time that can be bought and sold and therefore has, like
> any other commodity, a calculable equivalent in money), the cult of
> reason, and the ideal of freedom defined within the framework of
> an abstract humanism, but also the orientation toward pragmatism
> and the cult of action and success—all have been associated in
> various degrees with the battle for the modern and were kept alive
> and promoted as key values in the triumphant civilization estab-
> lished by the middle class. . . .
>   The "other modernity," literary Modernism, was from its
> romantic beginnings inclined toward radical, anti-bourgeois atti-
> tudes. It was disgusted with the middle-class scale of values and
> expressed its disgust through the most diverse means, ranging
> from rebellion, anarchy, and apocalypticism, to aristocratic self-
> exile. So, more than its positive aspirations (which often have very
> little in common), what defines cultural modernity is its outright
> rejection of bourgeois modernity, its consuming negative passion.[5]

We will have to consider the implications of this "consuming negative passion," since it is an undeniable feature of Modernism; but at first, in Modernism's "heroic era," it would be fairer to say that the various assaults on cherished forms and beliefs were joyous discoveries as much as they were complaints. Realism of setting, portraiture, and dialogue had to be violated if the novel was going to mirror the "new" reality, psychological life, more convincingly. Free verse in poetry and overt abstraction in painting allowed a degree of individuality into art that seemed to reflect the nature of perception more accurately. Certainly these new techniques "attacked" existing ones, but there was more than simple iconoclasm behind them. The world was more complex than the Victorian middle class believed or wanted it to be. Poetry, to speak only of that, became, as Eliot was to say much later, an "intolerable wrestle with words and meanings":

> Older and more traditional definitions of poetry—the spontaneous
> overflow of powerful feeling, the best words in the best order—
> were impatiently dismissed. Obsessive attempts to say "the unsay-
> able" made extreme demands on the mind's elasticity. Not only
> literature but all art of the period seemed to be intent on stretching

the mind beyond the very limits of human understanding. Human nature was "elusive, indeterminate, multiple, often implausible, infinitely various and essentially irreducible."[6]

It is true that much poetry of the time simply attacked the Victorians for their obvious failings. Pound, for instance, sometimes posed as a true-hearted Romantic so that he could belabor his stuffy contemporaries, as in "Salutation":

O generation of the thoroughly smug and thoroughly
uncomfortable,
I have seen fishermen picnicking in the sun,
I have seen them with untidy families,
I have seen their smiles full of teeth and heard ungainly laughter.
And I am happier than you are,
And they were happier than I am;
And the fish swim in the lake and do not even own clothing.[7]

Pound did not always belabor the late Victorian and Edwardian upper middle classes. His Chinese translations can be read as oblique criticisms of the culture of imperial Britain, but the criticism is so roundabout—the frontier guards only remotely resemble British troops in the trenches in World War I—that what is most impressive about these poems is their freshness and naïveté, as in "The River Merchant's Wife: A Letter":

While my hair was still cut straight across my forehead
I played about the front gate, pulling flowers.
You came by on bamboo stilts, playing horse,
You walked about my seat, playing with blue plums.
And we went on living in the village of Chokan:
Two small people, without dislike or suspicion.[8]

Here were several kinds of newness. Though the verse was free, it had a pronounced monosyllabic rhythm; and though there were none of the conventional properties of poetry like metaphor and simile or the grand rhetorical display of the feeling self, there was quite obviously a luminous depth of feeling. Not since the time of Chaucer had such trust been put in fact, in the image chosen for itself and not as grist for the synthesizing imagination. Though Pound took more obvious steps in other poems toward a colloquial vigor of speech, a poem like "The River Merchant's Wife" sounds much like a person thinking aloud or writing her most private thoughts in a letter.

In "Fabliau of Florida," Wallace Stevens not only dabbled in the new free verse (he would later abandon it), but also in highly imaginative renderings of reality.

> Barque of phosphor
> On the palmy beach,
> Move outward into heaven,
> Into the alabasters
> And night blues.
> Foam and cloud are one.
> Sultry moon-monsters
> Are dissolving.
> Fill your black hull
> With white moonlight.
> There will never be an end
> To this droning of the surf.[9]

Most disturbing to a practical mentality in this poem would have been the almost willful relationship to reality. Those who looked for Florida in "Fabliau of Florida" were naturally disappointed. Nothing like this was being written at the time in English, except possibly by Gertrude Stein in *Tender Buttons* (1914). The virtue in Stevens's poem lay in the poetry itself, the willing suspension of reality in a thick imaginative medium. With the nature of reality itself in question, poets like Stevens turned to the only solid ground left in human affairs, individual perception.

H. D.'s well-known little poem "Oread" was used for years to classify, not to say calcify, her as an Imagist.

> Whirl up, sea—
> whirl your pointed pines,
> splash your great pines
> on our rocks,
> hurl your green over us,
> cover us with your pools of fir.[10]

"Oread" is not so much a poem that uses an image as it is a poem that is an image. It does not discuss or explain; it is purely representative. Since it also avoids the metronome of regular meter, it qualifies in several ways as a representative Imagist poem. More important is its Modernist and post-Romantic celebration of natural energy and of the mind's ability to create meaning metaphorically. Whatever the sea is, finally, it is called upon—in ecstatic tones—to dominate us. The power of the imagination rivals that of the sea.

William Carlos Williams took other risks with conventional notions of poetry. He not only trusted the unadorned image to reveal beauty and truth (his first poems were Keatsian imitations); he trusted unadorned reality itself. His famous poem "The Red Wheelbarrow" drew perhaps the greatest derision of all early Modernist poems, greater even than *The Waste Land*, because of what looked like its pointless ordinariness.

so much depends
upon

a red wheel
barrow

glazed with rain
water

beside the white
chickens.[11]

Williams made the most radical departure of all because he was willing to turn his back on all existing ideas of culture and tradition, certainly those invoked by his peers. If Emerson's essays made it possible for him to find "an original relation to the universe" and an American version of the world, and if Whitman's example led him to trust the simple, abundant facts of that world, he did all of these things without donning the robes of seer or bardic father-of-us-all. The red wheelbarrow was first of all a red wheelbarrow, and it was right in front of us. "The Red Wheelbarrow" makes us wonder what sort of world it would be if everything were seen, as in some sense everything must exist, as clearly and inviolably itself.

All of these poems were written between about 1913 and 1921 and indicate the sense of exhilaration and discovery in what Frank Kermode has called the period of "paleo-modernism." The new work was certainly critical of existing attitudes, but in every case the old was swept aside so that something new could be given room to grow. It was not criticism for the sake of criticism, but criticism to make creation possible. Stein, Williams, H. D., Stevens, and others were hardly seized by a "consuming negative passion." Their careers, in fact, illustrate the opposite.

The negative passion was there, however. The years 1913 to 1921 are roughly the years of what was known as the Great War. It was not difficult for

many to see a connection between this cataclysm and the dominant, materialist values of Victorian and post-Victorian culture. The war was essentially
fought over the rise of German economic power and the British resistance
to it. Two empires struggled to hold, or increase their hold, on the world's
markets and resources. The Germans had developed the most impressive
scientific establishment of the time and were confident that life could be
improved through the direct, forceful application of scientific ideals. The virtues of the middle class—individual effort, inventiveness, competitiveness,
faith in progress and reason—all were easily converted, by both sides, into the
energy needed to fight a brutal and senseless war. Nothing caused a deeper
questioning of the nature of human beings than their eagerness and efficiency
in slaughtering one another, not the disappearance of the fixed Newtonian
universe in physics, not the disappearance of moral absolutism, not the discovery of the subconscious, of human evolution, or of class warfare. Pound
spoke more directly and savagely in "Hugh Selwyn Mauberley." The best of
his generation died for "a botched civilization," for a few "broken statues" and
"battered books."[12]

Side by side, then, with a Modernist exploration of the kinds and limits
of perception stood a vision of anarchy and despair, made most vivid in works
like *The Waste Land* and the novels of Franz Kafka. It is this vision that most
seriously challenges the optimism of the scientific and bourgeois worldview,
and it is this vision, this "consuming negative passion," that is customarily
implied by the word "Modernism." The idea of the modern, as Irving Howe
has said, is an idea of radical, not to say reactionary, isolation, a condition in
which people feel themselves cut off from each other and from all systems of
religion and philosophy.[13]

Oddly enough, this characterization of Modernism is fairly recent. For
one thing, the word "Modernism" was not used in the years 1910 to 1920.[14]
Many other words were used, but not "Modernism." For another, the gloomy
connotations of the word came from critics and writers who were decidedly
on the Left: Howe, Georg Lukács, Thomas Mann, David Caute, and others.
Mann once said that modern literature cultivated "a sympathy for the abyss."
The typical condition of Modernist literature became a cloying inwardness.
With nothing else to cling to, the modern sensibility clings to itself. From
such a perspective, the plunge inward in the stream-of-consciousness novel
or in Abstract Expressionist painting is easily seen as an abandonment of the
social world and an act of social irresponsibility. It does not matter to such
critics that, for instance, Virginia Woolf allows us to know more about the
inner workings of the female mind. Until recently, critics have not been able
to see that as an advance in perception with responsible, not to say radically
responsible, implications.

Howe says, further, that the Modernist dispenses with history and tries to live outside it. The typical Modernist implies that history is merely cyclical or, if headed in any direction, is headed toward some cataclysm. Pound believed, as his *Cantos* show, that history was a random succession of periods of enlightenment and darkness. Eliot ridiculed Emerson's hopeful view of history in "Sweeney Erect." Stevens seemed unaware of history. Williams and H. D. had to invent their own eclectic versions of it. Perhaps these are assorted ways of giving up on history, but when Howe and Lukács criticize writers for doing this, they do so as critics with a definite view of the way history works. History, to them, is progressive and scientific. Reason is at work in history, and to attack such a view or show an indifference to it is taken by them to be an evasion of the truth. A progressive politics requires a progressive and rational view of history as its foundation. Whether that view of history is truer than a view which says that the conditions of human existence are eternal and unchanging is finally a matter of belief.

Graham Hough has said, "For the most part . . . the poets have refused the great public mythologies of our time, and have evolved rival myths of their own, some grandiose and comprehensive, some esoteric and private, but none with any status in the world of organized scientific and historical knowledge by which the world conducts its business."[15] It would be wrong, however, finally to describe Modernist writers as some species of intellectual ostrich, lost in a Darwinian cul-de-sac of their own choosing or making, a view shared oddly enough by Marxist critics and the great bourgeois who were their targets. The pressures under which the Modernists wrote would have made any thinking person question "the world of organized scientific and historical knowledge by which the world conducts its business." More to the point, however, is that the Modernists opened up the world for us to see. They gave us strategies of perception and criticism which continue to be valid. They lit up the body of the world in ways we are still learning from. Not just reading or looking at or listening to, but learning from.

Edwin Arlington Robinson (1869–1935) began by writing fiction. His teachers in that art were European Naturalists like Zola. A case can be made, in fact, that Modernist poetry owes a large debt to the theories and techniques of nineteenth-century fiction. Robinson's poems, for instance, are almost always narratives. Even his sonnets are stories. Like Conrad and James, Robinson experimented with point of view. His famous poem "Richard Cory" is told from the point of view of a fellow citizen of Tilbury Town, a small town in Maine which Robinson invented, as many local colorists in fiction were doing at the end of the nineteenth century. The speaker, then, is as puzzled as the reader why Cory, who seemed to have every reason for being happy, should have committed suicide.

> ... we thought that he was everything
> To make us wish that we were in his place.
>
> So on we worked and waited for the light,
> And went without the meat, and cursed the bread;
> And Richard Cory, one calm summer night,
> Went home and put a bullet through his head.[16]

Cory was wealthy, so the poem takes part in the general criticism of materialism in post-Romantic literature, a criticism which it handed on to the poets of Modernism.

Robinson's poetry begins the turn toward Modernism in two other important ways. He has a strong sense of the limits of human aspirations, something that was very strong in Naturalists like Zola and Conrad. As "Richard Cory" suggests, Robinson was skeptical of the power of human reason and of the ability of people to know their world and manage competently in it. Finally, and this may be Robinson's most significant contribution to twentieth-century poetry, he used the language of everyday speech. This was unusual, especially in Robinson's early years, the 1890s, when poets were still trying to write a pretty, musical poetry in the manner of Tennyson or Longfellow. Nobody went home and put a bullet through his head in the poetry of Ella Wheeler Wilcox or William Vaughn Moody. Robinson's language was too colloquial and direct for poetry at that time, though not for the novel. When the new poetry arrived in roughly 1912, the year that *Poetry* magazine was founded in Chicago by Harriet Monroe, Robinson's manner as a formalist was well established. He did not join the makers of free verse, so his poetry seemed to belong to an earlier time. But this was an illusion. His contributions to modern poetry and to American poetry in general have been considerable.

Robert Frost (1874–1963) lived long enough into the twentieth century to have been not only premodern in his literary leanings but vocally antimodern. Frost's rejection of the new poetry, which is mostly a rejection of free verse, is stated forcefully in his review of Robinson's *King Jasper* in 1935, shortly after Robinson's death. It is a succinct and witty definition of the new poetry by a disbeliever.

> It may come to the notice of posterity (and then again it may not) that this our age ran wild in the quest of new ways to be new. The one old way to be new no longer served. ... Those tried were largely by subtraction—elimination. Poetry, for example, was tried without punctuation. It was tried without capital letters. It was

tried without metric frame on which to measure the rhythm. It was tried without any images but those to the eye; and a loud general intoning had to be kept up to cover the total loss of specific images to the ear. . . . It was tried without content under the trade name of poesie pure. It was tried without phrase, epigram, coherence, logic and consistency. It was tried without ability. . . . It was tried premature like the delicacy of unborn calf in Asia. It was tried without feeling or sentiment like murder for small pay in the underworld.[17]

As we shall see, it would be wrong to conclude from this witty defense of traditional poetry, as Frost almost seems to hope we might, that his poetry had nothing to do with Modernism.

Frost rarely wrote badly, but he wrote his best work in his first years. The decade 1910 to 1920 was his first and most productive, beginning with *A Boy's Will* in 1913. He was thirty-nine that year, so it is not too surprising that he was able to publish three more books in the next four years—*North of Boston* (1915), *Mountain Interval* (1916), and *A Way Out* (1917)—plus a *Selected Poem* in 1923.

Frost was born in California, so his decision to make himself into a New Hampshire farmer poet, at a time when the New Hampshire farmer was nearly a thing of the past and when the country was rapidly industrializing, resembles Thoreau's decision to live beside Walden Pond in a cabin of his own making. Frost had more than a little Emersonian self-reliance in him, in fact, as well as the typical Transcendentalist's dislike of materialism. He was hardly a Romantic, however. Like Robinson and a good many other writers of the late nineteenth century—Hardy, Housman, James Thomson, Conrad, Dreiser, Stephen Crane, to name a few—he was a religious skeptic and doubted the willingness or ability of human beings to care for one another. He may have disliked the formlessness of the new poetry, but he understood its spirit. His philosophic gloom and his antimaterialism are quite typical of what was later to be called Modernist writing.

A poem, said Frost, "begins in delight and ends in wisdom." It achieves a "momentary stay against confusion." Confusion, in other words, however that might be defined, was the norm, and delight was usually dispersed by thought or wisdom. *A Boy's Will* tries to capture "sheer morning gladness at the brim," but does so, as in "The Tuft of Flowers," by first dramatizing the isolation of human beings. "I went to turn the grass once after one / Who mowed it in the dew before the sun." The speaker never comes any closer to this "one," except to notice that he had spared a tuft of flowers in his mowing. He feels a "spirit kindred" to his own but never sees or meets the man. It is therefore both inspiriting and dispiriting to conclude:

And dreaming, as it were, [I] held brotherly speech
With one whose thought I had not hoped to reach.
"Men work together," I told him from the heart,
"Whether they work together or apart."[18]

From *North of Boston* on, Frost's poetry confronts this loneliness and isolation more convincingly. Like most Modernists, he sees much more silence
than brotherly speech between people. The first poem in *North of Boston*,
"Mending Wall," announces this clearly, but in "Death of the Hired Man,"
"Home Burial," "A Servant to Servants," "The Tear," and other poems, the
picture of humans reduced almost to animal silence is unmistakable and vivid.
"Mending Wall" manages to modify this Zolaesque Naturalism by letting an
idealist and rationalist speak the poem. He tries to instruct his neighbor, but
fails. Reason's arguments cannot alter the instincts and habits of the "old-
stone savage armed." If the neighbor is a sort of prehistoric figure, riddled
with superstition, he is also, as the speaker seems almost to learn, a man with
wisdom that a rationalist would never understand. Frost, however, does not
make the old farmer a noble savage, as an early Romantic writer might have,
but he is writing at a time when artists like Picasso and Braque were beginning to realize that primitive peoples were capable of great art and that the
primitive itself needed reexamination. There might indeed be something that
doesn't love a wall, but is it some innate goodness in nature that hates to see
divisions among people, as the speaker would seem to want to believe, or is
it a natural indifference or perhaps even a malevolence that destroys human
attempts at order and orderliness? Worse yet, are both conclusions true? In
this and other poems, Frost raises large questions and points toward conceiv-
able answers, but he can finally give no answer. Instead, he realizes a condition
of paradox in a world where only the most crude and fleeting communication
is possible. Later writers such as Lawrence or Joyce would use Freud to light
up this darkness. Frost is content to present it to us in vivid, realistic detail.

"The first poet I ever sat down with to talk about poetry," wrote Frost
years later, "was Ezra Pound [1885–1972]. It was in London in 1913. The first
poet we talked about, to the best of my recollection, was Edwin Arlington
Robinson."[19] Several parables of modern American poetry meet in such a
remark. First, Robert Frost was in London. Frost, in fact, spent several of his
formative years in England. Second, he was talking with his fellow American,
Ezra Pound, who by 1913 had made himself the most vocal force in a new
movement in poetry, soon to be given names like Imagism, free verse, the
New Intellectualism, and so on. Frost, of course, was not interested in any of
it. Pound had gone to London because it was the cultural center of the English-speaking world. Frost had gone not to London, but to England, pastoral

England, the country of Wordsworth. Pound and Frost met, however, and their talk went immediately to American poets and poetry, specifically to their near contemporary, Robinson, who was living the isolated life of the artist typical of America at that time, a life they were trying to avoid in the traditional manner by living abroad.

Ezra Pound was born in Idaho but grew up mostly in the Philadelphia area, where he met other poets of his generation like H. D., Marianne Moore, and William Carlos Williams. After college at Hamilton and a graduate degree in romance languages at the University of Pennsylvania, Pound took a job as a college professor. He was to last only six months at Wabash College, however, before the authorities dismissed him as a "Latin quarter type." He left the country immediately, in early 1908, and went to Venice where he published his first book, *A Lume Spento*. By September of that year he had moved to London, where he was to remain until late 1920.

It is hardly an accident that Pound's residence in London coincides almost exactly with the decade we are looking at, for no one person did more, or as much, to bring English-speaking literature into the contemporary world than Ezra Pound. He was not only instrumental in bringing Robert Frost to public attention, but it was through his efforts that writers like T. S. Eliot, James Joyce, Wyndham Lewis, H. D., William Carlos Williams, and others were brought into print. A flamboyant, determined polemicist for the "new" literature, Pound bullied and harassed editors into printing what he thought mattered, reviewed without a break for the whole time he was in London, and found time in all these activities to write some of the best poetry ever written in English. Chief among his literary labors was "persuading" Harriet Monroe that he should be foreign correspondent for the magazine *Poetry*, which she started in Chicago in 1912. Almost at once *Poetry* became the leading outlet for the new poetry. In his reviewing at this time, Pound made what nearly amounts to a systematic survey of the whole of culture, writing long series of reviews on music, art, drama, the literary press, classical translators, French literature, and many other aspects of world culture which he felt were relevant to the modern world. Pound was not content simply to be a poet. The condition of mind that would make significant poetry possible had to be created first. Editors, readers, writers, even politicians, needed to be convinced that the old world was dead and the old way of doing things outmoded.

Pound's reputation was quickly established by the publication, in London, of his third book, *Personae* (1909). It was published by Elkin Mathews, the "discoverer" of Yeats. In quick succession came *Exultations* (1909); *The Spirit of Romance* (1910), a treatise on the "pre-Renaissance literature of Latin Europe" and the first of his many studies of culture; *Provençal* (1910); *Canzoni* (1911); *Ripostes* (1912); *Cathay* (1915), his famous translations of Li Po;

Gaudier-Brzeska (1916), a study of the sculpture of a friend killed in the war; *Lustra* (1916); *Pavannes and Divisions* (1918); *Instigations* (1920), a book of essays; *Hugh Selwyn Mauberley* (1920), his "farewell to London"; and *Umbra* (1920). In this period, too, he was chosen by Ernest Fenollosa's widow to edit her husband's papers, and he began writing his *Cantos*.

Most critics are now inclined to dismiss the importance of the Imagist movement to Ezra Pound's career. His reasons for separating himself from it are complicated, but the truest thing to say is that the movement quickly developed a recognizable and easily imitated style with limited goals. By the time Amy Lowell had begun editing her Imagist anthologies in 1915, Pound was disaffected. He told her that he could not trust any "democratized committee" to maintain the standards of "Imagisme," as he preferred to call it, namely, "hard light, clear edges."[20] During its moment, however, Imagism exactly reflected the values Pound wanted for his writing and for writing in general, and the quickness with which it was imitated and institutionalized shows how wide its influence was.

Imagist theory is based on a few scattered pronouncements arrived at in 1912 by a group in London that included Pound, F. S. Flint, H. D., T. E. Hulme, and a few others. These pronouncements were written down in separate, short essays by Flint and Pound and, through the latter's position as foreign correspondent for *Poetry*, published in that magazine's March 1913 issue. The three points of what is sometimes called "the Imagist credo" were (1) "Direct treatment of the 'thing' whether subjective or objective"; (2) "Use absolutely no word that does not contribute to the presentation"; and (3) "As regarding rhythm: to compose in the sequence of the musical phrase, not in the sequence of the metronome." Add to this Pound's definition of the image—"That which presents an intellectual and emotional complex in an instant of time"—and the rationale for a poetry unlike any known before in English was complete. It would be a poetry that avoided talking about things; that is to say, it would avoid intellectualizing and generalizing. Instead, it would treat matters directly. Direct treatment meant "presentation," the thrusting of the reader into the middle of intellectual and emotional complexes without signposts or comforting explanations.

Imagist poems were intensely visual, and since they had little or no comment, they were often like photographs or still lifes in painting. Pound was to summarize this side of Imagism by saying, "Go in fear of abstraction." The avoidance of abstraction—or, to use another word, explanation—and the presentational method brought poetry in line with leading theories of prose fiction, notably the "dramatic method" described by Henry James. This may be one of the reasons why the language of poetry at this time took on a prose quality.

The main reason why poetic language changed, though, had to do with the second and third points of the Imagist credo. No word was supposed to be used in a poem if it had only musical or metrical value. That is to say, all words in a poem were to be scrutinized carefully and, if not needed, discarded. Pound was opposed to what he called the "slither" of late-Victorian and Edwardian verse, the pretty musicality for which Tennyson was well known. The Imagists were so anxious to get away from that sort of thing that they did away with the "metronome" altogether, that is, with conventional meter. In a single stroke, free verse was born.

Verse was not to be free of music, however. It was not to be an oddly aligned prose. The poet was to "compose in the sequence of the musical phrase," a delightfully ambiguous definition which at least theoretically allowed greater individuality to each poet and a greater range of musical possibilities in the language. Pound, whose ear was uncommonly sensitive and who was also well trained in meter, could create original movements and rhythms. But even more important, Pound believed that the image could speak more powerfully than any abstraction or explanation.

Another reason why Imagism did not hold Pound's attention for long was that it was a literary movement with exclusively literary ambitions. Pound wanted more than that. He wanted to reinvigorate culture and restore it to what he regarded as its proper relationship with political, social, and intellectual authority. In his view the British empire was unenlightened, and it was his hope to change that by creating an informed artistic intelligentsia which could then act, directly or indirectly, as the culture's eyes and conscience. Pound's later work and his later life make sense only if we see him trying to make what he called at the end of *The Cantos* a "paradiso terrestre." He was inevitably (and lamentably) drawn to leaders and forms of government which seemed to value the arts and were willing to use their authority, even despotically, to achieve the high aims of enlightened culture. He left England in December 1920 because that no longer seemed possible there, and in a very short time he had attached himself intellectually to Italian fascism in the belief that Mussolini cared for the arts. But that is a later story. Now we are concerned with the poetry Pound wrote under the double pressure of his high hopes and their defilement by World War I. In all of this poetry, though, we will hear, sometimes quietly, sometimes not, the committed cultural polemicist.

One of the ways Pound created authority for himself in doing this was to find and translate poetry from other cultures that had been in roughly the same straits as the British in his day. The poems in *Cathay* evoke the loneliness and sadness of people kept by war, business, or imperial affairs from the people and places they love. Pound resumed his attack by translation two years later when he published "Homage to Sextus Propertius." Imperial

Rome in Propertius's day was at its ostentatious worst, and Propertius simply turned his back on it. Not in rueful silence, however. He scorned the reigning culture, contented himself with modest comfort, and flattered the ladies. Through Propertius, Pound made the case over and over that bad writing, bad ruling, and ostentation are related matters.

Pound's aesthetics were always divided. Like Propertius, he thought that an art which praised the state was a false art. But an art which removed itself entirely from public awareness was doomed. This is the chief premise of his brilliant sequence "Hugh Selwyn Mauberley," his "farewell to London." Though there is much Pound in him, Mauberley is finally an ineffectual aesthete and hedonist. In "Mauberley," Pound again tries to place the artist in a significant relationship to social and political reality, and he records in vivid detail the threats in English society to the artist who wished art to avoid "the social inconsequence." The breadth of denunciations in "Mauberley" brings us as close as any poem in English before *The Waste Land* to the Modernist vision, but in Pound's case, this moment would prove to be an excuse to embark on a distinctly non-Modernist course, namely, to rebuild the world.

T. S. Eliot (1888–1965) shared Pound's dismay over the state of culture in the prewar years. As a student of Irving Babbitt at Harvard, he developed a critical attitude toward any form of Romantic optimism. Human nature was inherently flawed to Eliot, and the despair and misery he went on to record in his poetry served only to define and strengthen his conviction that human beings needed the support of a coherent Christian culture to lend purpose to their lives. Like Pound, he sought to acquaint people with what he called "the immense panorama of futility and anarchy which is contemporary history."[21] Like Pound again, in the last years of his life he all but gave up poetry for cultural polemicizing.

Eliot was born in St. Louis and attended Milton Academy and Harvard College, where he graduated in 1909. He began graduate studies in philosophy right away, spent the year 1910–11 at the Sorbonne, returned to Harvard to finish his studies, and in 1914 went to England, where by gradual process he settled down, married, and became a British citizen. He had written poetry as a young man, seriously enough so that when he went to Paris he went there more to visit the home of the Symbolist movement than to attend the lectures of Henri Bergson. He did finish his philosophical studies, but when he arrived in London in 1914 he was already carrying "The Love Song of J. Alfred Prufrock" with him. He found his way to Pound, who that winter would act as Yeats's secretary, and Pound knew at once what he had stumbled on. He wrote Harriet Monroe on 30 September: "He is the only American I know of who has made what I can call adequate preparation for writing. He has actually trained himself *and* modernized himself *on his own*."[22]

Between 1910 and 1920, Eliot published three books of poetry—*Prufrock and Other Observations* (1917), *Poems* (1919), and *Ara Vos Prec* (1920)—as well as two books of criticism, *Ezra Pound: His Metric and Poetry* (1917) and *The Sacred Wood: Essays on Poetry and Criticism* (1920). Like Pound, he would later be known as much for his criticism as for his poetry, but in his first years as a published writer, he was almost exclusively and most intensely a poet. Eliot was the most gifted poet of his generation, and he created not just new rhythms in the language but also landscapes and conflicts which had rarely been seen in English poetry. Whitman was the only other poet of the city in the English language, but his was the city of the open democratic masses. Eliot's city came from Baudelaire by way of the Decadents, and the people he found there were either coarse or cruelly oversensitive. "The Love Song of J. Alfred Prufrock" is at once the most vivid rendering of the late-nineteenth-century aesthetic sensibility and its most damning criticism. It undoubtedly influenced the writing of Pound's "Hugh Selwyn Mauberley."

The surprising thing about Eliot was, as Pound said, that when he appeared in the literary world, he was mature and fully formed. For one thing, he had a coherent worldview. Significant life took part in the city, where people were divided into the dispirited, lifeless poor, the insensitive merchants, and those from the class Eliot knew best, the pale harbingers of taste and breeding. None of these people merits much praise or pity. Eliot had a power of objectivity that occasionally makes him seem, especially in the early poetry, almost misanthropic. The merchants and commercial people, when they appear, are dismissed quickly and contemptuously and, alas, sometimes with what feels like anti-Semitism: "And the Jew squats on the window sill, the owner, / Spawned in some estaminet of Antwerp." This is not social satire but something like loathing.

If we feel that Eliot renders the lower and middle classes with unfair exaggeration, the same is not true of the members of his own class. A whole way of life, which must have been very close to Eliot's, is quietly dismissed in "Cousin Nancy," "The Boston Evening Transcript," or "Aunt Helen," who

> ... lived in a small house near a fashionable square
> Cared for by servants to the number of four.
> Now when she died there was silence in heaven
> And silence at her end of the street.[23]

In the family poems, the criticism is gentler, much closer to social satire. Occasionally, as in "Morning at the Window," Eliot's satirical guard comes down.

> The brown waves of fog toss up to me
> Twisted faces from the bottom of the street,
> And tear from a passer-by with muddy skirts
> An aimless smile that hovers in the air
> And vanishes along the level of the roofs.[24]

Suddenly we are in Eliot's unique territory, an imprecise but vivid realm of the subconscious where ethereal and sordid images mix freely to create an atmosphere of intense isolation and loneliness. One of the most modern aspects of Eliot's writing is this ability to objectify the subconscious. The technique of juxtaposing images in "Prufrock" may look as though it owes a debt to Imagist objectivity and concision, but Eliot reached that technique by way of French Symbolism and, of course, by patient attention to the workings of his own mind.

J. Alfred Prufrock is not just the speaker of one of Eliot's poems. He is the Representative Man of early Modernism. Shy, cultivated, oversensitive, sexually retarded (many have said impotent), ruminative, isolated, self-aware to the point of solipsism, as he says, "Am an attendant lord, one that will do / To swell a progress, start a scene or two."[25] Nothing revealed the Victorian upper classes in Western society more accurately, unless it was a novel by Henry James, and nothing better exposed the dreamy, insubstantial center of that consciousness than a half-dozen poems in Eliot's first book. The speakers of all these early poems are trapped inside their own excessive alertness. They look out on the world from deep inside some private cave of feeling, and though they see the world and themselves with unflattering exactness, they cannot or will not do anything about their dilemma and finally fall back on self-serving explanation. They quake before the world, and their only revenge is to be alert. After *Prufrock and Other Observations*, poetry started coming from the city and from the intellect. It could no longer stand comfortably on its old post-Romantic ground, ecstatic before the natural world.

Had H. D. (Hilda Doolittle, 1886–1961) died in the thirties, we would think of her as an interesting minor poet. As it is, she wrought a startling change in her work in the last decades of her life, and we now think of her as a major poet of this century. She published only one book, her first, *Sea Garden* (1916), in the decade 1910 to 1920, as well as two books of Greek poetry in translation. Growing up in the Philadelphia area, she met and fell in love with Ezra Pound, and though the episode is shrouded somewhat, she went to England in 1911 futilely thinking that she and Pound were to be married. At any rate she soon found herself among the Imagists. Her early poems, in fact, contain some of the most beautiful and characteristic poems of that short-lived literary movement. They are spare and almost purely presentative.

Whiter
than the crust
left by the tide,
we are stung by the hurled sand
and the broken shells.[26]

These early poems are also, as this fragment from "The Wind Sleepers"
suggests, breathless and urgent in a straightforwardly Romantic way. They
avoid the banalities of Romanticism, however, first by freeing themselves of
accentual-syllabic meter and second by relying almost entirely on the image.

The most striking thing about H. D.'s early poetry is its almost complete removal from the living world. Much of it evokes the culture of ancient
Greece. The poems are filled with the sea, sunlight, beaches, and, as in "Hunt-
ress," vaguely mythological beings and an incipient feminism.

Come, blunt your spear with us,
our pace is hot
and our bare heels
in the heel-prints—
we stand tense—do you see—
are you already beaten
by the chase?[27]

It is natural to ask why she should so severely limit her contact with the real
world, and the last poem in *Sea Garden* gives a plausible answer. "Cities"
refers to no city in particular, but it is clear that she is talking about the
modern city. The poem is spoken by a member of a "cell," a small group
of enlightened people who have taken upon themselves the task of guard-
ing some treasure of the past and preserving it for use or discovery in the
indeterminate future. By implication, of course, the present is ugly and
threatening.

And in these dark cells,
packed street after street,
souls live, hideous yet—
O disfigured, defaced,
with no trace of the beauty
men once held so light.[28]

Years later Eliot would call this act of preserving things of value in an
unsympathetic age "redeeming the time." The foreshadowing of Eliot

extends even to her using the word "waste" to describe the contemporary world ("Though we wander about, / find no honey of flowers in this waste"). She is not an imitator, but she, too, wanted to build what Pound called a "paradiso terrestre," in the belief that the modern world was contemptible and horrifying. As it turned out, her utopia was quite different from either Pound's or Eliot's, primarily because she was a woman. But, in her earliest work, she is imbued with something like a reformer's zeal. Imagism would have stifled such zeal, which is the main reason why no poet of consequence stayed an Imagist very long. Like the typical Modernist, she found this world insupportable, and her refusal to name it or even refer to it in her early poetry is perhaps the most radical act of any of these early Modernists.

William Carlos Williams's (1883–1963) first book, *Poems* (1909), was privately printed in his hometown, Rutherford, New Jersey. It was, for the most part, Keatsian imitations. He had gone straight from Horace Mann High School in New York City, in 1902, to the University of Pennsylvania Medical School. There he met Pound and H. D. He had already decided to be a poet by then, and whether because Keats had been a doctor or because he liked Keats's poetry, he labored over a long work in imitation of *Endymion*. Pound, at the time, was writing a sonnet a day.

The friendship between Pound and Williams was crucial to the latter because, through Pound's badgering, Williams was able to change his style completely in a short time. His second book, *The Tempers*, appeared in 1913, and his mature style was established—not perfected, but established. *Al Que Quiere* appeared in 1917 and a book of prose poems, *Kora in Hell: Improvisations*, in 1920. Williams became an Imagist, as it were, by mail. He stripped his language of generality and gush, abandoned the "metronome" of accentual-syllabic metrics (indeed, he went so far as to write prose poems), and schooled himself rigorously in objective writing, writing with as little comment as possible.

More important, Williams steeped himself in his given world. Nothing in Imagist aesthetics required the poet to describe what lay out the window, no matter what it might be, but Williams took the factual and visual implications of that aesthetic to its logical end. He made a virtue of what he called "the local." None of his expatriate friends and contemporaries—Pound, Eliot, and H. D.—was interested in such a thing. Those poets who did celebrate localities—Robinson, of Maine; Frost, of New Hampshire; Masters, of the rural Midwest; Sandburg, of Chicago—did so in the manner and under the influence of local-color Realism in fiction. Williams instead used Imagist techniques to bring his poetry closer to the realities of his place.

This meant two things. The focus of his attention was immediate and close:

There's my things
drying in the corner:
that blue skirt
joined to the grey shirt.[29]

And, as this excerpt from "Portrait of a Woman in Bed" shows, he would use a language that was as straightforward and unornamented as the things it described.

Williams came as close as anyone ever had to using the language of everyday speech for poetry, and it is his great contribution to American poetry to couple this aim with that of putting America, warts and all, into his poetry. This might make him sound like an American Kipling. Not so. He does not use American speech as a dialect. American speech, as he heard it, was his poetic language. It is useful to remember that Williams lived all his adult life in one house—9 Ridge Road, Rutherford, New Jersey—and, living close to New York City, he came into contact with dozens of writers, painters, and photographers who were trying to do what Emerson had urged in his "American Scholar" address, namely, forge an American consciousness and art. Williams would not become vocal and programmatic about America until the twenties, when he published *In the American Grain*, but the impulses were there in the teens. The Armory Show in New York introduced American audiences to the new post-Impressionist art, and it took place the same year *The Tempers* was published. Stieglitz was making photography into an art form. Painters like Sheeler, Demuth, Sloan, Marin, Luks, Bellows, and others were looking closely at American places and people. *Poetry* magazine was a year old in 1913. The *Little Review*, *Others*, and the *Dial* followed quickly. Williams was very close to all this activity.

By the time of *Al Que Quiere*, Williams had found his voice and his material. Some of Williams's best early poems are found in it: "Tract," "The Young Housewife," "Love Song," "El Hombre" (which Wallace Stevens put into his poem "Nuances of a Theme by Williams"), "Good Night," "Danse Russe," "Smell," and "Pastoral." At this point in his career, Williams joined most writers in trying to undo the stultifying effects of "the genteel tradition."

Gertrude Stein (1874–1946) continues to baffle critics, partly because her work is so varied, partly because it eludes comprehension, and partly because her poetry stands outside all traditions. She wrote poetry as though she had never read any, except Mother Goose. When Stein published her book of poems, *Tender Buttons*, in 1914, she had already published *Three Lives* (1909), a work of fiction which not only focused on the little-known lives of women, but did so through some of the first stream-of-consciousness narration ever written. Her next publication wasn't until 1922, when *Geography and Plays* appeared with a foreword by Sherwood Anderson. She wrote incessantly, however, and as the Yale edition of the *Unpublished Writings of Gertrude Stein* shows, she wrote more in the teens and twenties of what we would call—and what she sometimes herself called—poetry than at any other time in her life. Most of these poems are found in volume three of the unpublished writing, *Bee Time Vine and Other Pieces* [1913–27] (1953).

It is an exaggeration to say that Gertrude Stein stumbled into writing, but her serious writing did not start until 1903 at age twenty-nine, two years after she failed four courses at Johns Hopkins Medical School. By that time, she had traveled extensively and had settled in Paris. She quickly found her way, mostly as a buyer, into the world of post-Impressionist painting. She saw her first Cézannes in 1904, met Picasso in 1905, and a year later sat for him. No writer has ever been as much influenced by painting; and living when and where she did, that influence created distortions of perceptions and syntax which, almost a century later, keep much of her work startling and largely unread. In important respects, however, she is the perfect embodiment of experimental tendencies in Modernism.

Stein is one of her own best critics. Her monograph on Picasso was published in 1938, but it often obliquely explains what she was attempting in her writing. "In the nineteenth century painters discovered the need of always having a model in front of them, in the twentieth century they discovered that they must never look at a model ... The truth that the things seen with the eyes are the only real things, had lost its significance."[30] Similar realizations had helped make psychological portraiture necessary in fiction and in poetry had opened a door into Surrealism. In Stein's poetry, the effect was quite different. The pieces in *Tender Buttons*, for instance, which Virgil Thomson calls "still lives," were attempts to get away from the object. Stein said she wished "to describe a thing without mentioning it," as in "A Red Hat":

> A dark gray, a very dark gray, a quite dark gray is monstrous ordinarily, it is so monstrous because there is no red in it. If red is in everything it is not necessary. Is that not an argument for any use of it and even so is there any place that is better, is there any place that has so much stretched out.[31]

The abandonment of line and meter seems incidental. What delights or infuriates the reader is her indifference to logic, her incongruity and discontinuousness. Richard Bridgman calls these poems "explosively subjective."[32] Stein's word for it is the painter's word: abstraction. Or, as she calls it in *The Autobiography of Alice B. Toklas*, "disembodiedness."

Gertrude Stein, in her work, has always been possessed by the intellectual passion for exactitude in the description of inner and outer reality. She has produced a simplification by this concentration, and as a result the destruction of associational emotion in poetry and prose. She knows that in beauty, music, decoration, the result of emotion should never be the cause of emotion nor should they be the material of poetry and prose. Nor should emotion itself be the cause of poetry or prose. They should consist of an exact reproduction of either an outer or an inner reality.[33]

Playfulness, or as she calls it, "simplification," is probably the most conspicuous quality in Stein's work. We can see at once why she would have described Ezra Pound as "a village explainer." "Lifting Belly," one of the unpublished poems and one of her most playful and delightful, seems to be built from dialogue. Virgil Thomson calls it a "hymn to the domestic affections," and through its incongruities and apparent switches from inner to outer reality and back again reveals a liveliness of mind quite comparable to that in Milton's "L'Allegro," Smart's "Jubilate Agno," or Blake's *Songs of Innocence*.

> Lifting belly. Are you. Lifting.
> Oh dear, I said I was tender, fierce and tender.
> Do it. What a splendid example of carelessness.
> It gives me a great deal of pleasure to say yes.
> Why do I always smile.
> I don't know.
> It pleases me.[34]

It continues for another fifty pages. Does it have a beginning, middle or end, or is it all these things together at once? As Stein said in *Picasso*, "As the twentieth century is a century which sees the earth as no one has ever seen it, the earth has a splendor that it never has had, and as everything destroys itself in the twentieth century and nothing continues, so then the twentieth century has a splendor which is its own."[35] Few people read Stein's poetry these days, except as it has been absorbed and transmuted in the work of Frank O'Hara, Kenneth Koch, Allen Ginsberg, John Ashbery, and, by extension, a good many of the poets of our time.

None of the other American poets of this time became as prominent as Robinson, Frost, Pound, Eliot, and Williams. Other poets were widely known and admired at the time, some more than the ones I've mentioned, but time has not been kind to Amy Lowell, John Hall Wheelock, John Gould Fletcher, Conrad Aiken, and Vachel Lindsay. Their work has faded, much of it, it seems, forever. The same is not true, however, of Edgar Lee Masters and Carl Sandburg, and some accounting of them needs to be made.

Masters and Sandburg had many things in common. They grew up in the Midwest, away from the eastern centers of culture, away even from Chicago and St. Louis. They grew up in the era of Agrarian and Populist politics which, of course, were strongest in the Midwest. Sandburg came from a family of recent immigrants. And—a fact that cannot be ignored—they were male. In their different ways, they wrote a poetry that was proudly regional, that was democratic and forward-looking, and that made an effort to appeal to the common man. In all these things, their poetry was opposed to the new Modernist work which was urban and international, aesthetically intricate, politically and socially conservative, and difficult to grasp. The one thing both parties had in common was that they tried to make room in their work for what might be described as a "male consciousness." Whitman might have provided an example to them, but whether he did or not, it seems quite certain that both parties wished to rescue poetry from its reputation, cultivated and flaunted by the English Aesthetes and Decadents, as effete and unmasculine. When Pound shouted in "Sestina: Altaforte," "Damn it all! all this our South stinks peace," or when Sandburg announced that Chicago was "stormy, husky, brawling, [the] City of the Big Shoulders," it was part of a half-enlightened attempt to broaden the base of poetry. Such a similarity was too slight, however, to overcome the basic differences between these two kinds of poetry. Masters and Sandburg were the willing children of Emerson and the writers of Realist fiction in America. They were still trying to create an authentic American literature, one tied not only to the place but to its political ideals as well, and it is their principal glory and chief drawback that they succeeded.

Spoon River Anthology (1915) has found a permanent place in American literature, and though the rest of Edgar Lee Masters's (1868–1950) writing is less compelling, he will be remembered for his portrayal of small-town midwestern America in the days of subsistence farming and puritanical repressions, before the coming of radio, television, or the automobile. The poems in *Spoon River Anthology*, which take the form of epitaphs, were written over a short period of time, in something like a frenzy, and yet they sparkle with colloquial vigor.

> I went to the dances at Chandlerville
> and played snap-out at Winchester.[36]

Irony plays a large role in these poems. The whole world for Lucinda Matlock lay between Chandlerville and Winchester, two small towns unknown to the rest of the world. Masters's epitaphs, of course, give everyone the chance, in death, finally to tell the truth of their lives. The bland pieties of the traditional epitaph are replaced by the sorrows, secrets, and small triumphs of ordinary life. "Judge Somers" complains from the grave:

> How does it happen, tell me,
> That I lie here unmarked, forgotten,
> While Chase Henry, the town drunkard,
> Has a marble block, topped by an urn . . . ?[37]

Most of Masters's people lived their lives in this one small town, and their deepest feelings and most extravagant longings rarely extended farther than the end of Main Street. Yet Masters was able to create people who are fresh, direct, and complete. They are profoundly innocent and easily hurt, and, as in Greek tragedy, their experience is, without their realizing it, that of people everywhere.

Carl Sandburg (1878–1967) is remembered best for his poem "Chicago." It was the title poem of his first book, *Chicago Poems* (1916), a book which revived the almost forgotten legacy of Walt Whitman. *Cornhuskers* followed in 1918 and *Smoke and Steel* in 1920. No one had taken such risks with slang and colloquial language, not even Whitman, and no poet had looked as hard or as sympathetically at the lives of immigrant farmers and factory workers. The agrarian peasants of Whitman's day were almost gone. Sandburg lived in the midst of the first great industrial expansion in the United States, when the exploitation of workers was thought to be simply the operation of Darwinian principles in the social world. Sandburg was part newspaperman, part political organizer in his early days, and in 1910 he became private secretary to Emil Seidel, the Socialist mayor of Milwaukee. This was two years before the Socialists polled 900,000 votes in a national election, the highwater mark of political socialism in this country. When Sandburg asked the newspaper cartoonists in "Halsted Street Car" to "Take your pencils / And draw these faces,"[38] he was writing almost the way Eliot did in "The Preludes," the large difference being that he wrote in the language of the people he described and in the belief that their lives mattered.

Sandburg's work has not fared well among critics because it is too interested in its subject and not enough interested in the art and craft of making poems. At the same time, his poems show a remarkable honesty of perception and loyalty to his subject matter. His work makes clear how much is left out of our poetry, and his efforts to include the hoboes, millhands, farmers, pimps, whores, gamblers, and drifters of every description, not as exotic backdrop, but as human beings, will always earn him respect. Occasional poems flash brilliantly into our subconscious like the great photograph taken by a neighbor on his vacation. Here is "Soup" from *Smoke and Steel*:

I saw a famous man eating soup.
I say he was lifting a fat broth
Into his mouth with a spoon.
His name was in the newspapers that day
Spelled out in tall black headlines
And thousands of people were talking about him.
When I saw him,
He sat bending his head over a plate
Putting soup in his mouth with a spoon.[39]

Decades are not tidy, as I've said, so I will have to lump together here in a note some excellent poets, at least one and possibly two of whom are among the best American poets of this or any other century. E. E. Cummings (1894–1961), Robinson Jeffers (1887–1962), Marianne Moore (1887–1972), and Wallace Stevens (1879–1955) all published important work in the late teens. Moore published seventeen poems in 1915 alone in three of the most important magazines of that day, the *Egoist* (London), *Poetry*, and *Others*. Stevens began publishing his mature poems in 1914, including "Peter Quince at the Clavier" (*Others*, 1915), "Sunday Morning" (*Poetry*, 1915, five months after Eliot's "Prufrock" appeared there), and "Thirteen Ways of Looking at a Blackbird" (*Others*, 1917). Cummings relied almost exclusively on the *Harvard Monthly* until 1920, when he suddenly published twelve poems, an essay, and a review in the *Dial*. At any rate, Moore's first book, *Poems*, published in London by the Egoist Press, came out in 1921, Stevens's *Harmonium* (Knopf) in 1923, and Cummings's *Tulips and Chimneys* (Thomas Seltzer) in 1923. I have left them to be considered with the poets of the twenties.

Notes

1. T. S. Eliot, "Reflections on Vers Libre," *New Statesman* 8 (1917).
2. Eric Homberger, "Chicago and New York: Two Versions of American Modernism," in *Modernism 1890–1930*, ed. M. Bradbury and Jay MacFarlane (Harmondsworth, U.K.: Penguin, 1976), 159.
3. Woolf, "Mr. Bennett and Mrs. Brown," in *The Captain's Death Bed and Other Essays* (New York: Harcourt, 1973), 91–92. Originally published as "Character in Fiction," *Criterion*, July 1924, 409–30.
4. Matei Calinescu, *Faces of Modernity: Avante Garde, Decadence, Kitsch* (Bloomington: Indiana University Press, 1977), 41–42.
5. Ibid.
6. Jay McFarlane, "The Mind of Modernism," in *Modernism 1890–1930*, ed. Bradbury and MacFarlane, 72–81.

7. Pound, *Personae* (New York: New Directions, 1926), 85.

8. Ibid., 130.

9. Stevens, *The Palm at the End of the Mind: Selected Poems and a Play*, ed. Holly Stevens (New York: Random, Vintage, 1972), 46.

10. H. D., "Oread," in *The Norton Anthology of Modern Poetry*, ed. Richard Ellman and Robert O'Clair (New York: Norton, 1973), 73.

11. Williams, *Selected Poems*, ed. Randall Jarrell (New York: New Directions, 1963), 30.

12. Pound, *Personae*, 191.

13. Irving Howe, "The Idea of the Modern," in *The Idea of the Modern in Literature and the Arts*, ed. Irving Howe (New York: Horizon, 1967), 11–40.

14. See Calinescu, *Faces of Modernity*, for an excellent discussion of the history of concepts such as "the modern," "Modernity," and "Modernism."

15. Graham Hough, "The Modernist Lyric," in *Modernism: 1890–1930*, ed. Bradbury and MacFarlane, 318.

16. Robinson, *Collected Poems* (New York: Macmillan, 1937), 82.

17. Frost, *Robert Frost: Poetry and Prose*, ed. E. C. Lathem and Lawrence Thompson (New York: Holt, 1972), 346.

18. Frost, *Complete Poems* (New York: Holt, 1949) 31.

19. Frost, *Selected Prose*, ed. Hyde Cox and E. C. Lathem (New York: Holt, 1956), 64.

20. Pound, *The Letters of Ezra Pound 1907–1941*, ed. D. D. Paige (New York: Harcourt, 1950), 38.

21. Eliot, "Ulysses, Order, and Myth," in *Selected Prose*, ed. Frank Kermode (New York: Farrar, Straus and Giroux, 1975), 177.

22. Pound, *The Letters of Ezra Pound*, 40.

23. Eliot, *Collected Poems, 1909–1962* (London: Faber and Faber, 1963), 21.

24. Eliot, *The Complete Poems and Plays* (New York: Harcourt, 1952), 17.

25. Ibid., 16.

26. H. D., *Collected Poems of H. D.* (New York: Liveright, 1925), 18.

27. Ibid., 32.

28. Ibid., 59.

29. Williams, *The Collected Earlier Poems* (New York: New Directions, 1938), 150.

30. Stein, *Gertrude Stein's Picasso* (New York: Liveright, 1970), 3.

31. Stein, *Writings and Lectures: 1911–1945*, ed. Patricia Meyerowitz (London: Peter Owen, 1967), 158.

32. Bridgman, *Gertrude in Pieces* (New York: Oxford University Press, 1970), 104.

33. Stein, *The Autobiography of Alice B. Toklas* (New York: Harcourt, 1933), 259.

34. Stein, *Bee Time Vine and Other Pieces*, vol. 3 of *Unpublished Works of Gertrude Stein* (New Haven: Yale University Press, 1953), 67.

35. Stein, *Picasso*, 76.

36. Masters, *Spoon River Anthology* (New York: Macmillan, 1914), 229.

37. Ibid., 13.

38. Sandburg, *The Complete Poems* (New York: Harcourt, 1950), 6.

39. Ibid., 165.

ELEANOR COOK

From Etymology to Paronomasia:
Wallace Stevens, Elizabeth Bishop, and Others

Wallace Stevens was a paronomastic[1] by second nature, as well as by
family custom and the accident of historical timing. Age fifteen, he punned
on "condescension," complaining to his mother of condescension from
fellows in their twenties but surmising that eleven- to fourteen-year-olds
regarded his company as an "ascension."[2] Age fifty-six, he invented a pun
on the word "inarticulate": " . . . a dream they never had, / Like a word
in the mind that sticks at artichoke / And remains inarticulate" (OP 78).
He allowed himself a comment on this: "rather an heroic pun" (L 366, 27
August 1940). And age seventy-two, he wrote to a friend about Reinhold
Niebuhr: "an admirable thinker . . . but a dull writer." "Notwithstanding his
name, he is far from being Rhine Wein."[3] He was born to paronomasia. His
father was a punster: "Dear Wallace—just what election to the Signet signifies I have no sign. It is significant . . ." and so on to a total of eleven puns
(L 26, 21 May 1899). It was part of the times. Stevens' father was named
Garrett Stevens, his mother's maiden name was Zeller, and, yes, when they
married in 1876, a local Pennsylvania newspaper commented that Stevens'
father had "furnished his house complete from 'Zeller' to 'Garrett'" (SP 6).

Yet in the nineteenth century, though puns were immensely popular,
their presence in poetry was another matter. Lewis Carroll and Edward Lear
perhaps, but poetry properly so called? It was a time when the line of wit was

From *Connotations* 2, no. 1 (1992): 34–51. Copyright © 1992 by Waxmann Verlag GmbH.

less favoured than the line of vision, when the claims of charm poetry were paramount as against the claims of riddle poetry. As Northrop Frye observes in his essay, "Charms and Riddles," "Charm poetry . . . dominated taste until about 1915, after which a mental attitude more closely related to the riddle began to supersede it, one more preoccupied with the visual and the conceptual."[4] Paronomasia is related to charm verse, to follow Frye's argument, and also Andrew Welsh's in his *Roots of Lyric*,[5] but charm verse does not generate, does not display, obvious word-play—quips, quibbles, riddles—as in the metaphysical poets or Christopher Smart, let alone James Joyce. The paronomasia of Donne is (to offer a generalization) more spectacular than the paronomasia of Spenser, even though some techniques and functions are similar.

So also, some techniques and functions are similar in the work of Wallace Stevens and Elizabeth Bishop. (Bishop lived a generation after the high Moderns, including Stevens; he was born in 1879 and she in 1911.) But one would want to begin by saying that Bishop's kind of word-play follows a Spenser-Herbert line (she was devoted to the work of George Herbert). Stevens' kind of paronomasia occasionally does so (for example, in his visionary poems). But Stevens the witty and wicked paronomastic is the heir to Donne, to Byron, to Carroll, to Hopkins, and the like.

The *Oxford English Dictionary*, in good nineteenth century fashion, takes a low view of word-play. Definitions of pun and of paronomasia are more neutral, though, as it happens, they were published earlier (1909 and 1904 respectively; see the Introduction to the *OED*). The section including the term "word-play" was not published until 1928 but despite Eliot and Pound and Joyce and Stevens—perhaps because of them—it is very stern: "a playing or trifling with words; the use of words merely or mainly for the purpose of producing a rhetorical or fantastic effect," etc. ("play" *sb*. 7.b.). The three definitions are not altered in the second edition of the *OED*.

It is true that paronomasia has often excited warnings in rhetorical handbooks, chiefly about its overuse or its low status. "Marry, we must not play, or riot too much with them [i.e. words], as in *Paronomasies*," as Ben Jonson says (*Timber; or Discoveries*). Or, 1593, Peacham: "This figure [paronomasia] ought to be sparingly used"; antanaclasis "may fall easily into excesse" (*The Garden of Eloquence*). Or, 1730, Dumarsais: "On doit éviter les jeux de mots qui sont vides de sens." For him, Augustine provides a proper pattern (*Traité des tropes*). To which Fontanier later adds that paronomasia is better in Latin than in French ("ces jeux de mots ont en général moins de grâce dans notre langue que dans celle des Latins"; *Des figures du discours*, 1827). Quintilian, referring to Cicero, says that word-play is "non ingratae, nisi copia redundet" ("not unattractive save when carried to excess," as the Loeb translation has it; IX.iii.74). At the other end of a scale of significance, paronomasia might be built into the language by divine decree in order to teach us. As Augustine says: "it happened not by human design but perhaps by divine decision [etsi non humana industria, iudicio fortasse divino] that the grammarians have not been able to decline (or conjugate) the Latin verb *moritur* (he dies) by the same rule as other verbs of this form. . . . The verb cannot be declined in speech just as the reality which it signifies cannot be declined (that is, avoided) by any action" (*De civitate Dei* XIII.11[6]). Ernst Robert Curtius offers more examples in his *European Literature and the Latin Middle Ages*.[7] And, to leap forward to an English poet who admired Augustine, Coleridge delighted in word-play of every type and purpose.[8] The mid- to late-nineteenth century could not plead precedence for its low view of this rhetorical device.

I have used the term "paronomasia" throughout as a general synonym for punning and for word-play. That is, I have not distinguished such categories as, say antanaclasis. Nor do I distinguish the pun (low humour, below the salt) from word-play (a superior wit), as, for example, Freud distinguishes them.[9] Leo Spitzer noted in 1950 how the later term "pun" (used from 1662, says the *OED*) has come to include a whole series of earlier rhetorical figures for word-play.[10] Similarly with the modern use of "paronomasia," which has become an umbrella for word-play in general.

In treating paronomasia, it is possible to analyse types of puns, the most familiar division being between homonymic and semantic puns. It is possible to place paronomasia in a generic context as Frye and Welsh do, where it is associated with very early forms of writing, both charm and riddle. It is possible to consider paronomasia in relation to non-literary contexts, for example, logical or linguistic or psychological or, I dare say, neurological contexts. How is punning related to logical thought or, more widely, to rational thought? The answer, I suppose, would be: as Homer to Plato, to take that ancient quarrel as a pattern. How is paronomasia related to linguistic skills as they develop in an individual or in the practise of a society? Roman Jakobson observes: "In a sequence in which similarity is superimposed on contiguity, two similar phonemic sequences near to each other are prone to assume a paronomastic function."[11] How is paronomasia revealing psychologically? Freud, of course, is very fond of interpreting it. As for a neurological context, I am thinking of Oliver Sacks and the workings of memory, since punning develops very early in children and has mnemonic force. I am assuming that I don't need to spend time over the various types of argument that defend word-play.

My own interest lies in the area of poetics. Here, I think that a simple pun, one without further reverberation, would be classified as a scheme rather than a trope. But schemes can move toward tropes when they begin to tell fables about themselves. It is these fables, including their use of etymology, that interest me especially in the poetics of paronomasia.

I want to begin with one aspect of such fabling, and how it helps us to read twentieth-century poetry. The following question seems to me a useful one for reader and writer both. What words come with so venerable a history of paronomasia that no self-respecting modern poet can use them without making choices? That is, poets may use these words if they wish, but they must decide what to do about the standard paronomasia—whether to distance it, or merely to acknowledge it, or to carry on with it. I'm not, of course, talking about entire huge classes of possible puns, but rather about certain words where specific paronomasies (Jonson's handy word) have been used so often and/or so memorably that the words carry a punning sense. It takes great skill to extend the fabling history of such words. New puns are a delight, Stevens' on "inarticulate" and "artichoke," for instance. But re-capping or re-dressing altogether an old fable offers more challenge and more riches.

Let me start with the common word "turn" and the suggestion that a poet cannot use the word at the beginning or end of a line without thinking about the original descriptive energy of the word. Consider the following stanza from Bishop's poem, "Twelfth Morning; or What You Will":

The fence, three-strand, barbed-wire, all pure rust,
three dotted lines, comes forward hopefully
across the lots; thinks better of it; turns
    a sort of corner . . . [12]

Bishop has, in fact, given us not just one but a whole family of etymological connotations. The fence turns, turns the corner of a lot and those "lots" offer a variation of the standard pun on *stanza*, meaning "room," of which more in a moment. Those are fenced lots, so that the fence can turn with the line: "turns / a sort of corner." Well, so it is, there on the page, a sort of corner. And there it is, I think: this word that cannot be used at the beginning or end of a line, without remembering the tradition of word-play on "turn." "Turn," which is what "verse" means etymologically. "Turn," which is what "trope" means etymologically. "Turn," which in enjambment describes what the reader is doing, albeit with an eye rather than the etymological leg of enjambment, as it walks the line, and strides or limps or hops over the end of the line, and back, westward, to the start of the next line.

Stevens uses the word repeatedly at the beginning of a line in his well-known 1916 poem, "Domination of Black":

I heard them cry—the peacocks.
Was it a cry against the twilight

Or against the leaves themselves
Turning in the wind,
Turning as the flames
Turned in the fire,
Turning as the tails of the peacocks
Turned in the loud fire,
Loud as the hemlocks
Full of the cry of the peacocks?

If the word "turn" appears in mid-line, that, I think, is another matter. We should need a stronger signal for our paronomastic antennae to start waving.

Are there other such common words? I should think so. The word, "leaves," for example, also has an extended paronomastic family: (1) leaves of a tree (the common topos links them with the dead: Homer through Vergil through (in English) Milton and Shelley and so on; (2) leaves of a book; and (3) that which is left or leavings. These are standard and a poet can go on from there. Or a poet may decline the paronomasia on "leaves" but never in ignorance. An uninvited paronomasia is apt to commit a solecism.

In a stanzaic poem, the word "room" anywhere in the line wants testing, just in case the old pun on the Italian *stanza* is at work. Thus in Stevens, 1916, "Six Significant Landscapes," no. 6:

Rationalists, wearing square hats,
Think, in square rooms,
Looking at the floor,
Looking at the ceiling.
They confine themselves
To right-angled triangles.
If they tried rhomboids,
Cones, waving lines, ellipses—
As, for example, the ellipse of the half-moon—
Rationalists would wear sombreros.

"Square rooms"? We first read a conceptual analogy, then see that Stevens has not written a "square-room" stanza. That is, his stanza doesn't look square on the page, nor is it schematically square, for I suppose a square stanza is symmetrical, say four-by-four, a tetrameter quatrain. At least, that's what John Hollander suggests:

Why have I locked myself inside
This narrow cell of four-by-four,

> Pacing the shined, reflecting floor
> Instead of running free and wide?[13]

Modern poets are not the only ones to play on the word "room" in this standard manner. Hollander's "narrow cell" compacts two of Wordsworth's punning tropes for *stanza*, here a sonnet stanza: "Nuns fret not at their convent's
narrow room; / And hermits are contented with their cells." Wordsworth's
sonnet also speaks of "the Sonnet's scanty plot of ground."[14] (Lewis Carroll
might say of it: "I measured it from side to side, / Fourteen lines long and
five feet wide.") These are figures of right-angled rooms or plots, whether
square or rectangular. If you look at Stevens' stanza, you will see that he has
curved the unjustified right margin so that it is itself a half-moon ellipse or,
it may be, a sombrero. This kind of punning on *stanza* belongs also to a class
of visual word-play; Stevens' poem is almost a shape poem.

But then, so is Bishop's stanza or fenced lot. Look again, and you will
see a visual mimesis. The fence or "three dotted lines" comes forward as if in
an optical illusion such as Wittgenstein's famous example of the duck and the
rabbit. Here are three lines of print, and behold, a mimesis of the fence and a
prolepsis of what Bishop's own lines will turn into at the end: an ellipsis, three
dots, a kind of fence at the end of the stanza.

Stevens also punned on the marks for ellipsis in several letters to his
wife: " . . . (Notice my Frenchy way of punctuating? Très chic, n'est-ce pas?)
. . ." (16 August 1911).[15] Then, four days later: "I fell asleep over a French
book and had the most delightful dream. . . . [sic]."[16] The next pause offers
five dots, a progression of points (L 171). Two years later, "The cats have
grown very large!!! . . . ." (7 July 1913, L 179). Stevens implied they'd
been eating birds, so that the nine dots may have to do with the nine lives
of felines. This, by the way, is before Beckett's punctuating pun in his title,
"Dante . . . Bruno. Vico . . . Joyce" where each dot (not counting the period)
stands for a century. For word-play on the two dots that constitute an umlaut,
here is James Merrill in his poem, "Lost in Translation":

> The owlet umlaut peeps and hoots
> Above the open vowel.[17]

I've been speaking of common words charged with a history of etymological suggestiveness ("turn," "leaves," "room") and also of visual paronomasia.
Are there some less common words that require etymological or paronomastic awareness when we read twentieth-century poetry? I think so. Take the
words "immaculate" and "maculate." Here is the opening of Bishop's poem,
"Seascape":

> This celestial seascape, with white herons got up as angels,
> flying as high as they want and as far as they want sidewise
> in tiers and tiers of immaculate reflections;
> the whole region, from the highest heron
> down to the weightless mangrove island
> with bright green leaves edged neatly with bird-droppings
> like illumination in silver . . .
> it does look like heaven.

I pass by the ambiguity of "got up" meaning both "costumed" and "ascended." This pun opens up, in the most delicate way, the argument for a naturalistic origin for angels (like white birds, like swans, as Stevens suggests in *Notes toward a Supreme Fiction*). Bishop like Stevens is not a believer but she is usually quieter about her skeptical strain. "Got up," then, so that they can fly "in tiers and tiers of immaculate reflections," up to the highest heaven, if that echo sounds faintly in "the highest heron." "Immaculate" is here used in an etymologically pure way (from *macula*, or spot) meaning perfectly unspotted. Bishop delicately evokes older doctrinal uses, again as with "got up," setting them aside. (I'm also reminded of Dante's heaven in Bishop's "tiers and tiers of immaculate reflections"—of his "di bianco in bianco" [from tier to tier] playing against his "tanto bianco" [so white] in a flying passage in the *Paradiso* [XXXI.16, 14].)

And this is surely the point of the line about the "pure-colored or spotted breasts" of the "big symbolic birds" in her later, powerful poem, "Brazil, January 1, 1502":

> A blue-white sky, a simple web . . .
> And perching there in profile, beaks agape,
> the big symbolic birds keep quiet,
> each showing only half his puffed and padded,
> pure-colored or spotted breast.
> Still in the foreground there is Sin. . . .

"Pure-colored or spotted": this is the language of ornithological field-guides. It would sound peculiar to describe a song-sparrow or a wood-thrush as having a maculate breast. But it is, or should be, impossible to miss that history of "immaculate" and "maculate," which enables us to read the symbolism of the big symbolic birds.

As for Stevens, he was more irritated than Bishop with the language of whiteness, perhaps because he was more vulnerable. Pure poetry, if not doctrinally immaculate poetry, appealed strongly to him when he was young, and he reacted with proportionate bitterness later. See especially *The Man with the Blue Guitar*:

> The pale intrusions into blue
> Are corrupting pallors. . . .
> The unspotted imbecile revery. . . . (xiii)

"Unspotted" is the Germanic word corresponding to "immaculate." Stevens earlier in this sequence calls the moon "immaculate," which may just make us smile when we recall its spots. In *The Man with the Blue Guitar*, many a kind of whiteness is punningly evoked and dismissed. Words like "immaculate," Stevens implies, can themselves be lunatic ("imbecile") or even "corrupting." Word-play here enters an entire field of association, reminding us to test our whitest, unspotted, immaculate, moony, candid, pure ideals and idealization. We need to remember this when we read Stevens' canto on whiteness in *Notes toward a Supreme Fiction* (I.iii). The word "immaculate" does not itself remain immaculate in Stevens.

Eliot also liked the punning possibilities of the word, "immaculate," at least in the form of "maculate," which he used for "apeneck Sweeney":

> The zebra stripes along his jaw
> Swelling to maculate giraffe.

Stripes to spots, that is, and also distinctly spotted. "Still," as Bishop would observe, "Still in the foreground there is Sin," perhaps a shade relentlessly in this 1918 poem ("Sweeney among the Nightingales").

Another example of paronomasia may owe its modern prominence to Eliot, and that is the pun on Latin *infans* (unspeaking) and English "infant." Here is Eliot in 1919, in *Gerontion*:

> The word within a word, unable to speak a word.

Eliot's allusion to a sermon by Lancelot Andrewes is well known, as is Andrewes' punning paradox that the infant Christ is the Word who is "infans" or unable to speak.[18] The paradox of *fans atque infans* is listed in Lewis and Short, a dictionary in which Stevens said he delighted.[19] He adapted the double pun in the paronomasia of a fan and an infans in the poem "Infanta Marina." The lovely infanta is appropriately one of his muse-figures, that is, one who enables him to speak even if she herself is "infans," waving her fan, some palm-tree metamorphosed into a Florida infanta. Later infants in Stevens may also carry this paronomasia: "It is the infant

A standing on infant legs" (1949, CP 469). "Infant, it is enough in life / To speak of what you see" (1946, CP 365).

Bishop is too good a word-smith not to be aware of such histories. She acknowledges this at the end of her poem, "Over 2000 Illustrations and a Complete Concordance" (the reference is to a large Bible):

> Open the heavy book. Why couldn't we have seen
> this old Nativity while we were at it?
> —the dark ajar, the rocks breaking with light,
> an undisturbed, unbreathing flame,
> colorless, sparkless, freely fed on straw,
> and, lulled within, a family with pets,
> —and looked and looked our infant sight away.

"Infant" first because of the Nativity scene that is seen and not seen. Bishop once saw it in the old Bible, but has not seen it in her actual travel in biblical lands. "Our infant sight": a sight of an infant, of the infant. But sight itself is also infant in the sense that sight is always "infans" or unspeaking. We translate it into words. Yet how can we look and look our infant sight away? In different senses. As when we look away to our heart's content (Bishop's repeated "look" works to prolong this moment of looking). Or "look away" in the sense of removing "infant sight," averting our eyes? And if removing sight, then what follows? Speech, words? Or grown-up sight, and what would that grown-up sight be? In this simply worded but intricate paronomasia, Bishop has laid out our possible responses to the Nativity scene. It's remembered from a book. It's not to be seen by travelling to the area where it happened. It's desired. It might fulfil desire and at the same time necessarily translate desire into something ordinary and familiar, so that we would be back where we started in one way if not another.

Have the moderns invented new types of puns, as distinct from extending the repertoires of older types? If a portmanteau word is Lewis Carroll's invention, then the answer is yes. A portmanteau word is a paronomasia that presents the technique and the result all at once. Here is how puns work, it seems to say, and here is a new one, a neologism. "'Twas brillig and the slithy toves . . . ," etc. "Slithy"? "Slimy" and "lithe" come into our minds, thanks to Humpty Dumpty. They came into Stevens' mind too, but he decided to take Lewis Carroll one step back. Why not simply say "ithy"? As in "Analysis of a Theme":

> We enjoy the ithy oonts and long-haired
> Plomets, as the Herr Gott
> Enjoys his comets.

"Ithy" as in "slithy"? Or is it "ithy" with a short "i"? The short "i" seems
to invite words like "mythy" and "pithy," words that are more serious than
"slithy-ithy" words, portentous words, comets as omens. We recall Jove's
"mythy mind" in Stevens' well-known 1915 poem, "Sunday Morning." And
we recall E. H. Gombrich's persuasive play on the associations of "pong"
and "ping" in his *Art and Illusion*.[20] A long-i'd "ithy" seems to call for more
squiggly or whooshing Lewis-Carroll words: slithy, slimy, writhing, scyth-
ing. (Though there are, to be sure, "lithe" and "blithe.") But then there is
the prefix "ithy," from Greek *ithus* or straight, and not at all squiggly, as in
"ithyphallic" (the only example in the Oxford Concise), which described the
phallus carried in festivals of Bacchus as well as the metre used for Bacchic
hymns or generally for licentious poems (the trochaic dimeter brachycatalec-
tic). An "oont," by the way, is a camel.

There is a similar phenomenon in Stevens' late poem, "Long and Sluggish Lines":

... Could it be that yellow patch, the side
Of a house, that makes one think the house is laughing;

Or these—escent—issant pre-personae: first fly,
A comic infants among the tragic drapings,

Babyishness of forsythia, a snatch of belief,
The spook and makings of the nude magnolia?

. . . .

Wanderer, this is the pre-history of February,
The life of the poem in the mind has not yet begun.

Stevens' syntax tells us how to read the suffixes, "-escent" and "-issant. "
So does the Oxford Concise Dictionary, at least for one of them: "-escent,"
"forming adjs. denoting onset of a state or variation of colour etc. (deli-
quescent, effervescent, florescent, iridescent) ... pres. part. ... of vbs. in
-escere." The suffix "-issant" on the other hand makes no appearance in any
Oxford dictionary or in Webster either. But then, I have not been able to
find any word at all with this suffix, apart from one coined by Stevens himself: "The grackles sing avant the spring / Most spiss—oh! Yes, most spis-
santly. / They sing right puissantly" ("Snow and Stars"). This is also from a
pre-spring poem, a rather ill-tempered one (grackles are not happy birds in
Stevens). Stevens' seemingly invented suffix is itself a pre-history of words,

if we accept his own coinage as the first blooming "-issant" word that we have in English. "Spiss," though obsolete, is listed in Oxford and Webster; it means "thick, dense, close," including close intervals in music. Florio gives a form of it. But then we might hear a long "i" in "-issant," and hence a family of French words in this Ur-paronomasia.[21]

Paronomasia through neologism: this is one type of paronomasia that Bishop does not use, for she is not given to neologisms, whereas Stevens delights in them. His play with neologisms and with unusual words ("oonts") makes us listen for the paronomastic force of any unknown words as a way of defining them. It's a useful training. Such paronomastic testing of the unknown, together with the paronomastic history of the known, works to make us aware of the possible paronomasia in all our words—for all that, in our syllables, letters, and punctuation marks as well. Letters? Stevens' Alpha and Omega in his *An Ordinary Evening in New Haven*, for example. Or Anthony Hecht's recent brilliant pun on the "voiceless thorn," both the plant protuberance that breaks your skin and the Anglo-Saxon letter for a breathed rather than voiced "th" sound ("thorn" not "the"):

And the wind, a voiceless thorn
goes over the details,
making a soft promise
to take our breath away.[22]

An audible paronomasia may be noticed here: try sounding out "th," as in a soft wind, then stopping, as directed in the breath-taking pun of the enjambed last line. Hecht's crows are morticians; they do not "caw" but call out *cras* or "tomorrow," as Latin crows did. Language so tested and so paronomastic displays its own vitality. Words do have a life of their own, and paronomasia makes us acutely aware of this.

Stevens' instinct for word-play was part of his general delight in the history of words. Bishop also delighted in the diachronic life of words, their etymological family history, their various cognate relatives, and so on. In her work, words tremble with the energy of their own histories, and the potential for paronomasia is always there. Sometimes her word-play is made obvious, laid out for us. Sometimes it is hidden but it will rarely if ever be riddling. The subtleties and challenges are not combative, and the poems can be read without realizing how rich they are. Riddling paronomasia stops you short.

Nor does Bishop experiment with the limits of word-play. At least, this is what I think Stevens is doing in his poem, *The Comedian as the Letter C*, that difficult personal Bildungsroman. Yet her fewer and quieter examples of paronomasia are as remarkable as Stevens' own.

Stevens' paronomasia, especially in his early work, was also part of his revolt against the gentility and piety of the times, what he sardonically called "the grand ideas of the villages" in "The Man Whose Pharynx Was Bad." In the last fifteen or twenty years of his life, this shifted, as he centered his work increasingly on "the possibility of a supreme fiction, recognized as a fiction, in which men could propose to themselves a fulfilment" (L 820, 1954). The supreme fiction was to be, in effect, the heir and successor to Christianity. Bishop stays away from such questions. But she is like Stevens in working paronomastically to undo some effects of her religious heritage.

Andrew Welsh in his *Roots of Lyric* writes that "If Hopkins' oracle [in the poem, "Spelt from Sybil's Leaves"] is one form of poetry particularly suited to the play of language through various kinds of punning, perhaps the richest development of all the powers in the poet's language is the poetry of religious paradox."[23] We know this also from Herbert, and many a writer before and after Herbert. But if a word-play can affirm religious paradox, it can also undo religious paradox. Stevens knows this full well, and a whole taxonomy of paronomastic undoing (or what he would call "decreation") could be deduced from his work.

Yet another type of word-play is at work in Bishop's poem, "Twelfth Morning; or What You Will," a particularly interesting type which might be called allusive, though older readers would have found the term redundant, since one meaning of the word "allusion" used to be "a play upon words, a pun" (*OED* 2; the illustrative quotations range from 1556 to 1731). James Merrill, by the way, has remarked that modern poets may sometimes even substitute word-play for allusion: "The lucky 18th century reader—having read literally *tous les livres*—could be trusted to catch every possible allusion. This is no longer the case; some of us substitute word-play to make our texts resound."[24]

In Bishop's poem, allusive paronomasia allows her to speak back to Eliot, and to extend the fabling paronomastic history of the word "turn." For consider Eliot's use of the verb "turn," notably in *Ash Wednesday*, where "turn" at the end of a line comes close to being an Eliot signature. ("Because I do not hope to turn again . . ." etc.) Consider Eliot's "Journey of the Magi," the best-known twentieth-century poem in English on the subject of the Three Kings. And then consider Bishop's poem, set on the Feast of the Epiphany or the Three Kings, and centered on a black boy called Balthazár. Eliot: "three trees on the low sky, / And an old white horse galloped away in the meadow." Bishop: "the black boy Balthazár, a fence, a horse." "The fence, three-strand . . . the big white horse." If this were Eliot's poem, the number three in the three-strand fence would work differently. It would turn triune, perhaps trinitarian, an emblematic numerological punning. And Bishop's later question would sound much different:

Don't ask the big white horse, *Are you supposed*
to be inside the fence or out? He's still
asleep. Even awake, he probably
    remains in doubt.

If this were Eliot's poem, you would know for sure whether the horse were inside the fence or out, or, worse, sitting on the fence. Bishop does not foreground any of these effects. She keeps doctrinal and political matters peripheral to the main matter, which is song on this day of the epiphany, and a poor child in a small town in a remote area—rather like the original epiphany, we are given to understand. But her different paronomasia on "turn" itself turns Eliot's many turnings, alerting us to the different uses of the number three and of the white horse in her poem.

Bishop carries on other examples of word-play from Eliot and Stevens, both of whom are gifted allusive paronomastics.[25] Bishop has heard what they are doing, and signals that she wishes to do something different. To make such a challenge is easy but to live up to it is extraordinary. Bishop does so.

I want to end with an example from Stevens that I heard only recently, thanks to Bishop, who herself heard and repeated and enlarged this pun, speaking back to Stevens. Here is the opening stanza of Part III of Stevens' 1942 masterpiece, *Notes toward a Supreme Fiction*:

To sing jubilas at exact, accustomed times,
To be crested and wear the mane of a multitude
And so, as part, to exult with its great throat....

"Crested?" I previously recognized the metaphor of the multitude as a lion and the intricate word-play on *tuba-jubilate*, for one meaning of *juba* is "crest."[26] But I had not considered etymology sufficiently. The etymon for "crest" is Latin, *crista*, a crest, as on a bird or animal. Stevens thereby suggests another origin for the word "Christian" than the actual Greek origin, where Christ signifies "the anointed one," the equivalent of the Hebrew Messiah. He is using false etymology to suggest what is for him a true origin of the word "Christian," that is, a naturalistic origin. False etymology can be just as useful for poetic fables as true etymology.[27] Stevens' punning is genial enough; he is now past the satires of the twenties and early thirties. And he is writing on the third note to the supreme fiction, "It Must Give Pleasure." Bishop heard all this, I think. In her poem, "Brazil, January 1, 1502," she enlarges the etymological pun, and she is much sharper than Stevens.

> Just so the Christians, hard as nails,
> tiny as nails, and glinting,
> in creaking armor, came and found it all. . . .
> Directly after Mass, humming perhaps
> *L'Homme armé* or some such tune,
> they ripped away into the hanging fabric. . . .

Bishop has overgone Stevens, a rare feat. Here, not just one but all three Latin meanings of *crista* are at work: crest, as on a helmet, for Bishop is at pains to emphasize the armor;[28] crest, as on a bird, by analogy with the bird-women at the end; and crest, as in sexual use. Nor is Bishop's word-play genial. It sets all the Latinate uses against the Greek origin for the name of Christ, as Brazilian history itself would do, all too often, false etymology here becoming a true fable of false dealing.

* * *

A decade ago, we would be considering the deconstructionist challenge to older views of paronomasia. Now we are more likely to be considering a historicist challenge. Both concur in limiting the functions of word-play, as of all formal effects. It is the writers themselves who know the true seriousness in which paronomasia may partake, the true sense of *serio ludere*, the sense in which North Africans listened to Augustine's sermons, some sixteen hundred years ago.

> The African, particularly, had a Baroque love of subtlety. They had always loved playing with words; they excelled in writing elaborate acrostics; *hilaritas*—a mixture of intellectual excitement and sheer aesthetic pleasure at a notable display of wit—was an emotion they greatly appreciated. Augustine would give them just this.[29]

We who seem to have so much trouble with the space between *serio* and *ludere* have something to learn from these ancient Africans, as from our modern poets.

Notes

1. I have made a noun out of the *OED*'s adjective, "paronomastic." Or should I say "paronomasian"?

2. *The Letters of Wallace Stevens*, ed. Holly Stevens (New York: Knopf, 1966) 5 (23 July 1895); abbreviated in the text as L. Other abbreviations are: OP, *Opus Posthumous*, rev. ed., ed. Milton J. Bates (New York: Knopf, 1989), SP, *Souvenirs and Prophecies: The Young Wallace Stevens*, by Holly Stevens (New York: Knopf,

1977). Unless otherwise indicated, quotations from the poetry are from Stevens' *Collected Poems* (New York: Knopf, 1954) and may be located through the title index.

3. Unpublished Letter, 13 August 1952, to Barbara Church, Huntington Library. Quoted by permission of the Huntington Library.

4. Northrop Frye, *Spiritus Mundi: Essays on Literature, Myth, and Society* (Bloomington: U of Indiana P, 1976) 142.

5. Andrew Welsh, *Roots of Lyric: Primitive Poetry and Modern Poetics* (Princeton: Princeton UP, 1978).

6. *De civitate Dei* . . . , trans. Henry Bettenson, ed. David Knowles (Harmondsworth: Penguin, 1972) 521.

7. *European Literature and the Latin Middle Ages*, trans. Willard R. Trask from the 1948 *Europäische Literatur und lateinisches Mittelalter* (Princeton: Princeton UP, 1953, 1973) 299–301.

8. Cf. Owen Barfield, "Coleridge's Enjoyment of Words," in *Coleridge's Variety: Bicentenary Studies*, ed. John Beer (London: Macmillan, 1974) 204–18.

9. Freud's "puns" are "Kalauer," though James Strachey says the term is wider than in English. "Calembourgs" is offered in brackets. From *Jokes and Their Relation to the Unconscious* ("The Technique of Jokes"), vol. 8 of *The Standard Edition of . . . Sigmund Freud*, trans. and ed. James Strachey (London: Hogarth, 1905, 1960) 45.

10. "Puns," *JEGP* 49 (1950): 952–54.

11. "Linguistics as Poetics," in his *Language in Literature*, ed. Krystyna Pomorska and Stephen Rudy (Cambridge, Mass.: Harvard UP, 1987) 86.

12. Quotations from Elizabeth Bishop are taken from *The Complete Poems, 1927–1979* (New York: Farrar, Straus, Giroux, 1983).

13. "Others Who Have Lived in This Room," in his *In Time and Place* (Baltimore: Johns Hopkins UP, 1986) 37. The allusion works both schematically and thematically.

14. William Wordsworth, *The Poems*, ed. John O. Hayden, vol. 1 (New Haven: Yale UP, 1977, 1981) 586–87.

15. Unpublished letter, Huntington Library. Quoted by permission of the Huntington Library.

16. Unpublished portion of a letter, 20 August 1911 (L 171), Huntington Library. Quoted by permission of the Huntington Library.

17. James Merrill, *From the First Nine: Poems 1946–1976* (New York: Atheneum, 1984) 352.

18. See T. S. Eliot, "Lancelot Andrewes," *Selected Essays* (London: Faber and Faber, 1951) 349–50. See also K. K. Ruthven, "The Poet as Etymologist," *CQ* 11 (1969): 9–37, esp. 18.

19. See my *Poetry, Word-Play, and Word-War in Wallace Stevens* (Princeton: Princeton UP, 1988) 40n24. See also Richard Howard's richly paronomastic and allusive and funny poem on Stevens and Frost and the Lewis and Short Latin lexicon, " . . . *Et Dona Ferentes*," *Raritan* 8 (1989): 30–33.

20. E. H. Gombrich, *Art and Illusion: A Study in the Psychology of Pictorial Representation*, 2nd ed. (Princeton: Princeton UP, 1969) 370–71.

21. This French alternative was suggested by members of the Symposium on Paronomasia, chaired by Professor Inge Leimberg, Münster, July 6–8, 1992. Given Stevens' pleasure in the French language, it is very likely.

22. Anthony Hecht, "Crows in Winter," from his *The Transparent Man* (New York: Knopf, 1990) 65.

23. *Roots of Lyric* 251.

24. James Merrill, under "Comments," *UTQ* 61 (1992): 390.

25. See, for example, my "The Senses of Eliot's Salvages," *EinC* 34 (1984): 309–18. For Stevens, see my *Poetry, Word-Play, and Word-War*, chap. 4 and *passim*.

26. "Riddles, Charms, and Fictions in Wallace Stevens," in *Centre and Labyrinth: Essays in Honour of Northrop Frye*, eds. Eleanor Cook *et al.* (Toronto: U of Toronto P, 1983) 229–30.

27. Cf. the numerous examples given by Ruthven.

28. To Professor Inge Leimberg, I owe the observation that the "arma Christi" would include those very "nails" figuring in Bishop's description of tapestry and her metaphor of armor. The connection with the nails of the crucifixion is made by Bonnie Costello in her *Elizabeth Bishop: Questions of Mastery* (Cambridge, Mass.: Harvard UP, 1991) 148; Leimberg's suggestion helps to confirm this. To Professor Maria Elisabeth Brockhoff, I owe the persuasive argument that Bishop's word "fabric" is punning musically, as in German *Gewebe* (fabric) in the musical sense. The soldiers also "ripped away into the hanging fabric" of the Mass, tearing out from its entire *Tongewebe* the original secular song, "L'Homme armé"—tearing out not simply the melody, but, tragically, the militarism.

29. Peter Brown, *Augustine of Hippo* (Berkeley: U of California P, 1967) 254.

JAY PARINI

Robert Frost and the Poetry of Survival

Robert Frost (1874–1963) was among the great poets of this century—or any century. Only T. S. Eliot and Wallace Stevens, in his own lifetime, could be thought of as challenging voices. Nevertheless, as original as Frost was in his own extraordinary ways, his work can be read as a culmination of the tradition of plain-spoken poetry in which the natural world is mined for metaphors of spirit: a tradition mostly associated in English poetry with William Wordsworth, who at the beginning of the nineteenth century defined a poet as simply "a man speaking to men."

Frost was a competitive man, as his biographer Lawrance Thompson has shown. Two of his main rivals at the start of his career were Edwin Arlington Robinson (1869–1935) and Carl Sandburg (1878–1967). Robinson was a poet of considerable gifts whose dramatic lyrics are still underestimated by critics. As Roy Harvey Pearce has written in *The Continuity of American Poetry* (1961): "Robinson at his best transformed the characteristically egocentric nineteenth-century poem into a vehicle to express the exhaustion and failure of its primary impulse." Robinson showed that to renew the old-fashioned Romantic lyric, poets would have to come to terms with nature as it had been affected by the industrial revolution. They would have to deal with a mechanized, impoverished, soiled, even burnt-out world. In a beautiful poem called "Walt Whitman," Robinson wrote, "The master-songs are ended, and

From *The Columbia History of American Poetry*, Jay Parini, editor, and Brett C. Millier, associate editor, pp. 260–83. Copyright © 1993 by Columbia University Press.

175

the man / That sang them is a name." No more the mere celebration of man, nature, and machine that Whitman created in *Leaves of Grass*.

Robinson pioneered an American version of the dramatic monologue that had been popular in England throughout the century. He conjured a small New England town called Tilbury Town, which he peopled with such types as Richard Cory, Charles Carville, Minniver Cheevy, Luke Havergal, Aunt Imogen, and Eben Flood. He characterized New England, in his poem "New England," as a place "where the wind is always north-north-east / And children learn to walk on frozen toes." And his acerbic, depressive New Englanders seem always on the brink of survival. Some, such as poor Richard Cory, "a gentleman from sole to crown," do not survive: Richard Cory, "one calm summer night, / Went home and put a bullet through his head."

Frost was asked to write an introduction to a book of Robinson's poetry shortly after the poet's death. In a letter to a friend at the time of this request, he wrote of Robinson: "How utterly romantic the enervated old soak is. The way he thinks of poets in the Browningese of "Ben Jonson"! The way he thinks of cuckolding lovers and cuckold husband in "Tristram"! Literary conventions! I feel as if I had been somewhere on hot air like a fire-balloon. Not with him altogether. I haven't more than half read him since "The Town Down the River." I simply couldn't lend a whole ear to all that Arthurian twaddle twiddled over after the Victorians." For all this vitriol Frost nevertheless learned a good deal from Robinson, a debt he would never acknowledge.

Sandburg, too, had an influence on Frost. An almost exact contemporary, he "made it" before Frost, reciting his Whitmanlike poems in celebration of America across the country: "Chicago," "The People, Yes," "Grass," and others. Like Vachel Lindsay, whom he resembles in spirit, Sandburg sought a popular audience and developed a homey persona that played well in public—as Frost would later do himself. Sandburg learned a great deal, as Frost had, from Amy Lowell, H.D., and Ezra Pound, the Imagists, and his famous poem "Fog" became a model of sorts for a "modern" poem, as he describes it rolling in

on little cat feet.

It sits looking
over the harbor and city
on silent haunches
and then moves on.

Sandburg wrote that poetry is "a series of explanations of life, fading off into horizons too swift for explanations." This marries well with Frost's famous definition of poetry as "a momentary stay against confusion." Sandburg is always blither, more simple-minded, and "softer" than Frost. And in many ways Frost invented himself in contrast to a man like Sandburg, whose easy liberalism and identification with "the common man" struck him as false. Frost is the loner, the individualist, and his poetry is a poetry of survival.

* * *

Frost's accomplishments as a poet were hard won. A New Englander who spent some time in San Francisco as a child, he struggled for recognition for two decades after dropping out of Dartmouth and Harvard and marrying his hometown sweetheart, Elinor Miriam White. (Elinor and Robert had been tied for valedictory honors in their senior class at Lawrence High School, in Massachusetts.) Frost stumbled from job to job, farming in Derry and Franconia, New Hampshire, teaching school, loafing. He loved listening to his country neighbors, paying attention to what he called "their tones of speech." It was this tone that he would capture and transform in some of his best poems.

In 1912 at the age of thirty-eight Frost quit his job of teaching at Pinkerton Academy, a rural prep school in New Hampshire, and sailed to Britain with his wife and young children. He had pretty much in hand the poems of *A Boy's Will*, his first book, which takes its title from a poem by Longfellow. In fact, by this time he already had completed much of his second book, *North of Boston*. The Frosts settled in a little English village called Beaconsfield, and Frost set out to meet everyone who was important in poetry circles in Britain, such as Ezra Pound. He also met a young poet called Edward Thomas, who would have a profound influence on his work. Frost's rural subjects fit in nicely with the Georgian school of poets who were just gaining a wide audience in Britain, and Frost found a publisher rather swiftly. David Nutt brought out *A Boy's Will* in 1913.

Frost, as always, understood exactly what he was doing. He was writing pastoral verse—poems on rural subjects written for a well-educated "city" audience—much as Horace and Virgil had done in ancient Rome. In *The Pastoral Art of Robert Frost* (1960) John F. Lynen writes with savvy about what "pastoralism" means in Frost:

> Frost, like the writers of old pastoral, draws upon our feeling
> that the rural world is representative of human life in general. By
> working from this nodal idea he is able to develop in his poems
> a very broad range of reference without ever seeming to depart
> from particular matters of fact. He says nothing of other places

and other times—he gives us only the minute particulars of his
own immediate experience; yet ... the things described seem
everywhere to point beyond the rural world. The effect is to create
a remarkable depth of reference.

Frost, then, is not a naive chronicler of farm life in rural New England. He
is a poet fully aware of every influence, from the ancient writers of Greek
and Roman eclogues through the Romantics right up to his immediate
contemporaries. Furthermore, he was a "Modernist" in his own way, which
is why Ezra Pound—the ringmaster of literary Modernism—found him
interesting.

Shortly after the publication of *A Boy's Will* in England, Frost wrote a
memorable letter to his friend John T. Bartlett. In it he put forth a theory
of poetry that he called "the sound of sense." "I am possibly the only person
going who works on any but a worn out theory (principle I had better say)
of versification. You see the great successes in recent poetry have been made
on the assumption that the music of words was a matter of harmonized vow-
els and consonants. Both Swinburne and Tennyson arrived largely at effects
in assonation. But they were on the wrong track or at any rate on a short
track. They went the length of it." He separated himself from these writers,
who represented the reigning orthodoxy. "I alone of English writers have set
myself to make music out of what I may call the sound of sense."

The idea behind Frost's "sound of sense" theory is fascinating. "The best
place to get the abstract sound of sense is from voices behind a door that cuts
off the words," Frost explains. "It is the abstract vitality of our speech." In
other words, the specific denotation of the words, what we usually think of as
"content," is less important than the way the language moves something akin
to the "mind's ear."

Frost expanded in this same letter on how the "sound of sense" relates to
poetic meter. "If one is to be a poet he must learn to get cadences by skillfully
breaking the sounds of sense with all their irregularity of accent across the
regular beat of the metre." The metrical line is fixed, unnatural: a set number
of strong accents or "beats." Ordinary speech fits irregularity into the abstract
pattern of the meter. But the poetry in a line (another way of describing the
"sound of sense") is the product of the difference between the abstract metrical line and the natural flow of speech.

The obsession with ordinary speech and its relation to poetry is partly
what makes Robert Frost a modern poet. There is nothing of the elevation
of poetic style found in many Victorian poets in his work, nothing self-
consciously "poetic." The poetry resides in the plain sense of things, the articulation of moments of clarity and poise, the accumulation of what might be

called "wisdom" in the residuals of meaning that have accrued by the end of the poem.

Another aspect of Frost's theory—one he would hold for life—is his understanding of symbolism and how it functions in a poem. Frost liked to call himself a Synecdochist. "If I must be classified as a poet," he wrote in another letter, "I might be called a Synecdochist, for I prefer the Synecdoche in poetry—that figure of speech in which we use a part for the whole." A symbol is always synecdochal, which is to say that an image is meant to represent something larger than itself. The metaphorical aspects of the image are nonspecific, which gives them an aura of suggestiveness.

The poem "Mowing"—from *A Boy's Will*—is a good example of Frost's technique:

There was never a sound beside the wood but one,
And that was my long scythe whispering to the ground.
What was it it whispered? I knew not well myself;
Perhaps it was something about the heat of the sun,
Something, perhaps, about the lack of sound—
And that was why it whispered and did not speak.
It was no dream of the gift of idle hours,
Or easy gold at the hand of fay or elf:
Anything more than the truth would have seemed too weak
To the earnest love that laid the swale in rows,
Not without feeble-pointed spikes of flowers
(Pale orchises), and scared a bright green snake.
The fact is the sweetest dream that labor knows.
My long scythe whispered and left the hay to make.

Frost liked to write about working—physical labor—and he found in physical labor a synecdochal image: the "mowing" of the poem "stands in" for larger motions of the mind and spirit. That this is not just a poem about mowing hay should be obvious from the first line. Why was there "never" a sound beside the wood but one? Frost is separating this mowing from any purely physical act; the mowing is a mental action that isolates the poet (a favorite theme in Frost's work overall). The poet—and here "mowing" is analogous to writing poems—is thoroughly absorbed in the work that is productive of meaning. As if to reinforce the connection, the scythe is said to be "whispering." What does it whisper? Frost, in the Romantic tradition, does not place too much emphasis on the conscious aspects of literary production. A poet's meanings are "accidental." Thus, the mower says "I knew not well myself" what meaning was produced by his motion.

In typical Frostian fashion the speaker goes on to muse about possibilities: perhaps it was this or that. One sees a gradual unfolding of thought as image leads to image, as revelation produces revelation. As Lawrance Thompson notes in his early study of Frost called *Fire and Ice: The Art and Thought of Robert Frost* (1942):

> The central theme is built around this blending of the earnest love which derives satisfaction from the activities of the immediate moment. The extensions of the imagery suggest a much deeper emotional perception than that derived from a mere statement of the essential meaning. Objects and sounds, the grass, the woods, the mower, sunlight, the snake, the flowers—all these combine to accentuate the intense pleasure within the mower himself.

Clearly, the physical act of mowing is only part of the story.

Frost adored paradox, and the surface simplicity of his poems is often undermined by currents of paradoxical meaning that undercut the central, surface motion of the poem. In effect, the poems "deconstruct" themselves. In "Mowing" there is the surface meaning that concerns the act of haying. The satisfaction of the work is contrasted with the "dream of the gift of idle hours," the feeling of relief that the work is accomplished and the feeling that one might have gained something: gold, a job done. The poet of the surface quickly interjects his belief that "anything but the truth would have seemed too weak," thus celebrating the work itself as the goal. To extend the analogy to, say, poetry: the goal is the writing of the poem, not the resulting reputation of the poem or poet. Indeed, with an aphoristic compression worthy of Ralph Waldo Emerson, Frost's great precursor, Frost says: "The fact is the sweetest dream that labor knows." Nevertheless, the last line subverts this. "My long scythe whispered and left the hay to make."

The last line is pregnant with possibilities. "Left the hay to make" is a Symbolist's ideal moment: an image that ramifies in many ways, that carries beyond its immediate denotation. To leave the hay "to make" is to let it ripen in the sun. The result of the work—the nourishment of cattle, for instance—comes later: months later, perhaps, as the cows in the winter barn munch on the hay. But one can hardly avoid other echoes; "Make hay while the sun shines" is only one (and plays into the sexual metaphor implicit in "Mowing," where the analogy to making love is obvious enough). Perhaps the poet's work is an avoidance of seizing the moment elsewhere? That a man's complete meaning is derived alone, at work, without women, is a consistent theme in Frost and one that could be explored at length in all of his work. But, most telling, the last line of "Mowing" suggests that meaning is not at hand, that the goodness of the work is an after-echo, something that follows indeterminately. This undermines the poem's central theme, which is that the "fact" is the best thing. (Although, even here, one should stop to wonder why a fact is the sweetest *dream* that labor knows.)

There is almost no poem by Frost that does not yield to long and careful reconsideration. His work resists easy interpretation; indeed, it often seems that Frost designed the poems to fool the innocent reader into taking the "easy gold" of a quick interpretation. Almost invariably, these quick readings are wrong. Frost is plainly the most deceptive poet in the history of our literature. He himself once said in a letter that "any poem is most valuable for its ulterior meaning."

The quest for "ulteriority" is all part of the Frostian world. On the surface one finds the sentimentalized view of New England embodied in familiar images: dry stone walls, woodlots, lonely farmhouses, woods full of snow, fields of flowers, good-hearted country people. But only a very superficial reading stops there. An early poem like "Storm Fear" is typical of the Frostian view of man against nature:

> When the wind works against us in the dark,
> And pelts with snow
> The lower chamber window on the east,
> And whispers with a sort of stifled bark,
> The beast,
> 'Come out! Come out!'—
> It costs no inward struggle not to go,
> Ah, no!
> I count our strength,
> Two and a child,
> Those of us not asleep subdued to mark
> How the cold creeps as the fire dies at length,—
> How drifts are piled,
> Dooryard and road ungraded,
> Till even the comforting barn grows far away,
> And my heart owns a doubt
> Whether 'tis in us to arise with day
> And save ourselves unaided.

Frost's personae in his poems are often afraid of the natural world. There is none of the mystical urge to unite with nature one sometimes finds in Romantic poets. The nature of New England is inhospitable, something to be "got through." Frost—and his surrogates in his poems—want to stand apart from nature; the emphasis, always, is upon survival, the effort to "save ourselves unaided."

Frost's second book of poems, *North of Boston*, which followed a year after *A Boy's Will*, is perhaps his most brilliantly sustained collection. It contains half a dozen of his most famous poems: "Mending Wall," "The Death of a Hired Man," "Home Burial," "A Servant to Servants," "After Apple-Picking," and "The Wood-Pile." This last poem, one not often recognized as one of Frost's very best, is a remarkable example of the Symbolist work of his early period. It is about a man who is "out walking in a frozen swamp one grey day"—a typical situation in a Frost poem. The poet-as-loner is a frequent image, one that derives from the Romantic tradition (one thinks especially of Wordsworth here, who in a poem such as "Resolution and Independence" walks out in the countryside in search of instruction of a spiritual kind). The speaker in Frost's poem stumbles upon a cord of wood in the middle of a symbolic Nowhere: "a cord of maple, cut and split / And piled—and measured, four by four by eight." What was it doing out there, beyond the reach of human activity? There was no house in sight for it to warm, no other signs of humanity. It was just left there to "warm the frozen swamp as best it could / With the slow smokeless burning of decay."

Again, one searches Frost for "ulteriority," for the synecdochal meaning of the poem. What does the woodpile "stand for" in addition to its most literal, and important, level of meaning? It would be misguided not to recognize that, most crucially, this is a poem about a woodpile. One can almost hear Frost smirking at the critic who would too quickly leap to grab at metaphorical rings of interpretation. Nevertheless, the woodpile is clearly an object of human labor, the product of careful craftsmanship and sustained attention. It is, of course, very like a poem: something constructed for the sheer love of doing it, left by itself to "warm the frozen swamp as best it could." The natural world, left to its own devices, is pointless in Frost's deeply humanistic view of reality; indeed, one may well take William Blake's line as a gloss on all of Frost's poetry: "Without man, nature is barren."

In *North of Boston* Frost also began to experiment with the dramatic poem—the monologue or dialogue poem. An old couple, Mary and Warren, discuss the fact that "Silas is back" in "The Death of the Hired Man." Silas, an old hired man who has left Warren's employment, has come home to die. Frost catches the regional cant of these voices with eerie perfection:

"Where did you say he'd been?

"He didn't say. I dragged him to the house,
And gave him tea and tried to make him smoke.

I tried to make him talk about his travels.
Nothing would do: he just kept nodding off."

"What did he say? Did he say anything?"

"But little."

   "Anything? Mary, confess
He said he'd come to ditch the meadow for me."

"Warren!"

   "But did he? I just want to know."

"Of course he did. What would you have him say?
Surely you wouldn't grudge the poor old man
Some humble way to save his self-respect.
He added, if you really care to know,
He meant to clear the upper pasture, too."

On and on Mary and Warren struggle to come to terms with the fact that
"Silas is back." The final turn, of course, is that Silas is dead and the wran-
gling is all for nought. Frost had an astonishing gift for drama—indeed,
he is one of our best dramatic poets. And "The Death of the Hired Man"
remains among his most memorable efforts, as does "Home Burial," a
poem about a young couple trying to come to terms with the death of a
child.
      Anyone who imagines that Frost romanticizes country people and farm
life has not read his poems carefully. The world conjured in these poems is not
idyllic. Death, exhaustion, illness, marital bitterness, cold, and moral bank-
ruptcy are close at hand. Frost's poems are built upon darkness, and the world
he sees is one where sublimity, as in Wordsworth, is fostered by both beauty
and terror in equal proportions.
      A poem in *Mountain Interval* (1916), Frost's third volume, called "'Out,
Out—'" is among his strongest, darkest, and most exemplary poems about
country people. Its opening is memorable in every way:

The buzz saw snarled and rattled in the yard
And made dust and dropped stove-length sticks of wood,
Sweet-scented stuff when the breeze drew across it,
And from there those that lifted eyes could count

> Five mountain ranges one behind the other
> Under the sunset far into Vermont.

Frost's easy command of the blank verse line is breathtaking. The poem opens with an idyllic version of rustic country life, but it soon takes a turn into some of the darkest regions of this poet's emotional territory. The boy who is the subject of the poem is cutting wood with the buzz saw when his sister calls him in to supper. He turns quickly, and the saw cuts off his hand. The economy of the way Frost expresses himself here adds to the dislocation one feels:

> At the word, the saw,
> As if to prove saws knew what supper meant,
> Leaped out at the boy's hand, or seemed to leap—
> He must have given the hand. However it was,
> Neither refused the meeting.

In that "However it was" one locates a dark whimsicality that is part of the Frostian tone.

The narrative continues with succinct power. A doctor is called, and soon the doctor "put him in the dark of ether." But there is really nothing that can be done for the poor boy:

> He lay and puffed his lips out with his breath.
> And then—the watcher at his pulse took fright.
> No one believed. They listened at his heart.
> Little—less—nothing!—and that ended it.
> No more to build on there. And they, since they
> Were not the one dead, turned to their affairs.

The seeming callousness of those last lines are part of the Frostian effect. A casual reading might well give the reader the impression that Frost is portraying these people as pragmatic to a point of inhumanity. But the total meaning of the poem, framed by the title's quotation from *Macbeth*, goes beyond mere callousness. Frost invokes the tradition of tragedy, where "life is but a walking candle." It is as if these rude country folk understand the larger point and in some way transcend their humble circumstances in what William Pritchard calls the "weird, unforgettable bluntness" of the poem. They are deeply enthralled to the labor-value of the boy. His hand is gone, so there was "No more to build on there." The buzz saw, snarling and rattling, is a product of the mechanical revolution that has in effect ruined the lives of these people. It implies a world beyond the farm, an economic system that has diminished the world as a whole.

Mountain Interval also contains "The Oven Bird," one of Frost's unforgettable sonnets. Like "Mowing," it is a poem implicitly about the act of writing, about a bird who "knows in singing not to sing," which is to say that he must abandon the worn-out poetical diction and rhetorical conventions of his predecessors and offer a new kind of song. "The question that he frames in all but words / Is what to make of a diminished thing." The last two lines resonate with implications. What poet now writing is not faced with this dilemma? The world as we find it, much as the world Frost found, is sadly diminished, and the poet's job in the twentieth century has been what to make of this world, how to respond to its indignities, its savage and vengeful self-absorption, its greed, its abandonment of common decency and justice.

Perhaps the most haunting poem in *Mountain Interval* is "An Old Man's Winter Night," a poem about an old man dying in the wintry climate of New England and alone: "All out-of-doors looked darkly in at him / Through the thin frost, almost in separate stars." The poem meditates implicitly on the human condition as a whole, though it remains neatly, even maniacally, focused on the single old man here who "stood with barrels round him—at a loss." The old man is somehow made to bear the weight of all human loneliness, even though "a light he was to no one but himself / Where now he sat, concerned with he knew what, / A quiet light, and then not even that." The man's inner light, as it were, goes out as he sleeps; there is nothing left but the glimmer in the woodstove and the pale moonlight. The poem ends with a handful of deeply haunting lines:

> One aged man—one man—can't keep a house,
> A farm, a countryside, or if he can,
> It's thus he does it of a winter's night.

The word "keep" is central here, as elsewhere in Frost, carrying a freight of ambiguous meanings. The word's original denotation, in the Anglo-Saxon, is "to hold, to seize." By implication, a person's duty in life is to bear witness (as in the title of a late volume by Frost, *A Witness Tree*), to maintain a vigil. Frost's poet is a hermit who nonetheless lets his light shine, keeps the faith, holds steady against the chaos of the universe.

Critics such as Lionel Trilling and Randall Jarrell have stressed the darkness in Frost, his sense of the spiritual blight, and they were right to do so. But there is a side of Frost that might be called "twilight." It emerges in poems like "After Apple-Picking," "Hyla Brook," "The Sound of Trees," and in so many of the later poems. Frost is always the poet of survival, and survival for him entails the act of cognition itself. "After Apple-Picking" is, according to Reuben Brower and other critics, one of Frost's finest moments. It is a deeply strange poem, to be sure. It begins:

> My long two-pointed ladder's sticking through a tree
> Toward heaven still,
> And there's a barrel that I didn't fill
> Beside it, and there may be two or three
> Apples I didn't pick upon some bough.
> But I am done with apple-picking now.

Again, one must look beyond the surface of a Frost poem to make any real sense of it. First, the poem is not about the work of apple-picking but about the feelings that follow from it. "I am drowsing off," the speaker says in the monologue. And the poem begins to conjure a peculiar dream state, a twilight in which the poem moves between the real world and the dream world, between life and art. "I am overtired / Of the great harvest I myself desired," says Frost. Here is the exhaustion of composition, with its unbearable desire for something that can never be accomplished, since poetry is always a search for something beyond reach, a quest for a simulacrum of heaven, a place where the absolute is attainable and where all contrarieties are reconciled. Frost, still a young poet, displays an almost overwhelming burden of possibilities: "There were ten thousand thousand fruit to touch, / Cherish in hand, lift down, and not let fall." The last line quoted is heart-breakingly beautiful, the syntax imitating and embodying the action it mimics, with the asymmetry of the last phrase ("and not let fall") made wonderfully strange by its lack of parallelism.

Mountain Interval also contains the famous "Birches." In a fine book called *Robert Frost and New England*, John Kemp identifies this poem as the place where a different kind of Frost poem has its origins. These are the poems—and there are more and more of them as Frost's career unfolds—where the poet speaks as farmer-sage, as a homespun philosopher. The poem as a form of wisdom literature has an honorable tradition, of course, and Frost at his best does this kind of thing very well. "Good fences make good neighbors" is a line spoken by a farmer in "Mending Wall" that typifies his approach to poetry. In "Birches" there is no farmer speaking but Frost himself as farmer when he presents a totalizing statement in the last line of the poem, "One could do worse than be a swinger of birches." The calculated understatement here in some ways undercuts the poem, which is mostly a splendid monologue. Indeed, there are incomparable passages in "Birches," as in this image of the girls in the following lines:

You may see their trunks arching in the woods
Years afterwards, trailing their leaves on the ground
Like girls on hands and knees that throw their hair
Before them over their heads to dry in the sun.

The symbolic motion of the poem, too, is controlled with consummate artistry. The poem is about boys climbing birches (the sexual implications of this, as in "Mowing" and "Putting in the Seed," are wonderful to contemplate) to subdue them, to ride them to the ground. Indeed, the poem moves toward a remarkable statement: "Earth's the right place for love: / I don't know where it's likely to go better." These lines, according to James M. Cox in a strong essay called "Robert Frost and the End of the New England Line," are "Frost's greatest lines—lines which reveal the grace and loss and gain of all Frost's life and language."

   I think one may take Frost at face value in many of his wise utterances, as in the above instance. But Frost is dangerously canny, and—as such—he often means less than he says or, occasionally, the opposite of what he says. A crucial example is found in "The Road Not Taken," which ends with the often-quoted lines:

Two roads diverged in a wood, and I—
I took the one less traveled by,
And that has made all the difference.

A less than rigorous look at the poem may lead one to believe that Frost's "moral" is embodied in those lines; the poem is taken as a call to independence, preaching originality and Emersonian self-reliance. But the poem deconstructs its conclusion stanza by stanza. The poem's first three stanzas follow:

Two roads diverged in a yellow wood,
And sorry I could not travel both
And be one traveler, long I stood
And looked down one as far as I could
To where it bent in the undergrowth

Then took the other, as just as fair,
And having perhaps the better claim,
Because it was grassy and wanted wear;
Though as for that the passing there
Had worn them really about the same,

And both that morning equally lay
In leaves no step had trodden black.
Oh, I kept the first for another day!
Yet knowing how way leads onto way,
I doubted if I should ever come back.

The poem, in fact, stresses that there is no difference, or little difference, between the two roads offered—it is all in the mind. The second stanza claims that "the other" is "just as fair." The same stanza concludes that this same path is worn "really about the same" as the first road, presumably the more well-traveled road. Indeed, by the third stanza the point is confirmed: "And both that morning equally lay / In leaves no step had trodden black." What more evidence does a reader need? So what is the "one less traveled by" that makes "all the difference" to the speaker? The clue to the meaning of this poem lies in the two lines that open the final stanza: "I shall be telling this with a sigh / Somewhere ages and ages hence."

The poet will be telling his grandchildren, say, that he "took the road less traveled by" and that it "made all the difference." But he will be lying. The poem is, perhaps, about the tendency in this poet and, by extension, the tendency in all of us to romanticize our past, to lay claim to the "road less traveled," to glorify "the road not taken." But, indeed, the road not taken is *not taken* yet. The title itself embraces the dazzling and tantalizing ambiguity of this poem, which is infinitely more complex than first meets the eye. One should read this poem as a warning. Frost is saying: Don't take me literally.

Frost's fourth book, *New Hampshire* (1923), contains a number of Frost's best-known lyrics: "Fire and Ice," "Dust of Snow," "The Aim Was Song," "Nothing Gold Can Stay," "Stopping by Woods on a Snowy Evening," "For Once, Then, Something," and "The Need of Being Versed in Country Things." Frost's penchant for the brief lyric with an aphoristic bite is sharpened to a point of fire in many of these poems, which marry beautifully with W. H. Auden's chief requirement for poetry—that it be "memorable language." One never forgets a poem like "Dust of Snow":

The way a crow
Shook down on me
The dust of snow
From a hemlock tree

Has given my heart
A change of mood

And saved some part
Of a day I rued.

Here, Frost ties in with so many other Modernist writers in savoring the moment of sudden illumination, what Joyce called an "epiphany." But in Frostian fashion there is something underplayed as well; a mere change of mood is all that is celebrated, a shift in feelings. The poem also, by implication, presents a rather gloomy image of the poet as solitary depressive as he wanders in the wintry landscape ruing the day.

New Hampshire much more than *Mountain Interval* marks a beginning of the persona of Frost as philosopher of the common man, a persona that would eventually smother the poet. The long title poem "New Hampshire" is not, for instance, one of Frost's finer moments. Frost claims here to have "written several books against the world in general." He mentions having recently visited New York, where he gets involved in "converse with a New York alec / About the new school of the pseudo-phallic." Here is the onset of a frustrating Frostian stance: Frost as Reactionary. There is no doubt that Frost identified with political conservatism; what he takes aim at in his poems is anti-New. He hates anything that smacks of Freudianism. He hates Marxism. He is the New England equivalent of a Southern Agrarian, preferring small farming communities to large industrial cities. He hates the modern world, with its machines, its pace, its lack of values, its tendencies toward collective behavior. He is always the Emersonian or Thoreauvian Romantic, the individualist, falling back upon a stance of self-reliance. One mostly applauds these views, except when Frost gets cute, as he does increasingly in poems from "New Hampshire" on.

Frost would from now on alternate masks. He could still write in his powerful "realistic" mode, and many of his very best poems in this style lay ahead of him, including "Spring Pools," "Acquainted with the Night," "Design," "Provide, Provide," "The Silken Tent," "The Subverted Flower," "The Most of It," "Directive," "The Gift Outright," and "Choose Something Like a Star." But, increasingly, the books contained chatty, even verbose, presentations such as "The Lesson for the Day" and "Build Soil." The latter, for instance, rambles on in this vein:

Is socialism needed, do you think?

We have it now. For socialism is
An element in any government.
There's no such thing as socialism pure—
Except as an abstraction of the mind.

> There's only democratic socialism,
> Monarchic socialism—oligarchic,
> The last being what they seem to have in Russia.

This is Frost giving vent to hot professorial wind.

In 1920 Frost quit a teaching job at Amherst College to begin, as he wrote to his friend Wilbur Cross, "hurling fistfuls [of poems] right and left." He claimed to have "kicked himself free from care and intellectuality." He had recently won a Pulitzer Prize—the first of four he would receive in his lifetime—and was ready to dig in. The oddity is, of course, that Frost's digging in did not result necessarily in better poems. There was something self-satisfied in Frost that, in his lesser poems, hurt him. One sees this attitude reflected in a telling letter to a poet-friend, Kimball Flaccus:

> You wish the world better than it is, more poetical. You are that kind of poet. I would rate as the other kind. I wouldn't give a cent to see the world, the United States or even New York made better. I want them left just as they are for me to make poetical on paper. I don't ask anything done to them that I won't do to them myself. I'm a mere selfish artist most of the time. I have no quarrel with the material. The grief will be if I can't transmute it into poems. I don't want the world made safer for poetry or easier. To hell with it. That is its own lookout. Let it stew in its own materialism. No, not to Hell with it. Let it hold its position while I do it in art. My whole anxiety is for myself as a performer. Am I any good? That's what I'd like to know and all I need to know.

This attitude hurt Frost terribly in the long run. But there were marvelous reprieves from this selfishness, and Frost would time and again find himself engaged with the world in the generous way that is essential for the production of great poetry.

West-Running Brook appeared in 1928. It opens with "Spring Pools," one of Frost's most powerful and enigmatic lyrics.

> These pools that, though in forests, still reflect
> The total sky almost without defect,
> And like the flowers beside them, chill and shiver,
> Will like the flowers beside them soon be gone,
> And yet not out by any brook or river,
> But up by roots and bring dark foliage on.

As with so many of Frost's poems, the natural world is a source of metaphor, and metaphorical thinking is for Frost the most refined level of thought. As Margaret Edwards notes in an essay called "Pan's Song Revised" that was included in the first volume of *Frost: Centennial Essays* (1974), this poem regards nature as a cycle wherein the "purpose of destruction—in this case the absorption of the pools—is creation." Edwards continues, "The water will 'bring dark foliage on.' The pools make summer possible. And yet there is that note of regret for what the inevitable process will 'blot out and drink up and sweep away.'"

West-Running Brook also contains "Tree at My Window," a poem that meditates on the traditional Romantic conflict between subject and object, posed here as an opposition between "inner weather" and "outer weather." The poet, in classical fashion, addresses the tree:

> Tree at my window, window tree,
> My sash is lowered when night comes on;
> But let there never be curtain drawn
> Between you and me.

He goes on to contemplate this "thing next most diffuse to cloud" and says that not all the rattling of the leaves-as-tongues "could be profound." But he identifies with the tree, reaching for a reconciliation of subject and object through imaginative sympathy:

> But, tree, I have seen you taken and tossed,
> And if you have seen me when I slept,
> You have seen me when I was taken and swept
> And all but lost.

The poem moves toward an ingenious resolution in the final stanza:

> That day she put our heads together,
> Fate had her imagination about her,
> Your head so much concerned with outer,
> Mine with inner weather.

Thus, the human mind is mirrored by the natural world, and the natural world is, conversely, mirrored; the concern with "weather"—which one might identify with "mood" or "spirit"—connects the two worlds, draws them into the same cognitive sphere.

The demarcation of "inner" and "outer" worlds is discussed in lively terms by Frank Lentricchia in "Robert Frost and Modern Literary Theory" (in the *Centennial Essays* volume):

> Something in Frost wants to distinguish landscapes, to mark off "inner" from "outer," subject from object, human from nonhuman; perhaps it is because Frost feels so strongly that the outer landscape is not congenial to the self: the sash, at night, must be lowered, we must stay enclosed for our own good. All of which is to say that this poem, like so many poems by Frost, is grounded in a tough realist's view of things. Yet Frost gives us no unnavigable gulf between subject and object. The sash must be lowered, of course, but the curtain must never be drawn across the window. Thus, between self and not-self Frost places a transparency which allows for an interaction of sorts, as enclosed self and weathered tree take creative looks at one another.

The tree is like a person, in that it dreams and drifts in sleep; the speaker, treelike, is "taken and swept / And all but lost." So we get a complex sense of the relations between interior and exterior landscapes, with consciousness as "weather" serving as a kind of mediating space. (Lentricchia notes that John Dewey, like William James before him, believed that selfhood exists only as something potential until it is, in Dewey's words, "both formed and brought to consciousness through interaction with an environment.")

A Further Range appeared in 1936. As the title suggests, Frost was attempting to look beyond what he had done already in poetry. Unfortunately, the collection is weighted down with poems that, in retrospect, seem chatty and slight. Frost was by now on the college reading circuit in a busy way, moving from college town to college town and reciting his poems to large and appreciative audiences. He was rapidly becoming the quintessential American bard, and audiences looked to him for "delight" as much as "wisdom." Poems such as "Departmental" and "A Record Stride" are burdened with a fatal cuteness. The latter, for instance, ends with a sophomoric few lines:

> And I ask all to try to forgive me
> For being as over-elated
> As if I had measured the country
> And got the United States stated.

It is hard to forgive Frost for this kind of poetry.

Nevertheless, *A Further Range* contains "Design," arguably one of the best sonnets ever written by an American poet. It is a frightening poem, one that confronts the dire possibility that the universe is not only godless but that God is evil. In keeping with the Imagist tendencies in modern poetry, Frost centers the poem on a picture:

> I found a dimpled spider, fat and white,
> On a white heal-all, holding up a moth
> Like a white piece of rigid satin cloth—
> Assorted characters of death and blight
>
> . . . .
> . . . .
>
> A snow-drop spider, a flower like a froth,
> And dead wings carried like a paper kite.

The white spider—already a freak of nature—has landed on a white flower with a white moth in its grip. None of these three elements is normally white, which gives each of them an abstract eeriness. The fact that these elements are "mixed ready to begin the morning right, / Like the ingredients of a witches' broth—" is deeply ironic: indeed, the language parodies the language of breakfast cereal ads. What we get here is an image that combines death and blight. There is nothing life-enhancing about anything in this piece of nature.

In the sestet of the sonnet, where issues raised in the octet are traditionally resolved, Frost simply offers three haunting and unanswerable questions:

> What had that flower to do with being white,
> The wayside blue and innocent heal-all?
> What brought the kindred spider to that height,
> Then steered the white moth thither in the night?
> What but design of darkness to appall?—
> If design govern in a thing so small.

The poem is in many ways the key to Frost's universe, a poem so perfect in its execution that one cannot imagine a word placed otherwise. Frost's tone is deftly controlled throughout, with the poet's serious point balanced nicely by the parodic language of the first stanza. Ever aware of the linguistic roots of words, Frost is inwardly winking when he uses the word "rigid" to modify "satin cloth." Likewise, at the end, he is certainly aware (as a former Latin teacher) that the word "appall" means "to make white" in its root sense. And

Frost is delighting in the way he can wring an unexpected turn of meaning from the Classical argument from design.

That Frost was intimately familiar with English and American poetry is never in doubt: his work is full of quiet echoes of his predecessors. In "Design," for instance, one hears, a mock-echo of William Cullen Bryant's classic *To a Waterfowl*, in which Bryant meditates on the argument from design and writes of God as "He who, from zone to zone / Guides through the boundless sky thy certain flight." One also sees in this poem a careful working out of some ideas raised by William James, the pragmatist, as Richard Poirier argues in *Robert Frost: The Work of Knowing* (1977).

A Witness Tree appeared during the Second World War, in 1942, when Frost was sixty-eight. It is the last of his books where the strong lyric gift of the earlier books remains present in any substantial way. The book opens with "The Silken Tent," a seamlessly perfect sonnet composed of one sentence. The subject and verb of the sentence are completed after the first two words are uttered: "She is." The poem is a conceit, with the "she" compared to a silken tent in many different ways. The poem unfolds with a sureness and directness that takes away one's breath, especially as the sonnet moves into its concluding motion, in which we learn that "she" is bound by the cords that hold the tent in place but "loosely bound / By countless silken ties of love and thought / To everything on earth the compass round." And it is "only by one's going slightly taut / In the capriciousness of summer air" that any sense of bondage is made apparent.

The high standard of "The Silken Tent" is maintained in a dozen more of the lyrics in *A Witness Tree*. One of the lesser known of these is "Come In," a poem that might be considered archetypally Frostian in that the protagonist wanders out by himself in the woods or countryside, often at night, and encounters something along the way that gives him pause to meditate. There is usually a piece of Yankee wisdom at the end. "Come In" fits this pattern nicely. The poet encounters a thrush—a very Romantic thing to do! The thrush is frequently identified, of course, with poetry. Yet the poet-wanderer of "Come In" doesn't want to come in, or to be taken in by the poetry of the thrush:

But no, I was out for stars:
I would not come in.
I meant not even if asked,
And I hadn't been.

A few pages later one encounters "The Most of It," which is equal to anything else in Frost. In this poem the poet-wanderer "thought he kept the universe alone." Again, Frost uses the word "keep" in a special way; here, it has the haunting sense of "being responsible for." His reason for thinking himself so responsible is the Blakean one. "Without man, nature is barren." Frost's nature is indeed cold, and it often seems to lack the humanization that William Blake demanded. Frost's hero calls out across the lake, hoping for "counter-love" and "original response." But what he gets instead is the sound of a great buck that leaped out of the woods and swam across the water toward him:

> Pushing the crumpled water up ahead,
> And landed pouring like a waterfall,
> And stumbled through the rocks with horny tread,
> And forced the underbrush—and that was all.

The force of "The Most of It" resides in the ferocity of the vision of nature embodied in the crudely powerful buck. Here is raw energy without human purpose.

"The Subverted Flower," which comes soon after, deconstructs "human" nature in the same brutal terms, this time embodied in the sexual urge of an adolescent boy who is reduced by his drives to a dog who froths at the mouth and seems to "bark outright." The poem is a little drama, with boy and girl confronting each other in a ritual dance of sorts out in a field. The setting is lush:

> She was standing to the waist
> In goldenrod and brake,
> Her shining hair displaced.

He is standing with a flower in his hand: the flower being a thinly disguised phallus. Indeed, "he flicked and flung the flower." And he gets caught as the girl's mother approaches and is horrified by the crude sight that she is forced to witness.

The girl is frothing at the mouth, too, as the poem is brought to a compelling halt, with the three-beat meter pounding like a bass drum as the melody of the lyric plays lightly over the drumming triple beat:

> And oh, for one so young
> The bitter words she spit
> Like some tenacious bit
> That will not leave the tongue.
> She plucked her lips for it,

> And still the horror clung.
> Her mother wiped the foam
> From her chin, picked up the comb
> And drew her backward home.

With the noble exception of "The Gift Outright," an unusual and unusually panoramic Frost poem, *A Witness Tree* falls away in the second half of the collection. While most poets would be delighted to have written poems such as "Time Out," "The Lost Follower," or "The Rabbit Hunter"—to mention a few of the more interesting poems that may be found here—the compact fury of Frost's best work is missing.

Frost wrote two long dramatic poems in the mid-forties: *A Masque of Reason* (1945) and *A Masque of Mercy* (1947). The former is a witty digression on the theme of Job, while the latter's focus is Jonah. In each case the original Biblical story is replayed in a contemporary setting. But there is little real drama in these masques, which are digressive and pseudophilosophical in the manner of "West-Running Brook." Nevertheless, they are relatively unknown and deserve a wider readership than they have thus far gotten.

In 1947 *Steeple Bush* was published. Reviewing this collection in the *New York Times Book Review*, Randall Jarrell said that "most of the poems merely remind you, by their persistence in the mannerisms of what was genius, that they are the productions of someone who once, and somewhere else, was a great poet." This is sadly true, although Jarrell wisely excepted a poem called "Directive," which is Frost's attempt to write what M. H. Abrams once identified as "the greater Romantic lyric." It is one of Frost's finest moments, a poem of huge imaginative pressure that opens with some of this poet's most compelling lines:

> Back out of all this now too much for us,
> Back in a time made simple by the loss
> Of detail, burned, dissolved, and broken off
> Like graveyard marble sculpture in the weather,

And continues, building on these specific details:

> There is a house that is no more a house
> Upon a farm that is no more a farm
> And in a town that is no more a town.

"Directive" is both an elegy for a world lost in time and a program for the future. It is Frost's version of Wordsworth's "Tintern Abbey," and like that poem it begins with a journey backward to place where one once had inspiration. Frost, at the tail end of his poetic career, senses his own flagging powers. The focus is gone. The poet's language, once capable of being fired to a fever pitch, has cooled. But here the poet blows on the coals, which now break upon themselves and burn brightly one last time. The poet returns to a child's playhouse by a stream, where he finds a mock version of the Holy Grail. But here, in childhood, was the source of inspiration. Here in the woods by the stream was the origin of all poetry:

> A brook that was the water of the house,
> Cold as a spring as yet so near its source,
> Too lofty and original to rage.

These lines provide a marvelous gloss upon Frost's entire corpus. His verse was always too "lofty and original to rage." The poet finds here, briefly, that momentary stay against confusion that has always meant so much to him, these Wordsworthian "spots of time" where time dissolves.

Except for the Keatsian "Choose Something Like A Star," there are few other places in *Steeple Bush* where one can easily rest for long. And there is very little to commend *In the Clearing*, which appeared in March of 1962. But Frost was, after all, almost ninety by the time this last book appeared.

Looking over the entire career of Robert Frost, one sees a breathtaking vista. Poem after poem breaks ground in places where one might never have thought a house of stanzas (a "stanza" is, literally, a room or floor) could be erected, and Frost builds and builds. His work is full of permanent settlements. His language and tone, his angles of vision, are a huge part of American literature and consciousness. And he has provided inspiration for contemporary poets as diverse as Richard Wilbur, Donald Hall, Robert Pack, Peter Davison, and Seamus Heaney. One is tempted, with Frost, to conclude by repeating his own great lines ending "Directive": "Here are your waters and your watering place. / Drink and be whole again beyond confusion."

FURTHER READING

Frost, Robert. *The Poetry of Robert Frost*. Ed. Edwin Connery Latham. New York: Henry Holt, 1969.

Poirier, Richard. *Robert Frost: The Work of Knowing*. New York: Oxford, 1977.

Pritchard, William H. *Robert Frost: A Literary Life Reconsidered*. New York: Oxford, 1984.

Thompson, Lawrance, and R. H. Winnick. *Robert Frost, A Biography*. New York: Holt, Rinehart and Winston, 1981.

SUZANNE CLARK

Uncanny Millay

W riting sonnets in the era of high modernism, popular though she was,
Edna St. Vincent Millay courted oblivion. She has not, as it turns out, been
forgotten. But as we remember her, I want to account for her endurance
in terms that acknowledge, as she said: "Beauty is not enough" ("Spring").
I want to point out the difficult cultural work her poetry has done. The
work of Millay impacts literary studies more unconsciously than most, if
my experience is any marker. This is not because continuing interest exists
only in the popular domain, outside the university. Academics across the
country—male as well as female academics—can quote Millay for you when
you walk past in the hall, at the drop of a hat, at the slightest mention that
you might be working on her. What they quote probably depends on their
generation, but the memorability of her lines persists. She is not forgotten;
she is very much remembered, on the tip of so many tongues. But this is
more like a memory of the body than of the mind, the repetition of a kind
of unconscious evoked by her words, in the mnemonics of sound.

By speaking of the "uncanny," I mean to suggest the work of the unconscious, the ghostly reappearance analyzed by Freud, and the special functioning of women's fiction discussed by Hélène Cixous. Though the body
of her work has made its ghostly reappearance, Millay was dismissed from
the literary by a generation of critics. There were good reasons for keeping

From *Millay at 100: A Critical Reappraisal*, edited by Diane P. Freedman, pp. 3–26. Copyright
© 1995 by the Board of Trustees, Southern Illinois University.

199

Millay's impact out of mind, because her work challenges the gendered identity assumed by the modernist aesthetic.

Millay criticized gender roles and sexuality explicitly, in defiant lines that made her notorious in 1923 and that once again delight feminist students today. "I, Being Born a Woman and Distressed" is a love sonnet that concludes: "I find this frenzy insufficient reason / For conversation when we meet again." The poem is made especially notable for this generation by being included in Sandra M. Gilbert and Susan Gubar's edition of the *Norton Anthology of Literature by Women* (1,555–56). Millay also positioned herself firmly on the side of progressive politics, not only in her public life, but in poems like "Justice Denied in Massachusetts," on the Sacco-Vanzetti case. But such poems are not typical of her work; it cannot be said that most of her poetry thematizes a political feminism. I am interested, rather, in how she engages in a *poetic* politics as well. Within the modernist aesthetic, the speaker of a poem may be theatrical, figurative, and ironic without upsetting cultural assumptions about personal identity. The male poet (Wallace Stevens, for example) may write like a lady, but the rigorous separation of impersonal literary complexity from the reductiveness of ordinary life keeps the gender distinctions clear.

The modernist aesthetic separated literary language from ordinary language and, in particular, from the personal.[1] Millay's poetry, however, does not acknowledge this separation of life from art. Modernist critics including Cleanth Brooks, Allan Tate, and John Crowe Ransom claimed that Millay's poetry was not only too susceptible to the conventional but also too easily overwhelmed by sensibility.[2] Conversely, I wonder, doesn't Millay's poetry take the figurative, parodic—*conventional*—character of literary language and extend that rhetoricity to life, denaturalizing the personal? Her poems make visible through a theater of the personal how identity functions in culturally determined ways. If the social construction of male and female and the narrative of their sexual fates is produced by discourse, including literary discourse, this productivity is nevertheless hidden by the closure of identity. This cultural unconscious may therefore be exposed through doubling and parody—and, in Millay's case, in particular, masquerade. Literary techniques enable her to critique cultural ideology from inside its technology, at the level of producing subjects, that is, at the level of figuring through form certain possibilities for desire. In the displacement of the lyric subject from its singularity, Millay's poetry is "novelized," in Bakhtin's sense, moved away from the monologic.

Think about the performative context of Millay's work as America's best-known poetess. She would appear in a long gown for readings, her voice dramatic, her form girlish and attractive, more like a diva than like the gray-suited male poets. The self in her work is an actress performing, at once embodiment and interpretation. There is no separation of artist and person. She is neither inside nor outside the communal order because from inside she delineates the trying on of identities that might work a remedy to alienation at the same time that she denaturalizes this identity-making project and exposes its unconscious webbing as art. Masquerade functions as critique. Furthermore, allegorizing the forms of the imaginary, Millay tropes identity through personification, and the figures of personification define a specific poetics for her work. In other words, while the figure of masquerade may suggest a multiplicity of roles for a single person without really challenging the notion of a core identity, the figure of personification suggests that personhood itself is a trope. This is not to say that I see Millay in a new guise as a postmodern writer, because this play on the figures of identity takes place in the context of a historic body of language. The uncanny specters of a bardic tradition are evoked and embodied in this materiality of a voice. Or of a lyric *song*.

So Millay's poetry does not simply participate in the social construction of the personal, reinscribing love stories: her work troubles the process, sounding repetition in a new voice. Millay interrupts the closure of womanhood by her necessarily failed attempts to speak like a man, the equivalent on the level of sound of a cross-dressing. Without this kind of troublemaking, both the sounds of language and the familiarity of conventional stories and characters can work to reproduce and limit the possibilities for individual identity. Millay represents an unconscious that is at once of musicality and of cultural repetitions: a cultural unconscious. Millay's writing, even though it participates in the symbolic order, opens up a space for difference, for the uncanny return of the repressed, through disturbances of that order.[3] She makes the traditional resources of a male literary tradition uncanny, strange. The resurrections of literary traditions inhering in forms like the sonnet, in figure and phrase, extend to influence the cultural politics that depend on their keeping their place.

A reader might assume that any repetition of traditional forms would serve a traditional or conservative purpose, at least at the level of the unconscious, but Millay mobilizes their power to her own ends. Literature, in Millay's work, is not kept separate from the political questions of gender. The ideology of the aesthetic, as Terry Eagleton argues, has provided for capitalism and the middle class a way to produce self-governing subjects. Millay's poetry reveals the way the ideology of the aesthetic works, through the imaginary, as a cultural unconscious that is exposed in the critical discomfort she provokes.

It is the masquerade of personal identity that distinguishes Millay from modernist poets. T. S. Eliot said, in "Tradition and the Individual Talent," that we shall often find that not only the best, but the most individual parts of [a poet's] work may be those in which the dead poets, his ancestors, assert their immortality most vigorously. And I do not mean the impressionable period of adolescence, but the period of full maturity. (4)

Millay, too, writes with the sense of those poetic ancestors in her bones, and her style testifies to their influence. But Millay's poetry is not what Eliot had in mind. "The existing monuments form an ideal order among themselves, which is modified by the introduction of the new (the really new) work of art among them" (5). Millay threatens to introduce something new that unsettles the ideal order profoundly; she speaks among the poets as a woman.

Even though we encounter again and again in Millay the resurrected speech of dead poets, it is not with the effect of impersonality Eliot insisted upon. It is not in the form of an aesthetic influence, which leaves the person aside, intact. Rather, in Millay, the unassimilated speech of poetic history enters into an intertextuality that detaches the personal from its aura. Shortly, I will look closely at some examples of this—of appearances by Yeats and Ronsard in Millay's poems. Here what I want to make clear is how speaking as a woman while she speaks men's words might unsettle modernist impersonality. To retain the marker of gender is to resist that complete surrender of the ordinary embodied self that Eliot was advocating. Millay's poetry does not appear to practice "a continual self-sacrifice, a continual extinction of personality" ("Tradition and the Individual Talent" 7). The memorability of the poetic word involves effects of transference and identification that depend on personality. Poetry that mobilizes response like Millay's (the shared memories) discloses for us the uncanny powers that may account for the hold of ideology upon us and may offer a way to hold out *against* ideology.

Feminist criticism has often characterized its work as restoring the unconscious to consciousness, using writing to reorganize psychic space. In a related sense, Millay's poetry can be read as a restorative project that would propel the woman's uneasy figure into juxtaposition with the figure of the writer, shadowing the traditionally male-gendered creativity of the poet with another gender, another sexuality, another creativity. Millay's rhetoric of personification, her attentiveness to the question of Beauty, her violation of the modernist poem's autonomous objectivity raises a gendered poetic into view. When modernist critics such as John Crowe Ransom (of whom more later) called this a woman's poetic, however, they did not mean to be complimentary.

A ghostly body inhabits the poetry of Millay, a haunting image hovering between the fantasy and the impossible real, like poetry itself. It is the very figure of language and beauty, animated within the folded space of anamnesis or unforgetting where the past both is and is not recovered as the trace of embodied and sensuous experience. This figure invokes us as the subjects of the long book of literature, the realm where the apples are, Millay says, "half Baldwin, half Hesperides" ("To whom the house of Montagu was neighbor"). Readers, we are invited not to revere the poetic object but, as Millay writes in her sonnet to the feminist Inez Milholland, to "take up the song." The invitation to transference or identification makes a strong bond and opens literature out into the imaginary. The uncanny in Millay is the ghost of a cultural unconscious, the forgotten woman, but also the forgotten power of poetry. This imaginary power is forgotten by the most critical among us because it has seemed regressive, the mere slave of ideology—because identities have seemed to contemporary feminist and other critics either essentialist or fragmented and the politics of identity no question for poetry.

With the help of Millay, however, we can explore the role of literature in making identities and the difficult question of how the forgotten might use literary power. Because hers is not a narrowly aesthetic conception of literature, Millay dramatizes in both form and theme the way culture shapes individuals, what Teresa de Lauretis has characterized as the technology of subjects, beginning with herself. Does Millay know that she is problematizing the very idea of an identity by asserting the oxymoron of the woman poet? She seems to know that gender makes the cultural construction of selves as free, autonomous individuals questionable, that with gender we are plunged into the problem of the social, of empathy, of the love story, and of our entanglements with others, from mother to lover. What Millay may not know is that her challenge to the gendered identity of the poet might also problematize the very institution of literature as a separate aesthetic. As Cheryl Walker demonstrates, Millay cannot construct a space outside the commodification of culture, and indeed, by making the identity of the self the subject and the object of her poem, she enters that identity into the reifying forces of the culture around her.

The various appearances of a poetic avant-garde in the past two centuries have signaled a historical crisis in the personal and the literary alike. The school of Eliot, which led to the school of new criticism, tried to stabilize the crisis by insisting on separating the poem from the person. This formalist ideal of impersonal poetry had the virtue of calling attention to language, but at the cost of disavowing any connection between the situation of poems and of persons. The practice of an impersonal poetics kept the poetic/personal identity separate, away from the disruptive effects of an avant-garde discourse. Defamiliarization might call attention to literature without disrupting the family. The school of Eliot enlisted avant-garde poetics against a progressive politics, denying any rhetorical purpose for literature, denying especially that literature might have any connection with the way culture disciplines the body's emotions and desires.

Edna St. Vincent Millay's poems refuse to function within this aesthetic. Millay uses the traditional forms of poetry in a productive and radical challenge to the hierarchies of modernism. Millay's poems involve a different rhetorical situation for poetics, not based on self-contained symbols, but rather on figures—embodiments—that point outside themselves in an allegorical gesture. Millay's allegorical storytelling reproduces literature itself as a figure of reproduction. Her poems require a different view of literature altogether, and of language too, a view of literature that is interested in exploring the imaginative possibilities for different identities offered by the heterogeneity of language. There is an admitted doubleness to this productivity, an inevitable complicity with commodification and vulnerability to cultural definitions of self. Millay's work differs from the school of Eliot precisely because it does not deny the complicity of art with seduction or the way that beauty can betray. As Millay says: "Beauty is not enough."

If Millay was a public, contemporary figure who came to represent the new woman and who came to seem the voice of a rebellious generation, that image must be informed by how very seriously she took the historical and literary powers of language. This notion of literature as a public, not a private or separate art, contravened the dominant critical movement of her time. Are we, postmoderns, more receptive to such a sense of responsibility? Most especially, she challenged the critical agreements of the moderns not just by seeing herself as a public poet but by writing a poetry that moves the problem of female identity into the public domain. Though she used the leverage of all the history of literature, that very history carried with it the supposition of male authorship. Does Millay fully acknowledge the closure of poetry's high traditions against female authorship?

"Reader do not let me die," she wrote in "The Poet and His Book." Death and grief is a frequent subject in Millay's poems. But is it her own death she fears? More often than the familiar poetic search for immortality in verse, death is associated in her texts with the pain of losing someone else. This other may be the beloved but is also the person she addresses, the reader, and the very possibility of re-membering a community of readers. Precariously, Millay has constructed a body of work that might mediate the relationship of self and other and inscribe the woman as writer in a poem—and in a culture—where she might address empathetic readers. These repeated confrontations with death gesture toward a certain abyss, a black melancholy that does not believe in the power of poetry to resurrect intimate presence or the power of beauty to connect individuals. That abyss is both private and public for a woman poet. The authentic experience is not real, but uncanny, written, bringing the unconscious into contact with style, bringing the self through language into contact with another. The authentic experience is, in this sense, always only remembered, in the anamnesis that reverses the displacement of desire. Experience and identity are transitory, brought into being—or not—as the fate of the book will allow:

> Search the fading letters, finding
> Steadfast in the broken binding
> All that once was I!
> ("The Poet and His Book")

The transference from writer to reader operates according to an uncanny logic.

I am especially struck by the way personification tropes poetry as one of Millay's chief devices of style. This personifying impulse is rhetorical and melodramatic, not modernist. The persona or speaker, the interlocutor or the *you* to whom the poem is addressed, and the third party all may be figured forth as Love or Death or Beauty or Silence. These are figures of identity in Millay, embodiments that make evident the linguistic body that subtends persons and shadows forth the symbolic identity of all subjects as a kind of personification. Naming the person in the text would not make it more personal than the abstraction if self is an uncanny between-the-lines, not located in the word.[4] Even in the early poems, such as "The Suicide," "Kin to Sorrow," "The Dream," and "Indifference," personification often dramatizes the theme so that a word like *love* is a character more than a representation:

> I said,—for Love was laggard, oh, love was slow to come,—
> "I'll hear his step and know his step when I am warm in bed;
> But I'll never leave my pillow, though there be some
> As would let him in—and take him in with tears!" I said.
> ("Indifference")

The "him" of this poem balances between abstraction—"Love"—and a bodied and specific version of the lover.

Poetry is the act of love, and lovers its effect. Poetry tells the tales that bind us together because it is the persona we speak or write or draw or paint that represents the person for the other. This seems to be the theme of a sonnet from *The Harp-Weaver* that contrasts "the outward you" and the artist.

The poem describes that recurring moment in a relationship when there is no exchange of desire or when the audience simply is tired of listening. The loss, the poem says, is redeemed in this failure of a desire to connect with the once-loved other, the memory entailed by art. The rhetorical situation has lost its force: "And my gaze wanders ere your tale is through" ("Sometimes when I am wearied suddenly"). What makes the promise of love into an act? It becomes a performance that recurs as performance through the good offices of art: "So are we bound till broken is the throat / Of Song, and Art no more leads out the Nine." The history and tradition of literary language guarantees a kind of renewal of human bonds in the allegory of emotional figures: "Then I recall, 'Yet *Sorrow* thus he drew'; / Then I consider, '*Pride* thus painted he.'" This reliance upon the constructed subject of art—as compared to a constructed object—is precisely what critics of Millay would challenge. Such rhetoricity is something even Eliot was willing to consider as more than just bad writing in certain cases of dramatic character—in "'Rhetoric' and Poetic Drama," he cites Cyrano's "nose" speech—but Millay's critics do not read her as participating in theater. If the reader identifies with the impersonal speaker of modernist poetry, it is with the ironic indifference that frames emotional expression and not with the attachments of emotion.

Inviting the identification of the reader with emotion, Millay situates poetic speech between the mundane and the eternal, in the figures of Sorrow and Pride. It is not the movement when such sympathetic identifications would be easy that she portrays, but the moment of distraction when the tale loses its audience: " . . . when I am wearied suddenly / Of all the things that are the outward you." What song prompts is memory, and it is the memory of Art: "How first you loved me for a written line."

I myself first loved Millay when I was fourteen: my father read me "Oh World, I cannot hold thee close enough." His gesture of reading expected that I would understand how this poem spoke something my adolescent exuberance could move into, a capacious frame for that mobile excess of feeling. But when I learned how early Millay had begun to publish, how young she was when she wrote "Renascence," I despaired of becoming a poet myself, of ever being able to catch up to the poetic genius of Millay. At fourteen, I was already too late. Like so many, I never stopped loving her poems. Yet I, like so many, also associated her with adolescence and the identity crises of adolescence.

John Crowe Ransom promoted a critical tradition of characterizing her work as immature. Even sympathetic readers, including myself, thought of the figure of the girl in her poems as a mark of immaturity; Elizabeth Frank critiqued the girl in Millay as if all her poetry figured forth a single subject. The mistake here was to read her work as if the trying on of identity associated with the adolescent were something to give up with maturity and as if the multiple identities dramatized by her poems could be coalesced into the figure of a girl and labeled immature by their very multiplicity. I would like to suggest that Millay has more to do with the way literature, and especially the novel, is the locus of such a trying on of identities. Julia Kristeva has argued that the novel arises as adolescence comes into being, as just such a discourse, concerned with the "problematic incompleteness of young page-boys, picaros, delinquents, or terrorists—from Casanova to Milos Forman to Mad Max" ("Adolescent Novel" 8). The question of adolescence, she says, allows us to interrogate ourselves on the role of the imaginary and the "open psychic system" that echoes "the fluidity, i.e., the inconsistency, of a mass media society." Such an open structure we grant to the adolescent, but "the adult will have the right to this only as a reader or spectator of novels, films, painting . . . or as artist. I do not see, moreover," Kristeva adds, "what would prompt writing if not an 'open structure'" (II).

The narrative structures implicated in Millay's poetry are complex and various, open structures. The close attention to form especially evident in the sonnets could lead us astray if we read Millay's style as if it were an endorsement of conventional poetic hierarchies, especially of a stable, gendered speaking subject. We do her a disservice to read them monologically, as if they all proceeded from a single subject. This is to say that we need to read her outside a certain prematurely mature tradition of poetic reading in order to recover the aesthetic pleasure to which she invites us.

Millay's novelistic quality, signaled by the adolescent shifting of identity and the allegorizing to narratives, connects her not to the old authoritarian modes of poetic reading, which the school of Eliot, in a reactionary movement, resurrected, but to the increasing domination of a novelistic, polylogic discourse that would finally emerge with postmodernism.

Much after my first encounter with Millay, when I was in graduate school, I imagined I might study her verse. "No," advised my critical friends, "Edna St. Vincent Millay is simply not interesting." So I began my study of Millay asking perversely why the critics felt so convinced she was not "interesting." Despite her witty send-offs and her sustained irony about all the elements of literature usually called sentimental, she had been, I thought—along with the whole tradition of the sentimental—consigned to the stigmatized order of women's writing. Eventually, I wrote a book, *Sentimental Modernism*, about modernism and women writers, including Millay, in which I tried to confront those too-easy dismissals.

In the beginning of the twentieth century, as Edna St. Vincent Millay began to write, the ideal of a disinterested aesthetic increasingly dissociated the practices of art from everyday life and especially from the private extremities of domestic passions. Disconnected from sexual bodies, poetry could seem pure, liberated from the struggles of power and desire among males and females; poetry could seem objective, an objective correlative of distanced emotion. Modernist poetics posits an impersonal, ungendered, universal subject of aesthetic judgment, related to Kant's notion of the aesthetic and to the Coleridgean imagination. Disconnected from the history of the cultural aesthetic and its rootedness in gender, aesthetic judgments could seem disinterested at the same time that they discriminated against women.

Feminist criticism has challenged the discrimination imposed by the doctrine of disinterestedness. But the attempt of such criticism to valorize work like Millay's continues to run up against a stubborn appeal to the universal subject. Questions of gender emerge in such a rhetoric as partial, political, interested contingencies. The woman is the marked sex; if we admire Edna St. Vincent Millay as a woman poet, the rhetoric of universality makes it appear that only the woman poet has a gender, to say nothing of a body. Only a woman's poetry has this doubleness of gender and art; only a woman's poetry supplements art with this excess, an unseemly and suggestive sexuality. A woman's poetry violates aesthetic decorum to the extent that it attracts attention to her different sensibility. But this very attention to difference, this violation of a universal aesthetic, is precisely the point of feminist criticism.

This attention to difference was already in Millay's poetics. Millay's allegorizing dramatized the gendering of the imaginative desire that configures beauty, love, and death. Thus, she violated the repression denying the gendering of the aesthetic, the historical production of an aesthetic double bind. Coleridge once argued that the allegory was inferior art, since he conceived of the poem as a "unity in multeity," a self-enclosed system, autotelic. But that is a closure that would guard against the unmaking of subjects, while the allegorical impulse opens itself to external debate. Aesthetic autonomy works against open structures and the narrative impulse.

Millay violated an aesthetic that claimed universality as it struggled to dominate the politics of literary history. In the 1930s, the drive of formalist critics to establish a timeless foundation for modernist poetics had narrowed the field considerably, cutting down whatever work—black, proletarian, feminist—could not be reduced to formal universalism. Allen Tate, one of the poets of the Eliot school who became part of the formalist New Criticism, attacked the troubling presence of Millay, admitting that she was important in the history of radical change but claiming that her generation was past:

> Miss Millay is ... the spokesman of a generation. It does not behoove us to enquire how she came to express the feelings of the literary generation that seized the popular imagination from about

1917 to 1925. It is a fact that she did, and in such a way as to remain as its most typical poet. Her talent, with its diverting mixture of solemnity and levity, won the enthusiasm of a time bewildered intellectually and moving unsteadily towards an emotional attitude of its own. It was the age of The Seven Arts, of the old Masses, of the Provincetown Theatre, of the figure and disciples of Randolph Bourne. It has been called the age of experiment and liberation; there is still experiment, but no one is liberated; and that age is now dead. (335)

This characterization suggests how Millay is connected to a certain activism that Tate wants to separate from the literary tradition and declare a failure.

For the definition of their allegedly nonpolitical aesthetic, formalist critics like John Crowe Ransom reached back to Kant, to his characterization of the aesthetic as a "purposiveness without purpose" and the work of art as an autonomous object, an ontology. Art was distinctly different from everything else and especially from the language that connected it to matters of personal pleasure and taste or to personal qualities like sexuality, class, and race. Millay posed a formidable threat to this project. She was a powerful, well-regarded poet who had a reputation for wit and for bringing together erudition and the popular, but most of all, she did not keep either gender or sexuality out of her poems. She violated poetic impersonality by her figures of the personal. She threatened to blow open the whole cover-up operation that had quietly obscured and lost the telling connection between gender and the rise of the aesthetic manifested in Kant and claiming modernism as its own. In my earlier work on John Crowe Ransom "Poet as Woman," I read his attack on Millay as a blatant and outrageous example of the mostly hidden sexism in modernist poetics. On second thought, however, I am inclined to think that Ransom's essay represents something less individualized, an important and dangerous turn, a moment when—thanks to Millay—the figure of woman as poet had emerged into consciousness and the old Kantian ghost has to be invoked to reinforce not only the repression of gendering but the authority of a poetic hierarchy, to repress woman and the power of poetry together.

What Ransom did was to resurrect the old categories of the sensible and the intelligible and associate Millay with the sensible, a concept haunted by the feminine, where, as woman, she would naturally belong. If he could do this to Millay, he could silence the woman in women's poetry with the spectral gendering of philosophy's past. Though he does not say so, the position he names for himself would ally him not only with the intelligible, but with the sublime. That is, Ransom is conjuring up the ideology of the aesthetic, now become a kind of political unconscious. The ideology of the aesthetic, as

Terry Eagleton traces its course, began to coalesce in the eighteenth century together with the rise of the middle class and a set of cultural institutions that could seem invisible and ungendered as they regulated the body and desire.

In the eighteenth century, Edmund Burke constructed the conservative position around the responsiveness of the body: the beautiful is pleasing and the sublime is painful; the attractiveness of women is connected to the beautiful, to love, to being the object of desire. The capacity to endure the stronger passions of terror is dependent on reason, of course characteristic of men, and sublime. Even though Burke asserts a Lockean universality to the experience of the senses, and so to the basis for taste, the sublime goes beyond the senses, calling on the resources of reason to gain distance from the terror of death.

At first, Immanuel Kant, in his 1764 "Observations on the Feeling of the Beautiful and Sublime," kept the sublime aesthetic embedded in explicitly drawn categories of gender and class: women were identified with the beautiful, men with the sublime. However, by the time he wrote *Critique of Judgment* in 1790 after *Critique of Pure Reason* and following the direction established there, he would define the aesthetic as independent of interest, a disinterested and universal subjective judgment. That does not mean the gendering of the hierarchy vanishes, however; it is simply mystified. The beautiful is inferior to the sublime, and the beautiful remains feminine while the sublime is masculine. In the section called "Of the Distinction of the Beautiful and Sublime in the Interrelations of the Two Sexes," from the "Observations," Kant sets up the binary that Ransom seems to evoke to place Millay as a woman. It is important to see how here Immanuel Kant, later that very avatar of disinterestedness, sounds like Edmund Burke speaking: "Women have a strong inborn feeling for all that is beautiful, elegant, and decorated. Even in childhood they like to be dressed up, and take pleasure when they are adorned" (395). This characterization of the sexes goes on at some length, concluding that women "contain the chief cause in human nature for the contrast of the beautiful qualities with the noble, and they refine even the masculine sex":

> The fair sex has just as much understanding as the male, but it is a *beautiful understanding*, whereas ours should be a *deep understanding*, an expression that signifies identity with the sublime. . . .
> Laborious learning or painful pondering, even if a woman should greatly succeed in it, destroys the merits that are proper to her sex, and because of their rarity they can make of her an object of cold admiration; but at the same time they will weaken the charms with which she exercises her great power over the other sex. A woman who has a head full of Greek . . . or carries

on fundamental controversies about mechanics . . . might as well even have a beard. . . . (395)

In the later *Critique of Judgment*, Kant characterizes women as part of the sensible, the domain of the beautiful, but makes clear that the masculine sublime operates in a superior way as a kind of reverberation between the sensible and the intelligible—the sublime calls up the reason before the limitations of imagination. Thus, a disinterested aesthetic will by that very reverberation of the sublime legislate a gendered hierarchy of aesthetic value.

In Kant, and in the aesthetic history that follows, we do not have a simple gendering of cultural institutions with art and beauty identified with the woman while the culture of reason, science, and technology is for the man. Rather, within the aesthetic there may be a hierarchy of the beautiful and the sublime that also asserts the superiority of the masculine. If Millay challenges modernist aesthetics, she also threatens this pervasive cultural hierarchy. This is what Ransom reasserts when he writes "The Poet as Woman." Ransom is drawing on the ghostly authority of Kant here, echoing his language, relegating Millay to the "beautiful" and excluding her from the "sublime":

Man distinguishes himself from woman by intellect, but it should be well feminized. He knows he should not abandon sensibility and tenderness . . . but now that he is so far removed from the world of the simple senses, he does not like to impeach his own integrity and leave his business in order to recover it; going back, as he is often directed, to first objects, the true and tried, like the moon, or the grass, or the dead girl. (784)

Ransom was, if you read between the lines, acknowledging the danger, from his point of view, that readers were, in fact, taking the poet-as-woman seriously, the danger of sensibility as the threat of Millay. But his words suggest threat as well, that if he is directed to go back, the dead girl is the body he will discover.

What Ransom says he cannot quite find significant is a set of commonplaces that suggest not just the sentimental or the sensible but the space of female melancholy: the moon, the grass, the dead girl. Even though the dead girl is not actually so common a theme in Millay, there is a complex of love and grief that she does address. Feminist critics such as Leslie Rabine, writing about the romance, and Catherine Clément, writing about the melodrama of opera, have thought about what all those deaths of women in literature might mean. Rabine suggests that the principle of identity governing discourse since the Renaissance, what Kristeva calls the "ideologeme of the sign," has demanded that difference be erased, under the assertion of a single, governing meaning, the logic feminist critics have discussed as logocentrism. If Millay's poetry refuses to subscribe to such a principle of identity, partly by reaching back to historical literary strategies that did not assume such a logic, we know how difficult a refusal that might be. Clément concludes that the melodramatic scripts of opera continuously reassert patriarchal power but that the sound of the music does something else, transporting us bodily to another order entirely. The women in the operas die, but the music lives. What is Millay doing with her allegorizing and her musicalizing of the melancholy that so threatened Ransom (and that our male colleagues remember)?

Is she not giving us again and again the loss by which we enter into language, separating ourselves from a maternal boundlessness and taking up—as if entering into a masquerade—an identity, the subjectivity bound first by the image of the other and then by words? If I use Julia Kristeva's study, in *Black Sun*, of the connection between melancholy and the acquisition of language, I find a story that seems also to be told by Millay. Again and again she remembers the sensation of claustrophobic dependency and terrible loss, the rebirth into a separate speaking subject; again and again her readers retrace the temptation to refuse inevitable separation and refuse the moment when words replace absence with the conflict of meaning/not meaning. It is, in this story, a position of danger: a threat of death if the girl does not succeed in integrating loss into language.

Ransom most particularly gestures toward the scene of the dead girl. Is this really because Millay is too much involved with sensibility and not with intelligibility? Or because he does not want to imagine the fate of those whom language wastes in order to make meaning? What, for example, of the woman who does not fit into the story—or perhaps I should say the economy—of marriage and heterosexual love? Millay attacks that plot in particular, not only by stories of death but by taunts and barbs. Doing so, she challenges the very domain of the beautiful, set as it was in the private sphere, in the scenario of domesticity that I think Ransom is at pains to keep intact.

How does the dead girl come to be a tried and true commonplace? What interests Millay about dying for love is how the mundane detail intervenes, how female extremity seems ironically nothing more than a breach in decorum. In "The Pond," for example, "a farmer's daughter, / Jilted by her farmer beau" had fifty years ago drowned herself in a pond near the public highway. The juxtaposition of "farmer" and "beau" already gives us Millay's specific irony, the perspective by incongruity through which she sees, on the one hand, the romantic story of beauty and beau that alone seems to justify the jilted girl's hidden desperation, and on the other, the vernacular placidity of the pond, the farming life, and the wheels passing on the road. The poem's question asks us to imagine the way these two separate domains might be joined in the girl, setting up a terrible irony by the contrasting insignificance of the gesture that defines both her interaction with the public and the deadliness of her private grief:

> Can you not conceive the sly way,—
>   Hearing wheels or seeing men
>
> Passing on the road above,—
>   With a gesture feigned and silly
> Ere she drowned herself for love,
>   She would reach to pluck a lily?

What interests Millay is the "feigned and silly" gesture with which the girl might dissimulate her extremity. What interests Julia Kristeva is to restore our recognition of how extreme the death-in-life of female depression might be. What interests John Crowe Ransom is to assert that woman's melancholy is no more than sensibility, no more than the gesture of plucking the lily, perhaps.

Millay's poems designate a kind of maternal temporality that at once evokes longing and loss and yet also the irony of reproduction for its own sake, reproduction without progress. This storytelling about the personifications of Beauty, Death, and Love is precisely *not* the making-it-new narrative authorized by a modernism that would function as an avant-garde. Take, for example, Millay's "Spring" from *Second April*. In a period when the opening of T. S. Eliot's *Waste Land*, "April is the cruelest month," reverberated everywhere, Millay refuses to take a part in the debate about pessimistic or optimistic attitudes to history (as did, for example, Hart Crane). Instead, she moves the argument out of linear and into monumental time, hinting that the redemptive force of beauty arises ironically, precisely out of its signifying nothing: "To what purpose, April, do you return again? / Beauty is not enough." The force of Beauty's repetition is what I call maternal irony. The eternal return of life is the mortal body's great joke—and its consolation.

"Beauty is not enough" even though it is the symptom of resurrection: "It is apparent that there is no death." Rewriting the iconography of melancholy, Millay gives us an April like Ophelia who enters the stage "like an idiot, babbling and strewing flowers," but playing in something that is not a tragedy, not *Oedipus*, not *Hamlet*, a story in which death is not what provides the horizon of meaning for life. Millay's wit keeps the speaker of this poem located in a doubled space, where the idea that "Beauty is not enough" is both true and ironic. The concrete energy of April's vocabulary invades the discourse of melancholy—"Life in itself / Is nothing"—and makes the speaker appear a kind of Jacques, overtaken by the babbling and the comic as well.

Through personification, Millay again and again dramatizes a relationship of speaker and other that unsettles both subjects of the rhetorical situation: "For I am Nightmare: where I fly, / Terror and rain stand in the sky," she writes in "Some Things Are Dark"; "Desolation dreamed of, though not accomplished, / Set my heart to rocking like a boat in a swell" ("Desolation Dreamed Of"); "Time, doing this to me, may alter too / My anguish, into something I can bear" ("Sonnet"). Does she resurrect the old understanding that art addresses love and the death of love? If "Beauty is not enough," it is nevertheless more than a tale told by an idiot, signifying nothing—or that, signifying nothing, the poem nevertheless enacts a gesture that seizes the day. The poem remembers feeling, which is both female and public, impossible fantasy. This necessarily plunges Millay into the narrative space explored by women novelists where the question of affirming a kind of masculine power of symbol making is always at issue, where identities are imaginary, a work in progress. This narrative space contains the melancholy threat of emptiness and death. Nonetheless, literature offers the aesthetic pleasure of affirmation. If "Beauty is not enough," nevertheless poetry can seize the day, offering the transient but repeated pleasure of imaging experience, inscribing even the self imagining death into the public, imaginary realm.

Ransom invokes the sensible and the intelligible as qualities of gendered subjects, but Millay's ceaseless translation of subjectivity into narrative figure undermines his assertions of value as well as gender. Millay does not simply represent the value of the poet as woman, for where may the woman in the poem speak? Rather, her work shows us how a reversal of the Kantian categories also undoes their universality. The reception of her work suggests much about the operations of the modern aesthetic: how her poems replicate the way ideology dramatizes the subject and how well defended the institution of art is against admitting its politics.

If Millay's poems do not, for the most part, serve an avant-garde project of formal innovation, it is perhaps because they are involved in flagrant violation of another kind, apparently so threatening that critics such as Tate and Ransom had simply to deny the significance of what she was doing. Invoking the long history of love poetry, speaking uncannily with the voices of dead male poets, Millay writes about sexuality without the Freudian norm of reproduction and marriage. Her poems give us love, but it is before identity has been situated within heterosexual norms—not always homoerotic, but always provoking the limits of decorum. Love poetry has never really served the formulas of bourgeois marriage, which wants to install a respectable and stable private domain. Millay reminds us of this incompatibility. She has the shape of a love affair as a repeated cycle, from beginning to inevitable end. The point of rapture is not stability but a memorable break in time. This has some relationship to the nature of poetry. A number of her wittiest poems rework the *carpe diem* theme so that the discourse of the seducer and the poet are both intertwined with her female sensibility. *Fatal Interview* gives us the sonnet sequence and the love story as a dazzling tour de force of poetic reminiscence. In two sonnets, she takes up Ronsard's sonnet to Helen, the old favorite memorized by every child in French schools, which begins: "Quand vous serez bien vieille, au soir à la chandelle" ("When you are old, of an evening by candlelight"). Ronsard goes on to predict that you will marvel, singing his verses, that he celebrated you when you were young and beautiful: you will be old, bent over, regretting your disdain for love. Therefore, as the argument goes, "Cueillez dès aujourd'hui les roses de la vie" (line 14); gather the roses today. Yeats tried his hand at the same poem. He began, "When you are old and gray and full of sleep, / And nodding by the fire, take down this book," and concluded predicting that you will

> Murmur, a little sadly, how Love fled
> And paced upon the mountains overhead
> And hid his face amid a crowd of stars.

Yeats and Millay both diverge from Ronsard after taking the opening lines, with their resonance and their appeal to the remembrance evoked by poetry. Yeats, instead of noting how the poet marks his love with enduring fame, marks with irony the poet's changed relationship to the logic of *carpe diem*, his retreat to the heights. Millay re-marks the triumph of eros—with a flippant couplet asserting the lovers' rapture as solace for the passing of time. She begins with the appeal Ronsard makes to the passing of time: "When we are old and these rejoicing veins / Are frosty channels to a muted stream" (XXVIII). The argument concludes with a punning flippancy: "Be not discountenanced if the knowing know / We rose from rapture but an hour ago." Here the *carpe diem* rhetoric serves pleasure, but it also suggests a very modern defiance of propriety. The sexuality connoted by the Renaissance meaning of "knowing" resists the social intercourse of gossip, what the "knowing know." Is this gendered? In one sense, not. The lovers are "we"; the lover addressed could be a man or a woman; the speaker could be a man or a woman. The lover who speaks with the voice of the tradition is male. The more strongly we as readers insist on keeping the female poet in mind, as does Ransom, the more uncanny this male doubling becomes.

Later, another sonnet recalls the Ronsard poem, together with its conclusion: the memory of the poet's love must be a later source of pride. In this poem, Millay's debt is evident and her revision richly subtle. The poem begins: "If in the years to come you should recall, / When faint at heart or fallen on hungry days" (LI). Like Ronsard (who wrote the sonnet in later years), she imagines her love's power through poetry surviving her own death. Ronsard says: "I will be under the earth and a phantom without bones" (line 8). Millay proposes:

> Might not my love—although the curving blade
> From whose wide mowing none may hope to hide,
> Me long ago below the frosts had laid—
> Restore you somewhat to your former pride?

Whereas Ronsard's poem is a kind of open vaunting—"Ronsard celebrated me"—Millay's enacts a more modest recovery: "Indeed I think this memory, even then, / Must raise you high among the run of men." Nevertheless, the claim is there—and because the sonnet doubles Ronsard, it shadows forth this larger claim from the history of poetry, that Millay's poetry too will make memory powerful. The seductive moral of the *carpe diem* drops away and the implication of "seize the day" is associated not with the moment's sexual pleasure but with the celebration of the poet's victory over death. And here the beloved is clearly gendered ("among the run of men"). Though this does not even so imply that the poet is female, when the reader identifies the persona with a female poet, the claim itself is defamiliarized—the poet's vaunting persona becomes metaphorical, figurative, personification—part of a larger argument about love and poetry.

This poem, sonnet LI, is the next to final poem in *Fatal Interview*. The final poem, "Oh, sleep forever in the Latmian cave," inserts the sequence into the time of immortals. There is no shrinking from the role of the poet here. It is not love that endures but memory, the chain of remembrance uncannily evoked by poetic language. Did Millay understand the risk she was taking, not resisting but rather inviting the language of past poems to take her over? When it is a question of imaginary identity, can a woman enter into male speech?

This is a question about how ideology works to call up subjects in our culture. It is a question that involves not only psychic but also cultural history. Was there a place for the feminist new woman to enter into literature as a woman poet in the 1920s? In the 1950s? What about now? Is there any way to make a place except by writing? What we can clearly see, in retrospect, is how Millay was able to seize the day for a brief while in the 1920s, in a time of historical crisis, and how much of the ground she took was soon retaken by the counter-revolutionary New Critics. We can see that the question of the imaginary identity is a matter for public and political struggle. The double sense of strangeness and familiarity that marks the uncanny should alert us to the struggle over the terrain of the subject taking place in Millay's poetry.

The uncanny in Millay is a public unconscious, and it is bodied forth as the reader takes up the song. In her words, poetry speaks again, with an uncanny resonance precisely because it was a male tradition that would exclude it. Such speech is a kind of activism, a feminism on her part. Something returns not as remembrance but as the enactment of the empathy made possible by imaginary identifications. The death of the woman and the end of love haunt Millay's poetry, and yet she presses the reader past melancholy to the active engagement with text—and other. Does she write a poetry that expresses the kind of sensibility John Crowe Ransom is talking about? No. The melancholy scenario evoked by his list of "first objects"—the moon, the grass, the dead girl—suggests a kind of stasis that her theatrical presentation unsettles. She is not fixed in the attitudes of gender. Hers is neither cry nor epitaph. She seems quite conscious of the political ramifications of her work. She knows that she is writing in a style that is public and that violates the sequestering of the artist. She writes from the left, as a new woman, as a friend of Emma Goldman and Lola Ridge as well as Floyd Dell and Edmund Wilson. She writes as her independent mother's daughter and as the inheritor of feminist Inez Milholland's task. When she was in college, she and her friends greatly admired Milholland. Later, after Milholland's death, she became the second wife of Milholland's husband.

What do we do in memory of the women who came before us, whose places we uncannily occupy, whose work we hope to commemorate? In her sonnet to Inez Milholland, Millay acknowledges the limits of commemoration: "Upon this marble bust that is not I / Lay the round, formal wreath that is not fame." She tells us that the place of the female subject is empty: "I, that was proud and valiant, am no more;—/ Save as a dream that wanders wide and late."[5] And she proposes the remedy: "Take up the song; forget the epitaph."

Notes

1. This discussion of the difference between ordinary language and poetic language appeared in both Anglo-American and continental criticism. I. A. Richards and Philip Wheelwright both proposed a differentiation of conventional language from the figurative, mythical poetic language, a distinction that owed much to Coleridge's distinctions between fancy and imagination. The Russian formalists and the Prague school linguists developed a more theoretically rigorous analysis of poetic language around the function of defamiliarization. Millay's forms clearly fail to operate like modernist experiments, defamiliarizing at the level of the sentence. However, what I am arguing is that Millay makes the position of the lyric subject

strange, and that she therefore does not reinscribe the aesthetic distinction between literature and the personal.

2. I discuss Millay's relationship to sensibility, the sentimental, and middle-brow aesthetics at some length in *Sentimental Modernism*.

3. Julia Kristeva provides an especially helpful theorizing of the interaction of culture and individual through language. Her terms, the *semiotic* and the *symbolic*, point to the dialectic of body and law, the personal and the public, which underlies any subject at a moment of speech. See, in particular, *Revolution* and "Speaking Subject." This question of the subject has, of course, provided one of the central debates in literary theory in the last decade, with theorists from Althusser and Foucault (rewriting the Marxist concept of ideology as discursive formations) to Derrida to Lacan, together with feminists from Gilbert and Gubar to Butler, agreeing only that the individual is not the origin of individual identity. See, for example, Cadava, Connor, and Nancy, *Who Comes after the Subject?*

4. For a discussion of how the uncanny functions as a textual doubling, and not as a "real" referent, see Gardner Lloyd-Smith, *Uncanny American Fiction*.

5. The poem goes on: "Save as a wind that rattles the stout door, / Troubling the ashes in the sheltered grate. / The stone will perish; I shall be twice dust." At the Friday evening meeting of the Millay centennial conference, when we all gathered in the Surrey, Skidmore's Victorian mansion, to hear Nancy Milford read the last chapter of her biography of Millay, lights flickered, there were noises in the fireplace, and we heard a rustling at the open door behind her. Some said, "That was Norma." Others reminded us that the Surrey was said to be haunted. The next day, when I read this paper, its topic and its title seemed indeed twice "uncanny."

MARTIN HEUSSER

So Many Selves:
The "I" as Indeterminate Multiplicity

Naming the Unnameable

The following poem (CP 609), published as number 11 in the 1950 collection *XAIPE,* is one of the rare instances where Cummings explicitly accounts for the structure of the self in a poem. The self that we find here is introduced not so much as a disintegrated self, a self that never appears as a whole, but rather as an arrangement of constantly changing multiple selves:[1]

so many selves(so many fiends and gods
each greedier than every)is a man
(so easily one in another hides;
yet man can,being all,escape from none)

so huge a tumult is the simplest wish:
so pitiless a massacre the hope
most innocent(so deep's the mind of flesh
and so awake what waking calls asleep)

so never is most lonely man alone
(his briefest breathing lives some planet's year,
his longest life's a heartbeat of some sun;
his least unmotion roams the youngest star)

> –how should a fool that calls him "I" presume
> to comprehend not numerable whom?

"[E]veryone is born with a they in his we," declares Cumnnings in his Houghton notes, and the opening lines of the present poem substantiate this claim.[2]
A man consists of "so many selves" rather than one single self. These selves
are radically heterogeneous (consisting of "fiends" as well as "gods") and still
perfectly indistinguishable on account of their protean nature: "so easily one
in another hides" that they completely elude description. As they coexist in a
relation to each other that lacks any perceptible pattern, structure or hierarchy,
the self is in a state of perpetual anarchy. In a synecdochical way "hopes" and
"wishes"—for Cummings basic expressions of humanness and subjectivity as
well as signs of the presence of an individual—are likened to "tumults" and
"massacres." Unreasonable, devoid of any order and sensible purpose, they are
presented as chaotic multitudes subject to constant change.[3]

While all of this smacks of Nietzsche's *Nachlass* writings, Cummings'
strong emphasis on the multiplicity of selfhood also brings to mind David
Hume's notions of the "I." In the *Treatise of Human Nature* Hume argues that
it is fundamentally impossible for us to attain any idea of the self. For an idea
to rise, he argues, there must be a single, invariable impression—and that is
precisely what the self does not yield:

> Pain and pleasure, grief and joy, passions and sensations succeed
> each other, and never all exist at the same time. It cannot be, there-
> fore, from any of these impressions, or from any other, that the idea
> of self is deriv'd; and consequently there is no such idea. (*A Treatise
> of Human Nature* 1, 533)

Hume is unable to identify a self abstracted from the train of his emotions
and impressions. He explicitly repudiates the idea of the single, indivisible
self since there is "not any one impression" but rather an endless succession
of impressions:

> For my part, when I enter most intimately into what I call *myself*,
> I always stumble on some particular perception or other, of heat
> or cold, light or shade, love or hatred, pain or pleasure. I never
> can catch *myself* at any time without a perception, and never can
> observe any thing but the perception. (*Treatise* 1, 534)

Hume remarks ironically that "some metaphysicians" might perceive something within themselves which they are tempted to call the self. The rest

of mankind, however, he continues, "are nothing but a bundle or collection of different perceptions, which succeed each other with an inconceivable rapidity, and are in a perpetual flux and movement" (534). Hume claims that the notion of the "self" is—as that of "soul" and "substance"—nothing but a feint of the mind. To be exact, of course, what follows from his argument is not that there *is* no self but that we cannot *know* whether there is one and that the claim of its unity cannot be substantiated. The consequences are shattering nevertheless in that we can neither be at every moment intimately conscious of our self nor feel its continuation in existence.

While "so many selves" suggests an inherent kinship between Cummings' and Hume's (and Nietzsche's) notion of selfhood, it is clear that there is a basic difference between the two attitudes. Most importantly, Cummings is not a skeptic. He is not another in a long list of philosophers and artists who *deny* the existence of a substantial, single and indivisible self. Cummings writes in order to *find* the self, to get hold of it, to presence it. The problem is, however, that, despite his efforts, he does not succeed. As a result, we always find in his writing both the metaphysical as well as the Nietzschean self. Although Cummings continually fails in his attempts to produce the "i"—most manifestly in *i:six nonlectures*—, he does not simply replace the metaphysical notion of the self with a Nietzschean concept. Rather than reverting the traditional hierarchy by substituting e. g. multiplicity for unity, his notion of the self is constantly kept in a precarious balance between the *two* vanishing points. The question whether the self is a closed off totality or an open-ended, unlimited and illimitable entity is forever suspended in undecidability.

This does not mean that Cummings resigns in the teeth of adversity. To escape the impasse he uses his language, that is, his poetry, as a metaphor of the self. The strong rhetorical dimension in his writing is widely known—what has been neglected so far is its relation to questions of the self. Language itself, its structures and functions are directly involved in the poet's examination of the self. On the surface, or formally, this happens frequently in the guise of linguistic deviation. Cummings' straying from the norm always entails the substantial critique of tacit assumptions about apparently stable parameters or norms such as the "self."[4] In his deviant use of language, the poet brings to light rifts in the most fundamental notions of the "self," "unity" and "substantiality." No other poet makes it quite so clear that the *Ultima Thule* of the exploration of the self is language. And no other American Modernist poet plays so ruthlessly on the notion that the "I" might ultimately be nothing but a sign. To shed some light on the fundamental aspects of Cummings' notion of the self and how they are reflected in his rhetoric, we will now turn once more to "so many selves" for a closer look.

The simultaneous presence of the two competing notions of the self appears in condensed form in the final lines of the fourteen-liner. Since the whole poem consists of three quatrains and a couplet, it is modeled after a Shakespearean sonnet. Consequently, the concluding couplet sums up in epigrammatic manner the resolution of the *argumentum* presented in the preceding twelve lines. The last two lines show that the poet's quest for the self must end in an aporia, and they explain why this is so. Arch cause is his inability to reduce a multiplicity to a unity:

> –how should a fool that calls him "I" presume
> to comprehend not numerable whom?

One detail that easily passes unnoticed is the spelling of the first person singular pronoun. Until the mid-forties (*1 x 1*, 1944) Cummings uses both the standard spelling "I," as well as his own lowercase "i." After *1 x 1* the lowercase spelling prevails dramatically. Among more than 120 occurrences of the first person singular in the last three collections (*XAIPE*, *95 Poems* and *73 Poems*) we find only two uppercase versions, one of them in this poem.[5]

Cummings' choice of the capitalized form "I," in a phase of his writing where the lowercase "i" dominated by far, is highly significant. What is even more interesting in this context is that all the early versions of the poem, without a single exception, whether typescript or manuscript, have a lowercase "i."[6] Why the capital "I" in the published version? As the final couplet puts it, the act of calling a self an "i" and thus reducing an infinite multiplicity (a "not numerable whom") to an artificial unity, is foolish. To use the uppercase spelling (and thus literally capitalizing on an untenable notion) is even more unreasonable. Cummings' conspicuous use of the customary "I" thus forms—in ironical refraction—a salient critique of the traditional notions of the self, as expressed in the orthographic conventions of the English language.[7]

The notion of the unreasonableness of an unreflected use of linguistic conventions is further emphasized by the use of the word "presume." Particularly when used with the infinitive—as in the present example—"presume" means "to engage oneself in, without authority, venture, dare."[8] The mere use of the first person singular with its implied conjecture of a unified self constitutes an unwarranted assumption in Cummings' view. The self cannot be described—let alone presented—with the help of a language that aims to "comprehend," to grasp mentally, an infinite multitude.

When the poet himself is forced to name the unnameable, the "self," he does so by means of the nominalized interrogative pronoun "whom."[9] With this, Cummings' language expresses an attitude of precaution or modesty towards the self. In the light of the limited knowledge one may have of the self, anything other than the use of a question word would be preposterous speculation.[10] It is impossible to move beyond the question "whom do we mean when we refer to the self?" Cummings' deviant use of "whom" is noteworthy, particularly because it is not at all as isolated a phenomenon as it might seem.

There are numerous other passages in the *Complete Poems* where "whom" is used outside linguistic norms. These passages are very helpful points of orientation for the understanding of the word as it appears in "so many selves." Since the deviant use of individual words is a device Cummings employs very frequently, we shall now digress, exemplarily, and in some detail, on the deviant use of "whom." As a survey shows, all non-standard use can be said to fall into two groups. The first group is made up of those cases where the word appears as a relative pronoun with an uncertain, ambiguous or missing relation. The second category, which comprises far fewer poems, consists of those instances where "whom" is used as a noun.[11]

In the present context—that of "not numerable whom"—two passages from the *Complete Poems* are of particular interest. They illustrate how the deviant "whom" keeps appearing as a kind of trace marker for the contradictory and inexplicable nature of the self. One of these occurs in a strangely elliptic sentence, forming the end of CP 527:

> i rise which am
> the sun of whom

These lines offer a definition of the self which they undermine at the very moment they are making it. To begin with, the relative pronoun, "which," does so by occurring in a position where linguistic rules require "who" (after the personal antecedent "i").[12] This violation turns the "i" into a strangely quivering linguistic artifact, one that both is and cannot be the reference to a person. As the continuation of the sentence implies that "which" stands for the "sun," the depersonalization or dehumanization of the self is further intensified. An even more powerful disintegrative impulse stems from the deviant "whom" at the very end of the poem, which is responsible for the failure of the defining relative clause "which am / the sun of whom" to live up to its name. Chained to a hermaphrodite linguistic artifact—half question, half statement—the "i" must remain forever undefined in this poem.[13]

The second noteworthy appearance of "whom" can be found in the final lines of CP 534:

> crumb
> ling eye

```
-holes oUt of whe
reful whom(leas

tly)
smiles the
infinite nothing

of
M

an
```

After a moment of disorientation, we realize that the function of "whom" is most likely that of a relative pronoun. If we follow only its basic outline, the sentence reads "crumbling eyeholes out of whom smiles the infinite nothing of man." Such a reading, however, is severely disturbed and disrupted by typographical factors (line breaks, capitalization, missing space between words), as well as the insertion of two deviant lexical items—the adjective "whereful" and the adverb "leastly." Both the typographical as well as the lexical peculiarities are a strong echo of the violent fragmentation and relentless ellipsis which dominate the entire poem. From these deviations results a shift of emphasis from the whole to the part, which in turn foregrounds the independence of individual sentence parts: sentence boundaries lose their functionality and become irrelevant.

The poem thus invites and sustains readings across sentence borders as well as readings that disregard the totality of a sentence structure and remain confined to specific regions. For the last few lines of the poem this means that "whom" might equally be read as a noun. In this case, the "infinite nothing of man" smiles not only out of the "crumbling eyeholes," but also out of the word "whom." "Whom," the placeholder for "personality" or humanness, is devoid of any content, full of infinite nothing. It is furthermore characterized as "whereful," an adjective which takes up and, reciprocally, intensifies the semantics of absence and loss which are abundant in the immediate environment ("crumbling," "holes," "out"). Cummings frequently uses the suffix "-ful" in unorthodox word formations to denote "full of" or "an unusually high amount or degree."[14] "Whereful" is a coinage which occurs one more time in Cummings' work. In CP 819 we find it with an identical meaning in a similar environment as "my whereful / selves." Ingeniously exploiting the deceptive appearance of the suffix "-ful," with its ring of abundance or even completeness, "whereful" in both cases betokens the lack of identifiable structure or quality as well as the lack of presence.

What we have just observed is an important characteristic of Cummings' vocabulary, as well as a salient feature of his poetics. A large number of words exhibit an improper semantic usage that results in a blurred or obscured meaning. To arrive at a reasonably well-defined semantics, it is in such cases necessary to analyze carefully both the immediate context as well as related passages in which the word appears. As a rule, this involves a series of comparisons which allow the gradual narrowing down of a broad spectrum of semantic alternatives to a meaning that appears acceptable. Significantly, Cummings' semantic manipulations have two diametrically opposed effects. One is that words lose their conventional meaning and become in a way meaningless. Yet this does not mean that they cease to have any meaning whatsoever and that their use is purely arbitrary or random. Cummings only divests the words of their smug alleged definiteness or potential disambiguation and thus thoroughly undermines the unreflected notion of "meaning." His deviant use undercuts continually the tacit assumption that there is a fixed relation between a word and its meaning. He thus constantly refreshes the reader's (and probably his own) awareness of the complex individuality of words' meanings.[15] Although this cannot prevent a certain hypostatization of the Cummingsesque meaning of his key lexica (e. g. "sun," "star," "tree," "alive," "precise," etc.), it is obvious that the contrary is his intention. In order to be poetry, words need to be "alive." And they can only be "alive" in the sense Cummings uses the adjective—as long as they are individuals, as long as they are different from each other, even if they are morphologically identical.[16]

Concomitantly, this semantic variance has another consequence; namely that of allowing the poet to differentiate very finely individual word meanings. The reason for this effect lies in the fact that the immediate environment of a deviantly used word largely determines its meaning. The manipulation of such a word's environment therefore not only allows Cummings to alter its meaning but also lets him tune that meaning very finely according to the requirements of a particular passage. Even so, a strong element of insecurity about the precise meaning of a given word remains. It is in particular the key-words in Cummings' writing that are never translucent, and their usage inevitably forms at best an asymptote to their meaning. That it is often impossible to arrive at a satisfactory semantics for such terms has been a major source of critical irritation in the past.[17]

The passage from which we started out, "–how should a fool that calls him "I" presume / to comprehend not numerable whom?" gradually begins to yield up its considerable complexity. Rather than representing a momentary linguistic caprice of the author, "whom" is seen to illustrate essential qualities of the self as Cummings understands it. In either form, as a nominalized interrogative pronoun or as a relative pronoun, it plays on its own lack of specificity. In the former case, it is forged into a question whose object will never be known, in the latter, it futilely points at the ever-absent point of reference. How far "the fool that calls him 'I'" is from denoting and thus reaching the self is epitomized by the ungrammatical use of "him" instead of "himself." The absence of the "-self" illustrates morphologically (and thus iconically) the failure of the "I" to represent the self properly.

The Self as Part *and* Whole

It is only in the Houghton notes to this poem, however, that the full extent of Cummings' careful—if not anxious—attention to the linguistic representation of the self can be observed. On six sheets we find half a dozen different versions of "so many selves" together with more than three times as many variants of the couplet.[18] The latter are of particular interest here, because they form the logical conclusion, the *sequitur*, of the entire poem. Although the changes between the various versions are only minor, their number testifies to Cummings' alert awareness of the intricacies involved. Nearly all the modifications concern the definition or representation of the "i," placing particular emphasis either on infinity or multiplicity as its essential property. Epithets like "multitudinous," "illimitable" and "infinite" abound. What is especially remarkable about the different versions of the final couplet is their consistent reference to an illogical interference of the notion of the subject as multiplicity with the notion of the self as unity. The "self" of the last two lines leads an alogical double-existence as both *part* and *whole*. While in the final version this interference is barely perceptible in the oblique opposition between the "I" and the "not numerable whom," it is distinctly manifest in the Houghton notes as the following examples show:

> how shall any atom of an i presume
> to understand illimitable him

> —shall of him one(called i)atom presume
> to comprehend illimitable whom?

Both of these final couplets create the same fundamental logical inconsistency: the "entity" that undertakes the exploration of the self is characterized as merely a part of the whole it strives to comprehend. The "atom of an i" in the first version attempts to understand a self—referred to as "illimitable him"—of which it is but a small particle. The same basic constellation occurs again *mutatis mutandis* in the second example. Of course, this notion runs counter to the basic principles of Aristotelian (and with that of Western) logics which state that any entity is indivisibly equal to itself. A cannot be A and at the same time only part of A. In the face of this breach of logic, Cummings characterizes the self as being simultaneously *part* as well as *whole*. Helen Vendler is, thus, correct when she claims in her comments on the *Complete Poems* that there is "[s]omething . . . wrong with the relation of parts to wholes in cummings."[19]

There arises a strange tension between a sort of broad meaning that can be attributed to the couplets (the two unpublished ones as well as the one which appears in the final version) with relative ease and the way in which this meaning fails to appear stably in their constitutive elements.[20] Grossly simplified, the couplets form a rhetorical question whose answer is negative. A human "subject," they suggest, can—owing to its nature—never hope to understand itself. Interpretively, this is about as far as one gets without much hindrance. Yet as soon as one attempts to be more faithful to Cummings' wording, considerable difficulties arise. Because of the fundamental illogicality of the sentence, it is almost impossible to even paraphrase the couplets. Does Cummings implicitly compare the perspective of the human mind to, say, that of an atom and thus attribute our inability to comprehend ourselves to our diminutive nature? Or does he use the atom as an emblem of the partial, the infinitely fragmented? Is it therefore impossible for us to know ourselves because we are always hopelessly incomplete?

Another look at the two unpublished versions of the couplet shows not only that the relation between *part* and *whole is* elusive but that these categories themselves are ill-defined and thus highly unstable. Are "i" and "him" of the first example the same? Do they both refer to the *whole*? Are "him" and "whom" of the second example identical? Do they refer equally to the *whole*? Are not the "illimitable him" of the first example and the "illimitable whom" of the second more complete *wholes* than the "i" and the "him" respectively? Are perhaps the former the theoretical ideal, the model, while the latter remain actual but imperfect manifestations?[21] These questions force themselves upon the reader; they must be asked in view of the overt semantic differences between the various signs representing the self. The grammatically deviant use of "him" and "whom" in the second lines of the couplets produces a significant residual difference in meaning which prevents their equation with the "i" or "him" of the respective first lines of the couplets. But however differentiated an analysis may be, the text does not yield an unequivocal answer. Thus, the final lines are a linguistic echo of the overt claim the poem made at the beginning. The "I" consists of countless selves each of which "so easily . . . in another hides" that they can never be told apart.

Similarly, the term "atom" in the present context creates discomfiture rather than explanatory illustration. As it is used in the two couplets, "atom" suggests fragmentation, multiplicity, as well as incompleteness.[22] At the same time, however, an atom denotes a smallest indivisible (=άτομος) unity and as such represents the arch emblem of unity. Once more, multiplicity and unity, *whole* and *part* are sent into an unstillable oscillation.

The more thoroughly and carefully one tries to analyze these passages, the more difficulties arise. Instead of offering clarification on Cummings' understanding of the self, these notes take us only onto more labyrinthine tracks. It becomes clear that with increasing attention to detail, the distinction between *whole* and *part is* increasingly blurred, until the two can no longer be told apart. In an intricate moiré pattern, the self oscillates unstably between part and whole. That the "i" in the first example stands for the *whole* and in the second represents the *part* is neither whim nor negligence, but rather the expression of the illogical nature of the "i" according to Cummings. The "i" is as much *part* as it is *whole*.

There are two further subtle mechanisms on the language level which I would like to single out for consideration. Both of them form parallels with the linguistic structure of all variants of the final couplet and the meaning they convey. Firstly, the syntax of the sentences reflects iconically the condition of the "self": the object of the sentence is the object of the poet's quest. Syntactically, the "self" is—whether in the form of "illimitable him," "illimitable whom," or, as in the final version, of "not numerable whom"—the object of a sentence. All variants related to this version of the final couplet posit the self as an object of the desire to "understand" or "comprehend."[23] As a side effect of the linguistic requirements of this syntactical structure (i. e. of the presence of a subject and an object) a duplication of the self takes place. In accordance with the precondition for the cognitive act, the self, trying to understand itself, splits into two, turns from a subject into an object, and is subject and object at the same time.

Secondly, "him" and "whom," the objects of the sentences, are nominalizations, i. e. they are a personal pronoun and a question particle converted into a noun. That nominalization or substantiation of the words used to represent the self is a linguistic reflection of the poet's efforts at reifying that self, his attempt to make the self graspable, reachable and, ultimately, describable.[24] Yet the nominalization of the object of his quest is only partially successful. Morphologically, neither "him" nor "whom" are altered in any way. The nominalization is a purely functional effect on the syntax level; the original words remain the same. As a result, the object of the sentence leads a double life: it is and is not a noun, it is and is not a nominalization. The same unstillable oscillation is imparted to the self as the object of the poet's investigation, and so it, too, partakes of both lack of substance and substantiation. What is particularly interesting about the nominalization is that it is caused solely by the insertion of the adjectival epithets "illimitable" and (in the final version) "not numerable." It is the addition of the quality of *infinite multiplicity* that brings about the transition to the substantive. This has significant consequences for the definition of the self implied in the couplet. It is intimated that multiplicity is a basic requirement without which the self cannot exist "substantively." The evidence for the claim that self and multiplicity are linked with each other inseparably is situated on a linguistic level.

Unity Behind Multiplicity

In our investigation of "so many selves" we have so far been concerned primarily with those strong undercurrents in Cummings' language which hollow out the notion of the self as a unity. The self—tacitly connoted with unity, indivisibility—is seen as made up of an indeterminate multiplicity.

It is now interesting to see that another poem which seems to aim at precisely the same goal arrives at a surprisingly different result. In the process of establishing the self's multiplicity, this poem simultaneously creates a strong connotation of underlying unity. As in Nietzsche's *Zarathustra,* the notion of totality forces its way in with Cummings precisely at a moment when it is explicitly denied. The poem I have in mind is the early satirical "here is little Effie's head" (CP 117):

> here is little Effie's head
> whose brains are made of gingerbread
> when the judgment day comes
> God will find six crumbs
>
> stooping by the coffinlid
> waiting for something to rise
> as the other somethings did–
> you imagine His surprise
>
> bellowing through the general noise
> Where is Effie who was dead?
> –to God in a tiny voice,
> i am may the first crumb said
>
> whereupon its fellow five
> crumbs chuckled as if they were alive
> and number two took up the song,
> might i'm called and did no wrong

cried the third crumb, i am should
and this is my little sister could
with our big brother who is would
don't punish us for we were good;

and the last crumb with some shame
whispered unto God, my name
is must and with the others i've
been Effie who isn't alive

just imagine it I say
God amid a monstrous din
watch your step and follow me
stooping by Effie's little, in

(want a match or can you see?)
which the six subjunctive crumbs
twitch like mutilated thumbs:
picture His peering biggest whey

coloured face on which a frown
puzzles, but I know the way—
(nervously Whose eyes approve
the blessed while His ears are crammed

with the strenuous music of
the innumerable capering damned)
—staring wildly up and down
the here we are now judgment day

cross the threshold have no dread
lift the sheet back in this way
here is little Effie's head
whose brains are made of gingerbread

Primarily, the poem denounces the timid protagonist's violation of what
Cummings considers to be life's basic law, that one must live a life of actu-
ality rather than one of potentiality. With this, it also seriously questions
the standards of a puzzled, whey-faced God who grants life everlasting to a
human soul that was in the poet's eye "merely unalive."[25] What is of more
immediate interest in the present context, however, is the nature of Effie's

self. Effie, the timid "unalive" soul, is composed of "six subjunctive crumbs," helplessly divided, insubstantial. Yet around this notion of a disintegrated self there flutters a dimly visible self, a self that claims to be an integral whole, a totality. For one thing, the covert totality forces its way in through Cummings' vocabulary. The word "crumbs" that is used to describe the individual sub-selves suggests a totality as a vanishing point: the crumbs were once part of a whole. A crumb is a small piece, broken or fallen from cake, bread, or other baked products. The loaf of which the crumbs might be part remains unmentioned, however, the entirety is inscrutable and cannot be presenced, not even on Judgement Day. The crumbs speak each for themselves or for the other crumbs; at best they speak *for Effie*. But Effie as a *subject* never speaks herself. She has no voice. There is no Effie *qua* Effie: "my name / is must" whispers the last of the crumbs into God's ear "and with the others i've / been Effie who isn't alive."

Another hint at the hidden presence of an underlying totality is the violent image that likens the six crumbs to "mutilated thumbs." This image departs considerably from that of the meek subjunctive crumbs reporting humbly and modestly to God on the occasion of this apocalyptic roll call. Again, there is an underlying notion of a part-whole relationship in that the thumbs/crumbs are part of an unmentioned larger body. The qualification "mutilated" intensifies the notion of a hidden or potential wholeness as it describes the thumbs as either missing an essential (again unspecified) portion or being maimed and thus deprived of their full functionality.

A further trace of the potential totality of the self is contained in God's expectation to see "something" rise "as the other somethings did." The poem juxtaposes the "six crumbs" to "something," which forms again a vanishing point of the self—in the double sense of the word. On the one hand, it resembles that imaginary point in or outside a drawing where parallel lines meet. On the other hand, a vanishing point also designates the spot where something vanishes from sight, disappears, becomes invisible, or has eluded our perception. That is precisely how the "something" functions within the context of the poem. While "something" suggests the maladroitness of the six crumbs and insinuates that there should really be something else in their place, it fails to answer any more clearly the question what that "other" should be. All it can do is to suggest the necessity of an "otherness" without being any more specific about it. The hypothetical construction center of the self is also the point at which it disappears.

The Effie poem echoes the elusiveness of the self. It vacillates between union and disintegration. Cummings creates, as does Nietzsche, whenever he attempts to undermine the traditional concept of the self as a totality, a wholeness of the self. At the same time he is never able to track down and hold this totality fast for inspection or contemplation. It invariably turns out to be a fiction, an imaginary point of reference of the human self, a point that exists but as a necessity to our thinking. The consequences of this realization are spelled out in Hillis Miller's "Partial Portrait" of Walter Pater:

> If the magical appearance of unity to which we give the name "person" is always produced differentially, by the division or combat of contradictory forces, and yet exceeds anything which may be identified as in those forces ... then the momentary poise in a personification will always be divided against itself, folded, manifold, dialogical rather than monological. It will always be open, like all the master tropes of the great texts in the Western tradition, to multiple contradictory readings in a perpetual fleeing away from any fixed sense. (112)

It is against the background of these continually vacillating selves that Cummings' writing must be viewed.

The Self as Linguistic Entity

The treatment the self receives in the two poems we have considered is typical of numerous similar attempts throughout. Here, as elsewhere, we find a continual reflection of the properties of the "I" on a linguistic level. It is therefore appropriate that a few words be said about the function of linguistics in the analysis of Cummings' writing. Critics have realized the paramount importance of the systematic, careful inspection of Cummings' language for the interpretation of his work. But, unfortunately, his poetry is still widely regarded as a quarry for the linguist in search of deviation. As Richard D. Cureton stated in his 1979 essay on Cummings' use of deviant morphology, the poetry of E. E. Cummings presents an "irresistible challenge" for linguists who are interested in describing and analyzing the aesthetic use of language.[26] Although numerous linguistic analyses of Cummings' poetry have been published, most of them contribute little, if anything, towards a genuine understanding of his writing. Far too often these analyses are mere taxonomies of isolated phenomena, restricted to a discussion of a single poem or parts thereof.[27] While these approaches may yield valuable punctual linguistic insights, their scope is much too limited to contribute to the general understanding of his poetry. Fortunately, however, several notable exceptions to this rule have appeared in recent years. Two shall be mentioned here. One of the earliest of which I am aware is Irene Fairley's 1975 systematic, book-length study of Cummings' departures from standard linguistic use.[28] Another linguist who has very successfully dealt with Cummings' poetry is Richard Cureton.[29] In the conclusion to his excellent reading of CP 515, better known by its first line "anyone lived in a pretty how town," he sums up the fundamental deficiencies of many linguistic analyses:

> If the linguistic analysis of literary language is to make any contribution to our understanding of literature, this analysis, at some point, must be shown to be relevant to the larger aesthetic analysis of the work as a whole. While the formal analysis of literary language may certainly be used for other ends (e. g. as a testing-ground for linguistic theories, etc.) and, therefore, has some amount of inherent worth, it seems fair to claim that it only real- izes its ultimate value as a means to a larger end—the advancement of our understanding of language as art. ("'he danced his did': an analysis" 260)

Literary language is art, and no analysis must lose sight of the impact of the aesthetic effects on the reader. In the case of Cummings, this issue is con- tinually thematized. That its language continually relates to its own imma- nent aesthetics is a distinctive feature of his poetry. Particularly Cummings' lyrical poetry largely relies for its appeal on the poet's ability to bring to light again and again, in a continually changing manner, new and unexpected aesthetic aspects of language. By doing so, Cummings' rhetoric perpetually calls attention to its sign status, as well. It thus contains an element that is often not only overlooked but even flatly denied: a strongly developed philosophical strand. Although his language philosophy lacks the systematic development into a full-blown system, and although Cummings is surpris- ingly inarticulate whenever he tries to relate to it as to a conceptual under- pinning of his writing, its practical application is as systematic as it could possibly be: it informs, practically without exception, his entire writing.

Cummings exhibits a consistency and resolution to exploit the linguistic dimension of his writing, which has—perhaps with the exception of Mal- larmé and Joyce—remained wholly unrivalled.[30] That is why Cummings is frequently a very difficult poet, badly served not only by criticism, but also by his own accounts of what he was doing as a poet.[31] It has become clear that— contrary to widespread belief—the linguistic deviations of his language are by no means solely the result of playful facetiousness. While the ludic ele- ment doubtlessly plays an important part in this respect, linguistic deviation is more often than not highly functional. As he deals with illogicalities of the human sphere of experience, Cummings' language must necessarily become illogical in order to do its subject justice.

Cummings' implicit concern with the linguistic aspects of the self raises the question to what extent the "I" for him has the character of a linguistic convention or sign, in the Nietzschean sense, a "Formulirung unserer grammatischen Gewöhnung."[32] In fact, there are a number of indications that this may indeed be the case.[33] The poet's repeated substitution of one sign for the self by the next ("him," "whom," "me") is one of them. It raises the suspicion that one word (or "sign") may serve its purpose as well as another. However, since these signs obviously do not signify the same thing, they are not true signs of the self. They are seen both to refer and not to refer to the self. Through this unstillable oscillation Cummings continually asserts that there is no adequate sign for the self and any sign used to represent the self is necessarily catachrestic.[34] The published version of the couplet artfully plays on this issue in that "him" and "whom," both signs for the self, appear as phonetical variants of the same theme:

–how should a fool that calls him "I" presume
to comprehend not numerable whom?

Phonetically speaking, the mere change of a vowel turns "him" into "whom," makes of a definite reference an unanswerable question. This is to illustrate how close the defined or definable is to the indeterminate, the ungraspable, the incomprehensible.

It should not come as a surprise, then, when Cummings refers to the self as "Not to / be / / deciphered" in CP 361.[35] That it is impossible to read the sign "self" properly may mean two things: either the self is encoded so masterly that it cannot be decoded, or, and this is far more consequential, it cannot be decoded because there is *nothing encoded* in it; it is merely a perfectly arbitrary sign. In practice, Cummings never attempts to decide between these two notions—they are both present throughout his work. Whatever the "real" premises, the result is invariably the same: the "I," Cummings' language asserts over and over, is an ambiguous, obscure or illegible *sign*. It is a *sign* that continually invites decoding but can never be deciphered. Whether spelled with a capital or lowercase letter—or represented by any other sign—the "I" is but a linguistic convention. The "fool that calls him 'I'" is therefore also a fool because he assumes that *calling* himself an "I" would *make* him an "I." Whatever the nature of the "I," it is, Cummings insists repeatedly in the Houghton notes, a mystery that "cannot be known."[36]

Notes

1. The poem has not attracted more than casual interest. It is discussed in Lane (52–3) as well as in Rushworth Kidder, *E. E. Cummings: An Introduction to the*

Poetry (179–80). For a passing reference to the first stanza with regard to the interpretation of the *Enormous Room* see Harold T. McCarthy's chapter on Cummings ("E. E. Cummings: Eros and Cambridge, Mass.") in his *The Expatriate Perspective: American Novelists and the Idea of America* (123–35). In *E. E. Cummings: The Art of His Poetry*, Norman Friedman refers briefly to the first stanza (*18–19*) and to two individual lines (22, 70).

2. "Poetic Prose" (bMS Am 1892. 6 [93, #62]).

3. One of the early versions of the poem (bMS Am 1823.5 [319, n. p.]) refers to the mind as "so pitiless a massacre," extending the element of the unreasonable, unstructured and chaotic to human thinking and awareness in general. It is not only the mind that makes the self an exceedingly complex multiplicity; the body, too, defies any attempts at comprehension. It is "so absolute a chaos and profound" as one alternative early version has it.

4. Other traditional notions which Cummings undercuts with his idiosyncratic rhetoric include "time," "meaning," or "presence." What his poetry questions most relentlessly, though, is the tacitly assumed translucence of language.

5. The other capital "I" for the first person singular occurs in CP 774. There the purpose of the capitalization is twofold. It marks the kingbird's "royal warcry" ("I AM") as direct speech and emphasizes the assertiveness as well as the importance of the statement.

6. This and all subsequent references are to bMS Am 1823.5 (319), n. p.).

7. On Cummings' preference of the lowercase "i" see footnote 6 in Chapter 13. . . .

8. According to the *American Heritage Dictionary*. Cf. also the *OED*, which defines "presume" as "[t]o take upon oneself, undertake without adequate authority or permission; to venture upon."

9. For similar considerations on Cummings' use of "why" as a noun see Robert E. Maurer, "Latter Day Notes on E. E. Cummings' Language" (79–99, especially 91–6).

10. In his notes Cummings insists repeatedly on this attitude towards the self. The self and its essence, poetry, are mysteries which remain inscrutable. "I am here," Cummings declares in his notes for the "California lectures" he never delivered (. . .), "not to explain anything, but to celebrate something; & this something . . . was & is & always must remain a secret" (bMS Am 1892.7 [90, #422]).

11. In most cases, the word appears to be a relative pronoun with a relation that is either missing or difficult to establish (CP 300, CP 558, CP 584, CP 654, CP 777). Examples of poems where "whom" is used as a noun include CP 658, 716, 733 and 748. CP 637 is noteworthy, because it depicts the "whom" on the threshold of a noun: "the(whom we call / rose a)mystery."

On occasion, "whom" appears to be present merely accidentally ("a finding whom of girl," CP 565). The uneven distribution of these deviations is rather striking. They occur extremely rarely or not at all in the earlier collections (*Tulips and Chimneys, & [AND], XLI Poems*), while making up more than a third of all occurrences in the later poems. Perhaps this is an indication that the poet developed an increasing awareness of the problematic nature of the self as he grew older.

12. Relative pronouns agree with the "head" they refer to on the basis of a two-term "gender" system that differentiates between personal and non-personal words. "'[P]ersonality' is ascribed basically to human beings but extends to creatures

in the supernatural world (angels, elves, etc.) which are thought of as having human characteristics such as speech" (Quirk, et al. *A Comprehensive Grammar of the English Language* 1245).

13. A further twist in the indefinable identity of the "i" is added by the phonetic identity of "sun" and "son," which become indistinguishable in spoken language.

14. There are more than twenty different formations, most of which occur once only. They include e. g. "isful" (CP 456), "youful" (502, 832), "oneful" (537), "towerful" (CP 586), "sunful" (CP 607), "firstful" (669) and "muchful" (ETC 151). The single most frequent formation is "deathful" which appears four times in the *Complete Poems* (415, 567, 763, 768) and once in *ETC (14)*.

The abbreviation "ETC" here and in future quotations refers to *Etcetera: The Unpublished Poems of E E. Cummings*, the number gives the page on which the quotation occurs.

15. See also below, Chapter 11, "E. E. Cummings' Poetics" (219–40, passim).

16. "Aliveness" depends on being as well as on change, or eternal becoming. This aspect of Cummings' notion emerges very clearly from the only concrete definition of the term in the introduction to *Collected Poems* (1938). The present quotation is to CP 461–2 where the text has been included:

> Never the murdered finalities of wherewhen and yesno, impotent
> nongames of wrongright and rightwrong;never to gain or pause,never
> the soft adventure of undoom,greedy anguishes and cringing ecstasies
> of inexistence; never to rest and never to have:only to grow.

Kennedy defines "alive" as "a word which combines . . . concepts of identity and being ('is'), of movement, warmth, vigor, power, and joy" (*Dreams* 180).

17. Actually, Cummings' understanding of "poetry" as the recreation of a non- or extralinguistic phenomenon requires the presence of a certain amount of "non-referentiality" in his writing. . . .

18. This and all subsequent references are to bMS Am 1823.5 (319, n. p.). It is perhaps noteworthy that not only the mind—by and large regarded as the seat of the self—but also the body appears as a multiplicity in this poem. In several versions the body ("flesh") is called an "absolute chaos."

19. Originally published in the *Yale Review*, 62 (1973): 412–19, as part of "Poetry: Ammons, Berryman, Cummings," the essay is included in her *Part of Nature, Part of Us*, where the present quotation appears on page 323.

20. This discrepancy, which constitutes a basic quality of Cummings' poetics, has been observed on various occasions. Tanya Reinhart addresses it briefly though explicitly in "Patterns, Intuitions, and the Sense of Nonsense. An Analysis of Cummings' anyone lived in a pretty how town'" (86). The discrepancy is also a recurrent theme in the discussion of the line "he danced his did" in the *Journal of Linguistics* between 1965 and 1980 (see footnote 28 below). The linguists' difficulties to relate factually the "intuitive" meaning of the sentence to structural and semantic elements of the sentence would no doubt have amused, if not deeply satisfied Cummings.

Of related interest is also a relatively recent essay by Willie Van Peer entitled "Top-Down and Bottom-Up: Interpretative Strategies in Reading E. E. Cummings."

21. Kidder suggests that "not numerable whom" may also refer to the "infinite God" (*Introduction* 180). Although such a reading is not implausible, if the poem is regarded out of the context of the Houghton notes, the many extant alternative versions suggest that Cummings is primarily concerned with the definition of selfhood in this poem. One of these versions of the final couplet has "how should a fool that calls himself "I" / presume to rule such illimitable a whom." In these lines Cummings alludes to a widespread political metaphor of the self drawn on innumerable times from the antiquity to the present. Plato uses it in the *Republic*, Montaigne in the *Essays* and Nietzsche in the *Nachlass* (cf. also Appendix C).

22. The notion of the self as a very small, insignificant part is frequently linked with a notion of the diminutive strongly suggestive of a religious dimension: "mortal merely i," "a trifling socalled i," "some trifle of an i" (all bMS Am 1892. 6 [93, n. p.]).

23. To be precise, there are two genera of the final couplet in the Houghton notes, each of which occurs in numerous variants. The group I have analyzed in some detail above is the one which Cummings chose for the published version of the poem. Here the self appears as the object of the quest for self-knowledge. The other genus views the self *sub specie mortis* and asks the rhetorical question:

shall i(who am so infinite a he)
begrudge Death much the slimmest him of me

These lines, too, postulate the self as an infinite multiplicity. Addressing the problem of death as the possible annihilator of the self, they consolingly point out that death only affects a very minor part of the self ("the slimmest him of me" [bMS Am 1823.5 (319, n. p.)]). For this genus of the final couplet the multiplicity of the self is the basis for its immortality.

24. A thorough investigation of lexical conversion in Cummings' poetry has been conducted by Richard D. Cureton in "'he danced his did': an analysis," which appeared in the *Journal of Linguistics*. According to his terminology (based on U. Weinreich, "Exploration of Semantic Theory," *Current Trends in Linguistics* (ed. T. Sebeok), [396–477]), we are dealing here with a lexical conversion from a 'minor' category (i. e. articles, prepositions, conjunctions etc.) to a 'major' category (i. e. nouns, verbs, adjectives, adverbs). The result of such a conversion, according to Cureton, is twofold: (1) it is poetically effective because it adds meaning and (2) that meaning is fairly well defined. He, too, understands the conversion to a noun basically as an attempt at concretization: "nouns are, in some sense, *objects* (abstract or concrete)" (248, emphasis added).

25. The word "alive" has a double meaning here. On the one hand "who isn't alive" refers to Effie's physical death, on the other, it expresses Cummings' verdict on a human being whose life lacked essential insights and actions. This lack of true "aliveness" is reflected in the names of the six crumbs who made up Effie while she was alive. All of them are modal auxiliaries: "may," "might," "should," "could," "would," "must." But, Cummings insists, life is a "verb" (bMS Am 1892.7 [90, #20]), not a modal auxiliary. True expression of aliveness only comes to pass in the verb "be," in the finite present forms "am," "are," "is." The kingbird's "royal warcry" is a categorical "I AM" (CP 774)—an indicative and not a putative or "subjunctive."

Another poem that deals with the problematic of unaliveness is CP 412—"most(people / simply / can't)." Taking a similar angle of attack, this poem, too, relates the "unaliveness" to being caught up in a web of modal verbs. Unable to shake off "can't," "won't," mustn't," "shouldn't" and "daren't" the majority of mankind never actually "lives."

For a reading that stresses the religious implications of the Effie poem, see Lane (85–9). A good short reading is also Wegner (92–3).

26. "E. E. Cummings: A Study of the Poetic Use of Deviant Morphology" (213).

27. Under this category fall, among many others, the countless publications on the fourth line of Cummings' poem "anyone lived in a pretty how town" (CP 515). The (in)famous "he sang his didn't he danced his did" sparked a series of articles in the *Journal of Linguistics*, e. g. James Peter Thorne, "Stylistics and Generative Grammars," (1, 1965: 49–59); R. Fowler, "On the Interpretation of 'Nonsense Strings,'" (5, 1969: 75–83); Jan Aarts, "A Note on the Interpretation of 'he danced his did,'" (7, 1971: 71–73).

Other examples of similarly restricted analyses include Nomi Tamir-Ghez, "Binary Oppositions and Thematic Decoding in E. E. Cummings and Eudora Welty" or Klaus-Dieter Gottschalk, "E. E. Cummings: Orientale II. Eine Gedichtanalyse zur Einführung in die Linguistik." Such approaches, unfortunately, tend to propagandize Cummings' poetry as a playground for linguistic studies rather than consider them seriously as literary texts.

28. *E. E. Cummings and Ungrammar.* Cf. also her essay "Syntax as Style: An Analysis of Three Cummings Poems."

29. In several thorough analyses Cureton has admirably succeeded in bringing to light the aesthetic implications and intricacies of Cummings' language. I am thinking here of "E. E. Cummings: A Study of the Poetic Use of Deviant Morphology," "E. E. Cummings: A Case of Iconic Syntax" and "Visual Form in e. e. cummings' *No Thanks*," which appeared in *Word and Image*.

A pertinent investigation to be considered is Barbara Herrnstein Smith, *Poetic Closure: A Study of How Poems End*. Although her discussion of Cummings is limited to some brief comments on two of his poems (255–7), her general approach seems to me of great value. Hers is one of the few attempts at systematically investigating basic issues of language philosophy that allow a critic to make sound and reproducible statements about how poems function.

30. Of course, there have been experimentalist approaches, particularly during Cummings' early formative years—Gertrude Stein published *Tender Buttons* in 1914 and the Dadaists were active between 1916 and 1921—but Cummings' poetry differs decisively from such approaches. Although one can find in his writing an occasional juxtaposition of unrelated objects, words seemingly picked at random, a breach of logic, Cummings does not aim for arbitrariness or absurdity as a governing principle. . . .

31. It is Cummings' notes in particular that testify to his great concern with the philosophical implications of his writing. The copious notes for his published and unpublished plays, for instance, are brimming with ontological references. Cf., among others, bMS Am 1892.7 (51–2) "Notes for a play: Santa Claus and J[esus] C[hrist]," bMS Am 1892.7 (53) "Notes for a play: Science Scenes." Of great interest is also one of four little notebooks collected under bMS Am 1823.7 (40), in which Cummings explores the mechanisms of human sense perception and draws parallels between the eye, the mouth and the genitals.

32. Cf. Appendix C.

33. . . . Cummings insists that he and his writing are one and the same thing.

34. I am using the term here in the sense in which it appears in Hillis Miller's "Stevens' Rock and Criticism as Cure" (28):

> Catachresis is the violent, forced, or abusive use of a word to name something which has no literal name. The word also means, in music, a harsh or unconventional dissonance, a surd. Examples of catachresis are table "leg" and mother "tongue." Such a word is neither literal, since a table leg is not truly a leg, nor speech a tongue, nor figurative, since it is not a substitute for some proper word.

35. The poem constitutes a visionary description of the fate of the poet and his lover after their death. As the first half of the poem describes the decomposition of their bodies, "Not to / be / / deciphered" also plays on the notion that the lovers' "selves" or identities can no longer be discerned by human scrutiny, because their bodies have ceased to exist. . . .

36. bMS Am 1892.7 (90, # 370).

Chronology

1874	Robert Frost is born in San Francisco on March 26.
1878	Carl August Sandburg is born on January 6 in Galesburg, Illinois.
1879	Wallace Stevens is born on October 2 in Reading, Pennsylvania.
1883	William Carlos Williams is born in Rutherford, New Jersey, on September 17.
1885	Ezra Pound is born October 30 in Hailey, Idaho.
1886	Hilda Doolittle (H. D.) is born September 10 in Bethlehem, Pennsylvania.
1887	Marianne Moore is born November 15 in Kirkwood, Missouri.
1888	T. S. Eliot is born September 26 in St. Louis, Missouri.
1892	Edna St. Vincent Millay is born in Rockland, Maine, on February 22.
1894	E. E. Cummings is born on October 14 in Cambridge, Massachusetts.
1900	Sigmund Freud publishes *The Interpretation of Dreams*. Friedrich Nietzsche dies.
1904	Academy of Arts and Letters founded.
1907	Cubist exhibition in Paris.

1909	Pound publishes *Personae*. Williams publishes *Poems*.
1911	Pound publishes *Canzoni*. Elizabeth Bishop born February 9 in Worcester, Massachusetts.
1912	*Poetry* magazine founded in Chicago.
1913	Robert Frost publishes *A Boy's Will*. Marcel Proust publishes *Swann's Way*. Marcel Duchamp's *Nude Descending a Staircase* exhibited at the Armory in New York.
1914	Frost publishes *North of Boston*. World War I begins. Pound edits *Des Imagistes*.
1916	Sandburg publishes *Chicago Poems*. Frost publishes *Mountain Interval*. H.D. publishes *Sea Garden*.
1917	Eliot publishes *Prufrock and Other Observations*. The United States enters World War I. Pound publishes *Lustra and Other Poems*. Millay publishes *Renascence and Other Poems*. Williams publishes *Al Que Quiere!*
1919	Versailles Treaty is signed. Eliot publishes "Tradition and the Individual Talent." Sandburg publishes *Corn Huskers*, which wins Pulitzer.
1920	Pound publishes *Hugh Selwyn Mawberley*. Eliot publishes *The Sacred Wood*.
1921	Albert Einstein lectures in New York. Moore publishes *Poems*.
1922	Eliot publishes *The Waste Land*. James Joyce publishes *Ulysses*.
1923	Wallace Stevens publishes *Harmonium*. Williams publishes *Spring and All*. Cummings publishes *Tulips and Chimneys*. Frost publishes *New Hampshire*, which wins Pulitzer. Millay wins Pulitzer for *The Ballad of the Harp-Weaver, A Few Figs from Thistles*, and eight sonnets in *American Poetry*.
1924	H. D. publishes *Heliodora and Other Poems*. Eliot publishes *Sweeney Agonistes*. Moore publishes *Observations*.
1925	F. Scott Fitzgerald publishes *The Great Gatsby*. Harold Ross founds *The New Yorker* magazine. Eliot publishes *The Hollow Men*. Cummings publishes *XLI Poems*. Williams publishes *In the American Grain*.
1926	Cummings publishes *Is 5*. Moore becomes editor of *The Dial*.
1927	Martin Heidegger publishes *Being and Time*.

1928	Frost publishes *West-Running Brook*.
1929	Stock market crash initiates the Great Depression. Museum of Modern Art opens in New York.
1930	Hart Crane publishes *The Bridge*. Eliot publishes *Ash Wednesday*. Pound publishes *A Draft of XXX Cantos*.
1931	Cummings publishes *ViVa*. Frost receives Pulitzer Prize for *Collected Poems*.
1933	Eliot publishes *The Use of Poetry and the Use of Criticism*.
1934	Pound publishes *ABC of Reading*. Eliot publishes *After Strange Gods*.
1935	Eliot publishes *Murder in the Cathedral*. Moore publishes *Selected Poems*. Stevens publishes *Ideas of Order*. Williams publishes *An Early Martyr*.
1936	Frost publishes *A Further Range*, which receives Pulitzer. Spanish Civil War begins.
1937	Stevens publishes *The Man with the Blue Guitar*.
1938	Cummings publishes *Collected Poems*.
1939	Outbreak of World War II. Eliot publishes *Family Reunion*.
1941	Williams publishes *Broken Span*. Moore publishes *What Are Years?*
1942	Frost publishes *A Witness Tree*, which receives Pulitzer. Stevens publishes *Parts of a World*.
1944	Eliot publishes *Four Quartets*. H. D. publishes *The Walls Do Not Fall*. Williams publishes *The Wedge*. Moore publishes *Nevertheless*.
1945	World War II ends. Frost publishes *A Masque of Reason*. H. D. publishes *Tribute to the Angels*.
1946	Bishop publishes *North and South*. H. D. publishes *The Flowering of the Rod*. Williams publishes *Paterson (Book One)*.
1947	Frost publishes *Steeple Bush*. Stevens publishes *Transport to Summer*.
1948	Eliot wins Nobel Prize for Literature. Pound publishes *The Pisan Cantos*.
1949	Eliot publishes *The Cocktail Party*. Bishop appointed Consultant in Poetry at the Library of Congress.

1950   Millay dies. Williams wins National Book Award for *Selected Poems* and *Paterson (Book Three)*. Stevens publishes *The Auroras of Autumn*, which wins the National Book Award. Sandburg publishes *Complete Poems*, which wins Pulitzer.

1951   Moore publishes *Collected Poems*, which wins a Pulitzer and National Book Award. Stevens publishes *The Necessary Angel*.

1952   Williams appointed Consultant in Poetry to the Library of Congress but does not serve.

1954   Stevens publishes *Collected Poems*, which wins the National Book Award and a Pulitzer. Williams publishes *The Desert Music*.

1955   Pound publishes *Rock Drill*. Stevens dies. Bishop publishes *Poems: North and South—A Cold Spring*, which wins a Pulitzer.

1958   Frost named Consultant in Poetry to the Library of Congress.

1961   H. D. dies. Pound publishes *Thrones*.

1962   Cummings dies. Frost publishes *In the Clearing*. Williams publishes *Pictures from Brueghel*.

1963   Frost and Williams die. Williams is posthumously awarded a Pulitzer for *Pictures from Brueghel*.

1965   Eliot dies. Bishop publishes *Questions of Travel*.

1967   Sandburg dies. Moore publishes *Complete Poems*.

1969   Bishop publishes *The Complete Poems*, which wins National Book Award.

1972   Pound and Moore die.

1976   Bishop publishes *Geography III*, which receives National Book Critics Circle Award.

1979   Bishop dies.

Contributors

HAROLD BLOOM is Sterling Professor of the Humanities at Yale University. Educated at Cornell and Yale universities, he is the author of more than 30 books, including *Shelley's Mythmaking* (1959), *The Visionary Company* (1961), *Blake's Apocalypse* (1963), *Yeats* (1970), *The Anxiety of Influence* (1973), *A Map of Misreading* (1975), *Kabbalah and Criticism* (1975), *Agon: Toward a Theory of Revisionism* (1982), *The American Religion* (1992), *The Western Canon* (1994), *Omens of Millennium: The Gnosis of Angels, Dreams, and Resurrection* (1996), *Shakespeare: The Invention of the Human* (1998), *How to Read and Why* (2000), *Genius: A Mosaic of One Hundred Exemplary Creative Minds* (2002), *Hamlet: Poem Unlimited* (2003), *Where Shall Wisdom Be Found?* (2004), and *Jesus and Yahweh: The Names Divine* (2005). In addition, he is the author of hundreds of articles, reviews, and editorial introductions. In 1999, Professor Bloom received the American Academy of Arts and Letters' Gold Medal for Criticism. He has also received the International Prize of Catalonia, the Alfonso Reyes Prize of Mexico, and the Hans Christian Andersen Bicentennial Prize of Denmark.

PETER SCHMIDT is professor and chairman of the department of English literature at Swarthmore College. His work includes books on William Carlos Williams's poetry and experimental prose and on Eudora Welty's short fiction, plus an anthology co-edited with Amrijit Singh titled *Postcolonial Theory and the U.S.: Race, Ethnicity, and Literature.*

JEROME J. McGANN is a professor at the University of Virginia. Among his many titles are *Black Riders: The Visible Language of Modernism* and *The*

Point Is to Change It: Poetry and Criticism in the Continuing Present. He is also a poet and the editor of several volumes.

ROBERT PINSKY is a professor at Boston University and a former U.S. poet laureate. He is the author of many books of both poetry and criticism, for which he has won numerous awards. He is the poetry editor of *Slate* magazine.

MARK VAN WIENEN is an associate professor at Northern Illinois University. His publications include *Rendezvous with Death: American Poems of the Great War* and *Partisans and Poets: The Political Work of American Poetry in the Great War.* Additionally, he has contributed to the *Dictionary of Literary Biography.*

ROGER MITCHELL is a professor emeritus at Indiana University, where he also was director of the MFA program. He authored several volumes of poetry. For many years, he was the poetry editor of the *Minnesota Review.*

ELEANOR COOK is a professor emerita at the University of Toronto. Her titles include *A Reader's Guide to Wallace Stevens* and *Against Coercion: Games Poets Play.*

JAY PARINI is a professor of English and creative writing at Middlebury College. Among his many works are *Robert Frost: A Life* and *Why Poetry Matters.* He is a coeditor of the *Columbia History of American Poetry* and the editor of the *Columbia Anthology of American Poetry,* as well as other titles. He also is a poet and novelist.

SUZANNE CLARK is a professor at the University of Oregon. She is the author of *Sentimental Modernism: Women Writers and the Revolution of the Word* and is working on a manuscript called "The Natural History of Modernism."

MARTIN HEUSSER is a professor in the English department of Zurich University. He is the principal editor of several titles, including *Aspects of Modernism: Studies in Honor of Max Nänny* and *On Verbal/Visual Representation.* He is vice president of the European Association for American Studies.

Bibliography

Axelrod, Steven Gould, and Helen Deese, ed. *Critical Essays on Wallace Stevens.* Boston, Mass.: G.K. Hall, 1988.

Bagby, George F. *Frost and the Book of Nature.* Knoxville: University of Tennessee Press, 1993.

Baumann, Walter. *Roses from the Steel Dust: Collected Essays on Ezra Pound.* Orono, Me.: National Poetry Foundation; Hanover [N.H.]: Distributed by University Press of New England, 2000.

Bromwich, David. *Skeptical Music: Essays on Modern Poetry.* Chicago: University of Chicago Press, 2001.

Brooks, Cleanth. "*The Waste Land*: A Prophetic Document." *The Yale Review* 78, no. 2 (Winter 1989): 318–332.

Cook, Eleanor. *Poetry, Word-Play, and Word-War in Wallace Stevens.* Princeton, N.J.: Princeton University Press, 1988.

Crunden, Robert M. *Body and Soul: The Making of American Modernism.* New York: Basic Books, 2000.

Davie, Donald, ed. *Modernist Essays: Yeats, Pound, Eliot.* Manchester: Carcanet, 2004.

Dekoven, Marianne. *Rich and Strange: Gender, History and Modernism.* Princeton, N.J.: Princeton University Press, 1991.

Dembo, L. S. *Conceptions of Reality in Modern American Poetry.* Berkeley: University of California Press, 1996.

Dickie, Margaret. *On the Modernist Long Poem.* Iowa City: University of Iowa Press, 1986.

Diehl, Joanne Feit. *Elizabeth Bishop and Marianne Moore: The Psychodynamics of Creativity.* Princeton, N.J.: Princeton University Press, 1993.

Donoghue, Denis. *Words Alone: The Poet T. S. Eliot*. New Haven: Yale University Press, 2000.

Faggen, Robert, ed. *The Cambridge Companion to Robert Frost*. Cambridge; New York: Cambridge University Press, 2001.

Friedman, Norman. *Revaluing Cummings: Further Essays on the Poet, 1962–1993*. Gainesville: University Press of Florida, 1996.

Giorcelli, Cristina, ed. *The Idea and the Thing in Modernist American Poetry*. Palermo: ILA Palma, 2001.

Golston, Michael. *Rhythm and Race in Modernist Poetry and Science*. New York: Columbia University Press, 2008.

Gwynn, R. S., ed. *The Advocates of Poetry: A Reader of American Poet-Critics of the Modernist Era*. Fayetteville, [Ark.]: University of Arkansas Press, 1996.

Hakutani, Yoshinobu. *Haiku and Modernist Poetics*. New York: Palgrave Macmillan, 2009.

Hanscombe, Gillian E., and Virginia L. Smyers. *Writing for Their Lives: The Modernist Women 1910–1940*. Boston: Northeastern University Press, 1988.

Hart, Matthew. *Nations of Nothing but Poetry: Modernism, Transnationalism, and Synthetic Vernacular Writing*. New York: Oxford University Press, 2010.

Hatlen, Burton, and Demetres Tryphonopoulos, ed. *William Carlos Williams and the Language of Poetry*. Orono, Me.: National Poetry Foundation; Hanover: Distributed by University Press of New England, 2002.

Kaplan, Harold. *Poetry, Politics, and Culture: Argument in the Work of Eliot, Pound, Stevens, and Williams*. New Brunswick, N.J.: Aldine Transaction, 2006.

Leggett, B. J. *Early Stevens: The Nietzschean Intertext*. Durham: Duke University Press, 1992.

——. *Late Stevens: The Final Fiction*. Baton Rouge: Louisiana State University Press, 2005.

——. *Wallace Stevens and Poetic Theory: Conceiving the Supreme Fiction*. Chapel Hill: University of North Carolina Press, 1987.

Lentricchia, Frank. *Modernist Quartet*. Cambridge [England]; New York: Cambridge University Press, 1994.

Melaney, William D. *After Ontology: Literary Theory and Modernist Poetics*. Albany: State University of New York Press, 2001.

Miller, Cristanne. *Marianne Moore: Questions of Authority*. Cambridge, Mass.: Harvard University Press, 1995.

Paul, Catherine E. *Poetry in the Museums of Modernism: Yeats, Pound, Moore, Stein*. Ann Arbor: University of Michigan Press, 2002.

Perloff, Marjorie. *Poetic License: Essays on Modernist and Postmodernist Lyric*. Evanston, Ill.: Northwestern University Press, 1990.

Pratt, William. *Ezra Pound and the Making of Modernism*. New York: AMS Press, 2007.

Rae, Patricia. *The Practical Muse: Pragmatist Poetics in Hulme, Pound, and Stevens*. Lewisburg [Pa.]: Bucknell University Press; London; Cranbury, N.J.: Associated University Presses, 1997.

Rainey, Lawrence. *The Institutions of Modernism*. New Haven: Yale University Press, 1998.

———. *Revisiting* The Waste Land. New Haven: Yale University Press, 2005.

Rehder, Robert. *Stevens, Williams, Crane, and the Motive for Metaphor*. Houndmills, Basingstoke, Hampshire; New York: Palgrave Macmillan, 2005.

Rotella, Guy. *Reading and Writing Nature: The Poetry of Robert Frost, Wallace Stevens, Marianne Moore, and Elizabeth Bishop*. Boston: Northeastern University Press, 1991.

Schwartz, Sanford. *The Matrix of Modernism: Pound, Eliot, and Early Twentieth-Century Thought*. Princeton, N.J.: Princeton University Press, 1985.

Schwarz, Daniel R. *Narrative and Representation in the Poetry of Wallace Stevens*. New York: St. Martin's Press, 1993.

Smith, Stan. *The Origins of Modernism: Eliot, Pound, Yeats and the Rhetorics of Renewal*. New York: Harvester Wheatsheaf, 1994.

Stead, C. K. *Pound, Yeats, Eliot, and the Modernist Movement*. New Brunswick, N.J.: Rutgers University Press, 1986.

Stevenson, Anne. *Five Looks at Elizabeth Bishop*. London: Bellew, 1998.

Whiting, Anthony. *The Never-Resting Mind: Wallace Stevens' Romantic Irony*. Ann Arbor: University of Michigan Press, 1996.

Whitworth, Michael H. *Reading Modernist Poetry*. Chichester, West Sussex, U.K.; Malden, Mass.: Wiley-Blackwell, 2010.

Acknowledgments

Peter Schmidt, "*Paterson* and Epic Tradition." From *William Carlos Williams, the Arts, and Literary Tradition.* Copyright © 1988 by Louisiana State University Press.

Jerome J. McGann, "The *Cantos* of Ezra Pound, the Truth in Contradiction." From *Towards a Literature of Knowledge.* Published by the University of Chicago Press. Copyright © 1989 by Jerome J. McGann.

Robert Pinsky, "Marianne Moore: Idiom and Idiosyncrasy." From *Marianne Moore: The Art of a Modernist,* edited by Joseph Parisi. Published by UMI Research Press. Copyright © 1990 by Joseph Parisi. Reprinted with permission of the author.

Mark Van Wienen, "Taming the Socialist: Carl Sandburg's *Chicago Poems* and Its Critics." From *American Literature* 63, no. 1 (March 1991): 89–103. Copyright © 1991 by the Duke University Press.

Roger Mitchell, "Modernism Comes to American Poetry: 1908–1920." From *A Profile of Twentieth-Century American Poetry,* edited by Jack Myers and David Wojahn. Copyright © 1991 by the Board of Trustees, Southern Illinois University.

Eleanor Cook, "From Etymology to Paronomasia: Wallace Stevens, Elizabeth Bishop, and Others." From *Connotations* 2, no. 1 (1992): 34–51. Copyright © 1992 by Waxmann Verlag GmbH.

Jay Parini, "Robert Frost and the Poetry of Survival." From *The Columbia History of American Poetry,* Jay Parini, editor, and Brett C. Miller, associate editor. Copyright © 1993 by Columbia University Press.

Suzanne Clark, "Uncanny Millay." From *Millay at 100: A Critical Reappraisal,* edited by Diane P. Freedman. Copyright © 1995 by the Board of Trustees, Southern Illinois University.

Martin Heusser, "So Many Selves: The 'I' as Indeterminate Multiplicity." From *I Am My Writing: The Poetry of E. E. Cummings.* Copyright © 1997 by Stauffenburg Verlag Brigitte Narr GmbH.

Every effort has been made to contact the owners of copyrighted material and secure copyright permission. Articles appearing in this volume generally appear much as they did in their original publication with few or no editorial changes. In some cases, foreign language text has been removed from the original essay. Those interested in locating the original source will find the information cited above.

Index

Jakobson, Roman, 161
James, Henry, 113, 139
James, William, 192, 194
Jarrell, Randall, 185, 196
Jay, Gregory S., 35
Johnson, Samuel, 26
Jolas, Eugene, 44–45
Jonson, Ben, 160, 162, 176
"Journey of the Magi" (Eliot), 170
Joyce, James, 18, 44, 77, 160, 164, 233
   Ulysses, 9
Jubilate Agno (Smart), 26
"June" (Sandburg), 121
"Justice Denied in Massachusetts" (Millay), 200

Kafka, Franz, 138
Kant, Immanuel, 91, 208–209, 214
   Critique of Judgment, 210–211
   Critique of Reason, 210
   "Observations on the Feeling of the Beautiful Sublime," 210
Kearns, Cleo McNelly, 35
Keats, John, 8, 12, 14, 31
   "The Fall of Hyperion," 7, 13
   influence of, 36, 38, 75, 137, 197
"Keeping Their World Large" (Moore), 27
Kemp, John
   Robert Frost and New England, 186
Kenner, Hugh, 18, 24
Kermode, Frank, 137
King Jasper (Frost), 140
King Lear (Shakespeare), 36
"Kin to Sorrow" (Millay), 205
Kora in Hell (Williams), 8–10, 54–55
Kreymborg, Alfred, 48
Kreymborg, Williams, 48
Kristeva, Julia, 207, 211–213

La Follette, Robert, 118
La Fontaine, Jean, 26–27
Large Glass, The (Duchamp), 49

Last Night of Paris (Soupault), 57
Lauber, John, 93–94, 96
Lauretis, Teresa de, 203
Lawrence, D.H., 16–18
Lear, Edward, 159
"Leaves of Grass" (Whitman), 38, 176
Lentricchia, Frank
   "Robert Frost and Modern Literary Theory," 192
"Lesson for the Day, The" (Frost), 189
"Letter to N.Y." (Bishop), 105
Lewis, Wyndham, 77
Lincoln, Abraham, 117
Lindsay, Vachel, 176
   and populism, 131–132
Locke, John, 210
Longfellow, Henry Wadsworth, 140, 177
"Long and Sluggish Lines" (Stevens), 168
"Lost" (Sandburg), 124
"Lost Follower, The" (Frost), 196
"Lost in Translation" (Merrill), 164
Lowell, Amy, 176
   on Sandburg, 121–123, 128
   Tendencies in Modern American Poetry, 121
Lukás, George, 138–139
Lynen, John F.
   The Pastoral Art of Robert Frost, 177

Macbeth (Shakespeare), 184
Malatesta, Sigismundo, 85, 96
Mallarmé, Stéphane, 233
Mann, Thomas, 138
"Manuelzinho" (Bishop), 111
"Man Whose Pharynx Was Bad, The" (Stevens), 170
"Man with the Blue Guitar, The" (Stevens), 166
Mariani, Paul, 14, 49
   William Carlos Williams: A New World Naked, 7

264   Index